GIGANTIC BOOK OF

WINNING SCIENCE FAIR PROJECTS

Bob Bonnet & Dan Keen

Main Street
A division of Sterling Publishing Co., Inc.
New York

Library of Congress Cataloging-in-Publication Data

Bonnet, Robert L.
  Gigantic book of winning science fair projects / Bob Bonnet and Dan Keen.
    p. cm.
  Includes index.
  ISBN 1-4027-2923-5 (pbk.)
  1. Science projects--Juvenile literature. 2. Science projects--Competitions--Juvenile literature.
I. Keen, Dan. II. Title.
  Q182.3.B6735 2005
  507'.8--dc22

                                                                2005005847

10 9 8 7 6 5 4 3 2 1

Published by Sterling Publishing Co., Inc.
387 Park Avenue South, New York, NY 10016

© 2005 by Sterling Publishing Co., Inc.

This book is composed of material from the following Sterling titles:
Science Fair Projects Energy © 1997 by Bob Bonnet and Dan Keen
Science Fair Projects Chemistry © 2000 by Bob Bonnet and Dan Keen
Science Fair Projects Physics © 1999 by Bob Bonnet and Dan Keen
Science Fair Projects with Electricity & Electronics © 1996 by Bob Bonnet and Dan Keen

Distributed in Canada by Sterling Publishing
%o Canadian Manda Group, 165 Dufferin Street
Toronto, Ontario, Canada M6K 3H6
Distributed in Great Britain and Europe by Chris Lloyd at Orca Book
Services, Stanley House, Fleets Lane, Poole BH15 3AJ, England
Distributed in Australia by Capricorn Link (Australia) Pty. Ltd.
P.O. Box 704, Windsor, NSW 2756, Australia

Illustration Credits
Alex Pang: pages 13–93, 352 (top)
Frances Zweifel: pages 97–264, 351, 352 (bottom)
Karen McKee: pages 269–348

Design by StarGraphics Studio

Sterling ISBN 1-4027-2923-5

For information about custom editions, special sales, premium and
corporate purchases, please contact Sterling Special Sales
Department at 800-805-5489 or specialsales@sterlingpub.com.

TABLE OF CONTENTS

CHEMISTRY

PHYSICS

ELECTRICITY & ELECTRONICS

INTRODUCTION TO
SCIENCE FAIR PROJECTS

Because safety is and must always be the first consideration, we recommend that all activities be done under adult supervision. Even seemingly harmless objects can become a hazard under certain circumstances. If you can't do a project safely, then don't do it!

Respect for life should be fundamental. Your project cannot be inhumane to animals. Disruption of natural processes should not occur thoughtlessly and unnecessarily. Interference with ecological systems should always be avoided. Ethical rules must be followed also. It is unethical to hypothesize that one race or religion is better than another.

Science is the process of finding out. "The scientific method" is a procedure used by scientists and students in science fairs. It consists of several steps: identifying a problem or stating a purpose, forming a hypothesis, setting up an experiment to collect information, recording the results, and coming to a conclusion as to whether or not the stated hypothesis is correct.

A science project starts by identifying a problem, asking a question, or stating a purpose. The statement of the problem defines the boundaries of the investigation. For example, air pollution is a problem, but you must set the limits of your project. It is unlikely that you have access to an electron microscope, so an air pollution project could not check pollen in the air. This project might be limited to the accumulation of dust and other visible materials.

Once the problem is defined, a hypothesis (an educated guess about the results) must be formed. Hypothesize that there is more dust in a room that has thick carpeting than in a room that has hardwood or linoleum flooring.

Often, a hypothesis can be stated in more than one way. For example, in considering a project to gather data for using rocks to store and release heat during the night in a solar heated home, you might test to see if one large rock or many smaller rocks are better for giving off stored heat for a longer period of time. This could be stated in two ways: Hypothesize that one large rock will give off stored heat for a longer period of time than an equal mass of smaller rocks. Or, you could state the opposite: Hypothesize that smaller rocks will give off stored heat for a longer period of time compared to one large rock of equal mass. It does not matter which way the hypothesis is stated, nor does it matter which one is correct. The hypothesis doesn't have to be proven correct in order for the project to be a success; it is successful if facts are gathered and knowledge is gained.

Then you must set up an experiment to test your hypothesis. You will need to list materials, define the variables, constants, and any assumptions, and document your procedure so that you or someone else will be able to repeat the experiment at another time. Finally, from the results collected, you must come to a conclusion as to whether or not the hypothesis is correct.

When choosing a science fair topic, pick something that is interesting to you, that you would like to work on. Then all your research and study time will be spent on a subject you enjoy!

For presentation at a formal science fair, consider early on how you can demonstrate your project. Remember, you may not be able to control certain conditions in a gym or a hall. Decide how to display the project's steps and outcome, and keep a log or journal of how you got your results and came to your conclusion (photographs or even a video). Something hands-on or interactive often adds interest to a project display. As a fairgoer, what would your hands be itching to do? Now is the time to pass on some of that enjoyment.

NOTE TO PARENTS

There are many benefits in store for a child who chooses to do a science project. It motivates the child to learn. Such an activity helps develop thinking skills; it prompts a child to question, and learn how to solve problems. In these activities, the child is asked to make observations using all the senses and to record those observations accurately and honestly. Quantitative measurements of distance, size, and volume must be made. Students may find a subject so interesting that, after the project is completed, they will want to do more investigation on their own. Spin-off interests can develop, too. In doing a science project about energy conservation, while using a computer to record data, a child may discover an interest in computers.

The authors recommend that parents take an active interest in their child's science project. Apart from the safety aspect, when a parent is involved, contact time between the parent and child increases. Such quality time strengthens relationships as well as the child's self-esteem. Working on a project is an experience that can be shared. An involved parent is telling the child that he or she believes that education is important. Parents need to support the academic learning process at least as much as they support Little League, music lessons, or any other growth activity.

Parents should take the time to help the student in reading, understanding, and completing these educational and fun projects. Adults can be an invaluable resource that the child draws upon for information, as older people are given the opportunity to share their own learning and life experiences. Transportation may be helpful and appreciated, such as taking the child to a library or other places for research. One student in our school, doing a project on insects, was taken by his parents to the Mosquito Commission Laboratory, where he was able to talk with professionals in the field.

Bob Bonnet & Dan Keen

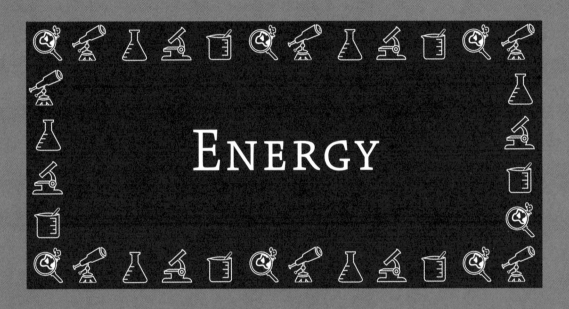

ENERGY

INTRODUCTION TO
ENERGY

Welcome to the fascinating world of energy! This section explores projects in energy and the physics of energy. The term "energy" is difficult to give a meaning to, since it is found in many forms and is closely linked to "forces" (magnetism, gravity, wind, etc.). Physicists define energy as the ability to do work, and they define "work" as the ability to move an object over a distance.

Forms of energy include solar, mechanical, chemical, electrical, moving fluids (both gases and liquids, etc.), heat, light, sound, pressure, thermal, nuclear, electromagnetic waves, respiration (living things get energy from foods, and muscles do work), and the forces of weather, gravity, and magnetism.

Energy can be transferred from one object to another; a rolling marble strikes a stationary marble and causes it to start rolling. Energy can be converted from one form to another, such as light energy to heat energy. Albert Einstein is known for the formula $E = mc^2$ he put forth in 1905, stating that matter can be changed into energy and energy into matter.

Energy is said to be either "kinetic" or "potential." Potential energy is "stored-up" energy—something that has the ability to do work. Kinetic energy is the energy of movement, when work is actually being done. Potential energy can be converted into kinetic energy, and vice versa. Energy from sunlight is stored in trees (potential energy), which can be burned in a fireplace to produce heat (kinetic energy). Roll a rock up a hill (using kinetic energy), and set it on the hilltop (potential energy), where, because of gravity, it has the potential to do work (when it falls).

SHRINKING CUBES

CHANGING THE SUN'S LIGHT INTO HEAT ENERGY

PURPOSE Imagine a sunny day at a picnic. You pour a glass of cola soda to drink. Your friend fills a glass with a lemon-lime soda he likes. You both take one ice cube. Which ice cube will last longer?

OVERVIEW Sunlight turns into heat energy. Things that are dark in color absorb more light energy than those that are lighter, so they become hotter. Will the darker soda collect more sunlight and melt the cube faster?

YOU NEED
- 2 same-size clear drinking glasses
- clear-colored soda drink
- dark-colored soda drink
- a table by a sunny window
- 2 sets of same-size ice cubes
- a dark room

HYPOTHESIS Hypothesize that the kind of soda itself (flavor, sweetness) does not affect the melting of the ice cubes.

PROCEDURE Take two same-size clear glasses, fill one with a clear or light-colored soda and one with a dark-colored drink. Fill each glass to the same height, not quite to the top. Place the glasses in a sunny window for a half hour. Then, take two ice cubes of equal size and drop one into each glass. Which of the two ice cubes lasts longer? Why?

To prove that our assumption is correct, do the experiment again. This time, set both glasses of soda in a dark room instead of in the sun. If both ice cubes take the same amount of time to melt, then the sodas had an equal effect on the ice cubes, and our assumption is correct.

Test out other drinks: orange juice, red punch, lemonade, ginger ale. Try carbonated/noncarbonated, diet (sugar substitute)/high sugar, with/without solids (pulp), etc.

RESULTS & CONCLUSION Write down the results of your experiment. Come to a conclusion as to whether or not your hypothesis was correct.

SOMETHING MORE What else about a drink might affect the melting speed of ice cubes? How can you find out if it does?

FROSTY'S SUNSCREEN

WARDING OFF THE SUN'S HEATING RAYS

PURPOSE Will putting a "hat" or kerchief on your snowman's head help shade him from the sun and keep him around longer?

OVERVIEW It's fun to build a snowman and have it stand guard in your yard all winter long. But rising temperatures and the sun's heat are not kind to snowmen. It can quickly make them melt away.

YOU NEED
- a sunny day with snow on the ground
- large black plastic bag
- large white plastic bag

HYPOTHESIS Hypothesize that either the bag color will affect the melting, or that it will not have an affect on the melting.

PROCEDURE On a sunny day when there is snow on the ground, build two identical snowmen. Fold a large black plastic (trash) bag into a kerchief or hat and place or tie it on the head of one snowman. You might need to use snow or small twigs to help hold it in place.

Fold a large white plastic bag as you did the black bag and place it on the head of the other snowman. Again, keep it in place by tying or using snow or small twigs.

As the day goes by, check each snowman to see if there has been any melting. If so, which one's head shows the most melting?

RESULTS & CONCLUSION Write down the results of your experiment. Come to a conclusion as to whether or not your hypothesis was correct.

SOMETHING MORE Plastic bags often come in other colors—blue, red, and green, for example. Would using these colors as hats make any difference in keeping a snowman around longer? Would using no kerchief make a difference? (If there's not enough snow available to make several large, whole snowmen, just make large snowball "heads" and wrap same-size sections of the different-colored bags on them for this experiment.)

GETTING STEAMED

WATER VAPOR PUT TO WORK

PURPOSE To learn about steam energy.

OVERVIEW Steam is water changed into a gas by heat energy. We use the energy of steam to do many things. Steam has been used to power boats and trains. Steam turbines generate electricity when steam pressure pushes against blades or paddles connected to a shaft and turns the shaft. On the other end of the shaft is an electrical generator.

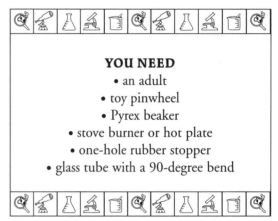

YOU NEED
- an adult
- toy pinwheel
- Pyrex beaker
- stove burner or hot plate
- one-hole rubber stopper
- glass tube with a 90-degree bend

HYPOTHESIS Hypothesize that creating steam, heat energy, will in turn create mechanical energy.

PROCEDURE Get a Pyrex beaker, a one-hole rubber stopper, and a glass tube with a 90-degree, or right-angle, bend. These items can be purchased inexpensively at a science store or borrowed from your science teacher at school.

Never work around a hot stove without an adult with you. Be very careful! The stove burner, the beaker, and the escaping steam will be hot. Do not touch them!

Pour some water into the beaker. Insert the rubber stopper in the top; then ask an adult to gently push one end of the bent glass tube through the hole in the stopper.

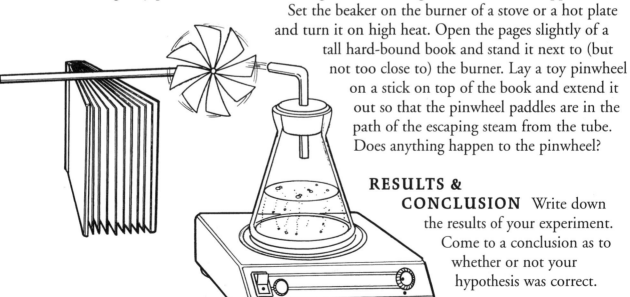

Set the beaker on the burner of a stove or a hot plate and turn it on high heat. Open the pages slightly of a tall hard-bound book and stand it next to (but not too close to) the burner. Lay a toy pinwheel on a stick on top of the book and extend it out so that the pinwheel paddles are in the path of the escaping steam from the tube. Does anything happen to the pinwheel?

RESULTS & CONCLUSION Write down the results of your experiment. Come to a conclusion as to whether or not your hypothesis was correct.

HOT STUFF

HEAT ENERGY FROM DECOMPOSITION

PURPOSE Can grass clippings be of any use?

OVERVIEW Heat energy is given off when organic things (material that was once alive) decay. Many people who plant gardens have "compost piles" to make fertilizer for feeding the garden. A compost pile is a small area, often boxed, filled with dead or dying plant and animal leavings such as peels and scraps from the kitchen, fallen leaves, grass clippings, manure, hay, and other things that rot. The material is stacked and allowed to decay for months, as it turns into rich fertilizer. As it decays, heat is given off.

YOU NEED
- freshly mowed grass clippings
- a warm, sunny day
- lawn rake
- clock or watch

HYPOTHESIS Hypothesize that the longer grass clippings are out in the sun, the more heat energy they will give off.

PROCEDURE When your lawn or your neighbor's lawn is mowed, gather some grass clippings by using a lawn rake. Make a pile of grass clippings 1 foot (30 cm) high and about 1 foot (30 cm) in diameter. Place the pile on the lawn in a bright, sunny spot. Let it sit in the sunlight.

 After two hours, use the rake to make another pile of grass clippings and place it next to the first one. Both piles should be the same size. Wait ten minutes. Then push one hand into the middle of each pile. Does the inside of one pile feel warmer than the other? If so, which pile feels warmer, the one you just raked or the one that has been sitting in the sunlight for two hours?

RESULTS & CONCLUSION Write down the results of your experiment. Come to a conclusion as to whether or not your hypothesis was correct.

SOMETHING MORE Do you think grass clippings can be used to make a good habitat or nest for some animals?

BOTTLED GAS

STORED CHEMICAL ENERGY (CO₂) IN SODA

PURPOSE To find out what happens when you pour a carbonated soda into a glass slowly. What happens when you pour fast?

OVERVIEW Carbon dioxide (CO_2) is a colorless gas. Humans and animals breathe out carbon dioxide. It is also formed when things made of carbon, such as charcoal, wood, and coal, are burned.

Energy is used by the food industry to dissolve carbon dioxide into water; this adds the fizz to carbonated soda drinks. As long as the soda bottle remains unopened or the opened soda is kept tightly capped, the carbon dioxide stays dissolved. But as soon as the cap is taken off the bottle, the carbon dioxide starts to expand and escape (this is chemical energy).

HYPOTHESIS Hypothesize that the release of carbon dioxide is what makes the bubbles in soda, and gives it a foamy head.

PROCEDURE We can see if there is energy being released by making the expanding carbon dioxide do work.

First, stretch a balloon several times in all directions. Blow it up as big as it will go, then let all the air out. Doing this will make the balloon easier to inflate.

Open a bottle of carbonated soda (read the label if you aren't sure whether the drink is carbonated). Remove the cap and stretch the opening of the balloon over the mouth of the bottle. Carefully, shake the bottle to release carbon dioxide from the soda. What happens to the balloon?

RESULTS & CONCLUSIONS Write down the results of your experiment. Come to a conclusion as to whether or not your hypothesis was correct.

SOMETHING MORE Do you have an unopened bottle of soda that has been stored for a long time? Put the balloon over its mouth when you do open it. Does the balloon inflate? What does that tell you about the CO_2 in the soda, and the plastic container or tightness of its cap?

ROLLING STOCK

POTENTIAL ENERGY, MASS, AND GRAVITY

PURPOSE If two objects are raised to the same height, which has more energy stored in it (required more energy to move), the lighter object (less mass) or the heavier one (more mass)?

OVERVIEW Energy used to move an object up to a height is stored in the object as "potential energy" because gravity pulls downward on the object and will cause it to move.

HYPOTHESIS The bottle with more mass will store more energy.

YOU NEED
- 2 two-liter plastic soda bottles
- books
- ruler
- 2 boards, about 1 × 4 feet (30 × 122 cm)
- water
- an adult

PROCEDURE Stack several books on the floor, making two piles the same height, about 1 foot (30 cm) tall. Make two ramps by propping one end of each long board up on a stack. Shelf boards work well if you have them; if not, have an adult help you find two same-size boards, or cut two boards from a section of plywood.

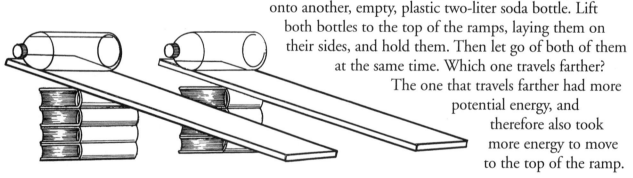

Fill a plastic two-liter soda bottle with water and screw the cap on tightly. Screw the cap onto another, empty, plastic two-liter soda bottle. Lift both bottles to the top of the ramps, laying them on their sides, and hold them. Then let go of both of them at the same time. Which one travels farther? The one that travels farther had more potential energy, and therefore also took more energy to move to the top of the ramp.

RESULTS & CONCLUSION Write down the results of your experiment. Come to a conclusion as to whether or not your hypothesis was correct.

SOMETHING MORE The bottle that travels farther also has more "momentum." Momentum is a force that moves an object. It is the product of mass times velocity. The bottle filled with water has more mass than the empty one. Now, why do you think it is hard to stop a moving train quickly?

A ramp is an "inclined plane," a type of simple machine. Research inclined planes.

STORMY WEATHER

DETECTING THE ENERGY RELEASE OF STORMS

PURPOSE Storms happen all the time; what force is behind a storm?

YOU NEED
- a storm
- pencil and paper
- AM radio

OVERVIEW Tremendous amounts of energy are released every minute around the world by the earth's weather system. Lightning, wind, hurricanes, and tornadoes are powerful energy producers. It is said that lightning strikes somewhere on earth 100 times each second! A lightning bolt is thought to release as much as 100 million volts of electricity, with the bolt reaching a temperature as high as 50,000° Fahrenheit (27,760° Celsius).

HYPOTHESIS A storm will release a lot of energy which can affect the radio.

PROCEDURE Next time it storms, look out your windows.* Make a list of evidence that energy is being released by the storm. Remember, energy "works" (the ability to move something over a distance). So, what do you see: trees moving, leaves stirring, the flag and rope on a flagpole whipping around, sand blowing, a clothesline jiggling, a can rolling noisily down the street, or paper flying through the air? Is smoke from chimneys rising straight up, or bending or scattering? Are there fierce-looking waves on a large, nearby lake? Is sea water spraying from the tops of rough ocean waves?

If it is raining, is the rain falling straight down or at an angle? What is happening when the rain hits the ground? Is a heavy rain causing streams down streets and across yards? Is there evidence of erosion—soil being pushed by the moving water?

Open a window a bit and listen. Write down the sounds of energy release. Do you hear the wailing of the wind? If it is a thunderstorm, do you see lightning and hear the crash of thunder that follows? Using your AM radio, can you detect the crackle and static of radio frequency energy released by the lightning?

RESULTS & CONCLUSION Write down the results of your experiment. Come to a conclusion as to whether or not your hypothesis was correct.

*Storms can be dangerous. Make your observations from the safety and comfort of your home. If lightning is *nearby*, do not use the telephone, and move away from windows.

BRICK TRICK

TRANSFER OF HEAT ENERGY IN A SOLID

PURPOSE Can heat move through solid matter?

HYPOTHESIS Heat energy can be transferred, or move *through* an object or *from* one object to another.

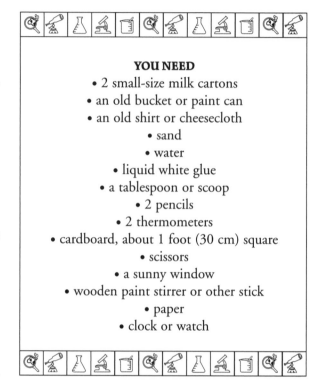

YOU NEED
- 2 small-size milk cartons
- an old bucket or paint can
- an old shirt or cheesecloth
- sand
- water
- liquid white glue
- a tablespoon or scoop
- 2 pencils
- 2 thermometers
- cardboard, about 1 foot (30 cm) square
- scissors
- a sunny window
- wooden paint stirrer or other stick
- paper
- clock or watch

PROCEDURE Lay two empty small-size (pint) milk cartons on their side, with the spout openings facing upward. With scissors, carefully cut the top side off each carton. The cartons will serve as molds to make two bricks.

First, using the cartons as measuring containers, fill one and a half pint cartons with sand and pour it into an old bucket or paint can. Add 6 ounces (¾ cup) of liquid white glue and 2 ounces (¼ cup) of water. Mix thoroughly. Then spoon the mixture into an old shirt or a large piece of cheesecloth, and squeeze out any excess water. Place the mixture into each milk-carton mold. In each one, push a pencil halfway into the brick, near one end, and leave it there.

Place the bricks in a sunny window for a few days, until they harden. Roll the pencils that are in the bricks between your fingers a few times as the bricks dry, so the pencils will be easier to remove later. When the bricks are dry and hard, take the pencils out of the bricks. Put a thermometer in each hole left by the pencils.

In a room that has a sunny window, place one brick near the window, where it can get sunlight. Position it so that the end that has the thermometer stuck in it is away from the window. Cut a piece of cardboard to fit over the brick, making a sunshield, so that the front half of the brick is in sunlight but the back half is in shade. Place the other brick on a table in the same room, but away from the sunlight.

RESULTS & CONCLUSION Read and write down the temperatures showing on both thermometers. Every five minutes, read and write down the temperatures again. After one hour, compare the temperatures you recorded for both bricks.

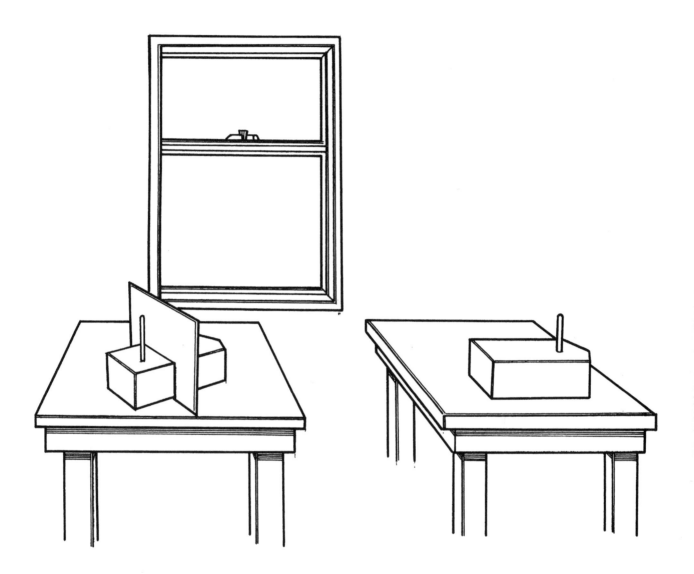

SOMETHING MORE

1. Did the one in the sunny window show a warmer temperature?
2. Did heat from the sunny side of the brick travel through the brick to the other end?
3. What was the "rate of heat transfer," that is, how fast did the heat move through the brick (one degree every five minutes, two degrees every five minutes, three degrees every five minutes . . .)?

SAILS ALOFT

USING WIND ENERGY TO POWER A BOAT

PURPOSE To explore how different designs affect a sailboat.

OVERVIEW From mankind's early days, sails have been used on boats to harness the energy of the wind. Let's make small sailboats, using quart-size milk cartons, and experiment with different shapes and sizes of sails.

HYPOTHESIS The type of sail will affect how a sailboat moves.

PROCEDURE Lay an empty quart milk carton on its side, with the spout-opening upward. With scissors, cut off

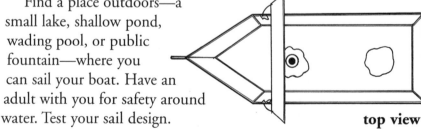

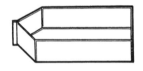

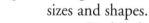

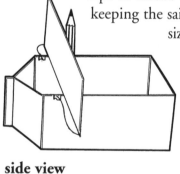

YOU NEED
- stiff paper
- thread
- pencils
- modeling clay
- string
- scissors
- quart milk cartons
- adhesive tape
- body of shallow water
- an adult

the top half of the carton lengthwise to make a boat.

Near the front (pointed end), place a small mound of modeling clay. To make a mast, push the eraser end of a pencil into the clay. A small amount of clay may be needed near the back of the boat to keep the boat balanced. Tape a 1-foot-long (30 cm) piece of string onto the back of the boat so it will drag in the water (this will help hold the boat on course).

Cut a sail out of a piece of paper and tape it to the pencil mast. You may need tape or thread to hold the bottom ends of the paper to the sides of the boat, keeping the sail tight in strong winds. Make several boats using sails of different sizes and shapes.

Find a place outdoors—a small lake, shallow pond, wading pool, or public fountain—where you can sail your boat. Have an adult with you for safety around water. Test your sail design.

side view

top view

RESULTS & CONCLUSION Which sail design do you think will make the boats go fastest? Write down the results of your experiment. Come to a conclusion as to whether or not your hypothesis was correct.

SALT OR NOT?

COMPARING SOLAR ENERGY STORAGE IN SALT AND FRESH WATER

PURPOSE Does the ability of water to hold the heat energy it has collected differ if the water is salt water or fresh water? Does a saltwater lake cool differently than a freshwater lake when the sun sets?

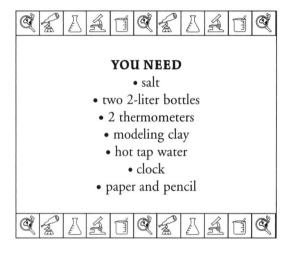

YOU NEED
- salt
- two 2-liter bottles
- 2 thermometers
- modeling clay
- hot tap water
- clock
- paper and pencil

OVERVIEW Compared to air, water is slow to change temperature. If the weather has been hot for a few days, and the water in a swimming pool is warm, one night of cooler temperatures will not change the temperature in the pool very much. It will still be almost as warm the next day.

HYPOTHESIS Hypothesize that either saltwater or freshwater will retain heat more, or that there will be no effect of the salt in the water.

PROCEDURE Fill two 2-liter soda bottles with equally hot water from your kitchen sink (let it run a bit until you get a constant temperature). Add eight teaspoons of salt to one bottle. Stir to dissolve the salt thoroughly.

Instead of screwing the caps on, lightly place a ball of modeling clay over the mouth of each bottle. Carefully push a thermometer into the bottle through the clay, so that the bulb of the thermometer is in the water. Make sure you can read the temperature on the thermometer, then press the clay against the thermometer to hold it in place. Do this to both bottles.

RESULTS & CONCLUSION Every ten minutes, read the thermometers and write down the temperature readings. After two hours, compare the temperatures you recorded. Did they both lose heat energy at the same rate?

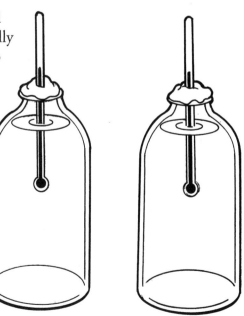

THINGS ARE HEATING UP

GRAPHING SOLAR ENERGY COLLECTION IN MATERIALS

PURPOSE & OVERVIEW As the sun beats down on the earth, heat energy is absorbed by everything on the surface. What gathers more of the sun's heat energy: air, water, sand, or stone?

HYPOTHESIS Which do you believe gathers more of the sun's heat energy?

PROCEDURE Find four large glasses or, using scissors, carefully cut the top half off four clear 2-liter plastic bottles. (Place the discarded tops in a recyclables trash container.) Stand a ruler upright on a table alongside the container (glass or bottle bottom). Four inches (10 cm) above the table surface, mark the container using a small strip

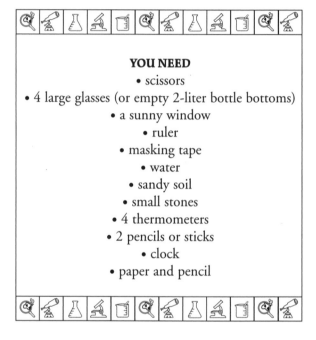

YOU NEED
- scissors
- 4 large glasses (or empty 2-liter bottle bottoms)
- a sunny window
- ruler
- masking tape
- water
- sandy soil
- small stones
- 4 thermometers
- 2 pencils or sticks
- clock
- paper and pencil

of adhesive tape. Place the top of the tape at the 4-inch height. Do this for all four containers, then write the contents of each container on the tape (air, water, sand or soil, stones). The tape will serve as both a label and the fill-to mark for the containers.

Leave one container empty ("filled" with air). Fill another to the 4-inch mark with water. Fill a third up to the mark with sandy soil. The bulb of each thermometer must be placed, hanging, in the middle of each container, not touching the sides or bottom. For the containers of air and water, suspend the thermometers by placing a section of tape at the top of the thermometer and over a pencil or stick placed across the top of a container. The thermometer bulb should be hanging about 2 inches (5 cm) from the bottom of the container. Carefully push a thermometer down partway into the sandy soil. For the fourth container, hold a thermometer inside the container with one hand so that the bulb is 2 inches (5 cm) below the fill line. With the other hand, gently place small stones, about ½ to 1 inch (1–2.5 cm) in diameter, up to the container's fill line.

Set the four containers in a sunny window. After one hour, measure the temperature of each material by reading the thermometers. Write down the temperature readings and compare them.

Take all four containers out of the sunny window and place them somewhere in the room that is out of direct sunlight. Every five minutes for thirty minutes, read the temperatures on the thermometers and write them down in a list. Thirty minutes later, after an hour has passed, record the final temperature readings. Which container lost heat the fastest? Which material continued to give off heat the longest? Was this also the same material that gathered the most heat?

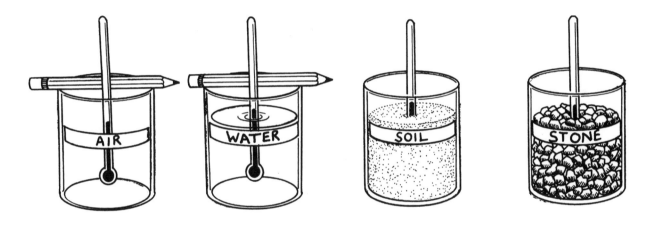

RESULTS & CONCLUSION For your project display, make up four simple graphs; see sample for Air. Across the top (X-axis) put in the time of the readings (every 5 minutes). List temperatures going down the chart (Y-axis). Then enter your own time—temperature readings of each tested material on its chart. Come to a conclusion as to whether or not your hypothesis was correct.

WANT, HELP, NEED

CATEGORIZING HOME ELECTRICAL APPLIANCES

PURPOSE To examine the energy usage of our homes.

OVERVIEW Many appliances in our homes or apartments save us work and make our lives healthier, happier, and easier. But it also takes energy to run them, usually electrical energy.

YOU NEED
• paper and pencil

HYPOTHESIS Hypothesize that many things in our homes require energy to run them.

PROCEDURE Making up a list, search through each room of your home and look for things that use electrical energy (the refrigerator in the kitchen, a hair dryer in the bedroom, lamps in the den, a TV set in the living room). Be sure to include such things as smoke alarms, flashlights, and portable radios, which work off electrical energy stored in batteries.

Once your list is complete, think about each item on your list, and decide if that energy-user is a *want* (you like and want it), a *help* (makes your life easier), or a *need* (necessary in your household).

A need is something that you really must have in order to have a healthy, safe, and working home. If your home is not connected to your city's water system, you probably have a well. In that case, an electric water pump would be necessary to you, supplying water for cooking, cleaning, washing, and personal hygiene.

Consider a help to be something in your home that it is good to have, but that you could do without if you had to. A flashlight would be something you would put in the help category. It's handy to have one in your home in case there is an electric

power failure, which might happen during a storm, but day to day you could live without it.

A want is something we have in our home simply because we like it. Usually its purpose is to make our life more enjoyable. A video game may be very entertaining, but it is not necessary to our health or survival.

Some items may fall under a different category for different homes. Although a telephone answering machine is usually just a convenience (a want), if someone is running a business in the home, an answering machine may be more of a help or even a necessity, or important business calls could be lost.

Don't forget to check outside your home, too. See if there are any energy-using devices in your yard, such as a swimming-pool pump or security lighting, that should be added to your list.

RESULTS & CONCLUSION Write down the results of your experiment. Come to a conclusion as to whether or not your hypothesis was correct.

YESTERDAY'S ENERGY

CONSERVING FOSSIL FUELS

PURPOSE Are there simple ways that we can help conserve energy in our homes?

YOU NEED
• paper and pencil

OVERVIEW Fossil fuels are sources of energy that we find within the earth. We release the energy from such fuels as oil, coal, and natural gas by burning them. These fossil fuels are the remains of animal life and vegetation (energy in the form of trapped sunlight) that have been within the earth for millions of years. At the current rate, we are using up our resources of fossil fuels faster than the earth can make more. Unless we use these fuels more wisely, we will someday run out.

Is your home heated by the burning of fossil fuels? You can save natural gas or heating oil by not letting heat escape through open or drafty doors or windows in cold weather. Can you reduce the need for heating by trapping some of the sun's warming solar energy indoors?

The gasoline that cars run on is made from fossil fuels, so automobile manufacturers are always working to make their cars more fuel-efficient. By driving more slowly and not using cars as much when they don't need to, car owners can help conserve gasoline, too.

How else can we help save fossil fuels? Many electrical power plants make electricity by burning fossil fuels. Are there electrical energy-users you could do *without* to help save electricity?

HYPOTHESIS Little changes could be made in our daily routine to help conserve energy without making our lives hard.

PROCEDURE On a sheet of paper, make a list of appliances that use electricity, such as a hair dryer, electric toothbrush, air conditioner, and a clock. In a second column beside the appliance, write down ideas for doing the same task without using electricity. In a third column, note whether the energy-saving way would be "a little inconvenient," "very inconvenient," or "a real hardship."

RESULTS & CONCLUSION Write down the results of your experiment. Come to a conclusion as to whether or not your hypothesis was correct.

SOMETHING MORE Are there other things to consider about energy usage? You might think of replacing a 100-watt bulb with a 60-watt bulb to save energy. But if the bulb lights the cellar stairway, would it be bright enough to make going down the stairway safe?

ONE IF BY LAND

COMPARING LAND AND WATER SOLAR-HEAT STORAGE

PURPOSE What loses heat faster—a body of water or the land near it?

OVERVIEW The sun warms our planet. As the earth turns and night falls, the surface the sun has warmed begins to cool, radiating the heat energy absorbed during the day.

HYPOTHESIS Hypothesize that either the body of water or the body of land will lose heat faster.

YOU NEED
- string
- 2 thermometers
- long pointed stick
- body of water
- a sunny day
- pencil and paper
- an adult

PROCEDURE Find a lake, pond, or large swimming pool. *Note:* Always have an adult with you for safety when you are working around deep water.

Tie string to each thermometer. At the end of a sunny day (about 5:00 p.m.), poke a hole 1 to 2 feet deep (30–61 cm) into the ground near a body of water with a long stick. A stake from a game of horseshoes or croquet works best. Lower one thermometer into the hole and tie the other end of the string to the stake. Then, hold the other thermometer in the water. Several minutes later, pull up both thermometers and read and record the temperatures.

RESULTS & CONCLUSION Take temperature readings every hour as the sun goes down and record your measurements on a chart. Compare the changes in temperature over time. Which lost heat faster, the land or the water? How do you think this affects the night temperatures of a town located at the edge of a large body of water? Were water and land both heated to the same temperature when you took the first reading?

TESTING THE WATERS

AN INVESTIGATION OF SOLAR HEAT DISTRIBUTION

PURPOSE Does the water in a small lake evenly distribute the sun's heat energy, so that the temperature of surface water is the same as the water several feet down?

OVERVIEW It is easy to take a lake's temperature near the shoreline. All you need to do is place a thermometer into the water at the edge of the lake. To read the real temperature of the lake's surface and some distance below is harder. The thermometers should be placed near the middle of the lake, or at least well out into it, not near the shore. This can be done without going out in a boat or into the water by constructing a small "boat" from wood, with one thermometer hanging below it and dragging a second, floating, thermometer off the back or stern of the boat.

> **YOU NEED**
> - thumbtacks or nails
> - 6-inch-long (15 cm) piece of wood (1 × 2 or 2 × 4)
> - fishing rod and reel
> - string
> - a thermometer
> - a thermometer that floats (an aquarium thermometer)
> - metal washers
> - a lake or pond
> - paper and pencil
> - an adult

HYPOTHESIS Hypothesize, or guess, which you think will be warmer, the water on the surface of a small lake, the water several feet down, or the water at the edge, along the shoreline.

PROCEDURE First, find a standard-size piece of wood about 6 inches long (15 cm) to serve as the boat that will tow the heat-measuring instruments. Tie a long piece of string to the regular thermometer and fasten the other end to the boat, using a thumbtack or nail. The thermometer should hang down at least 2 feet (61 cm) from the wooden boat. Tie a short piece of string to the thermometer that floats. Fasten the other end of the string to the boat also. Floating thermometers are often used in fish tanks and can be found at aquarium supply stores or pet shops.

Now that you are ready, ask an adult to take you and all your equipment to a nearby pond or lake and stand by to help with this experiment.

First, you need to find out the temperature of the lake at the shoreline. Bending carefully on the shore of the lake, place the thermometer in the water. Wait about three minutes to give the thermometer a chance to reach the proper temperature. Then remove the thermometer and immediately read and write down the temperature that it is registering.

To get the wooden boat out into the lake, lay it securely on the beach at the edge of the water or have your helper hold it there. Fasten the end of a fishing line from a fishing pole to the boat with a thumbtack. Slowly let out the line as you walk around the shore of the lake. (A helper could hold the boat and release it at your signal, when you get into position on the other side.) Carefully reel in the fishing line, dragging the boat and its "instruments" to a spot near the middle of the lake (or at least to a spot where the water is deep). Wait three or four minutes to allow the thermometers to properly change temperature. Then, reel the boat in as quickly as you can, and read the thermometers. The thermometers must be read before they begin to change temperature. The shoreline where you stand to reel in the boat should have sandy or a soft bottom, because quickly dragging the thermometers over a rocky bottom might break them.

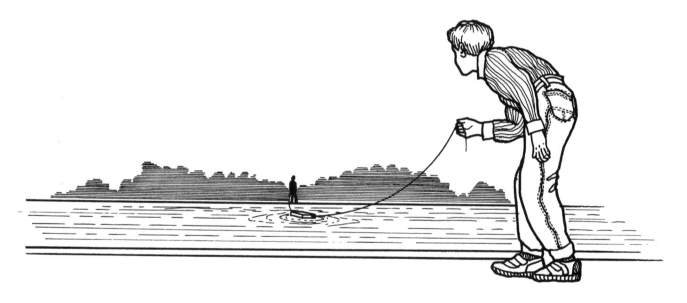

RESULTS & CONCLUSION Write down the results of your experiment. Come to a conclusion as to whether or not your hypothesis was correct.

OUR TOWN

TRANSFORMING AND TRANSPORTING ENERGY

PURPOSE The light that comes from the lamp you read by in the evening is the result of energy changing forms several times and being transported over a great distance.

OVERVIEW It all starts at a power plant. Energy from one of several sources is converted into electricity. Some plants burn fossil fuels (coal, oil, or natural gas), converting the solar energy stored in those fuels into heat. The heat is used to make steam that turns the shaft of generators (mechanical energy) to make electricity. Hydroelectric power plants use running water to turn the generators. Nuclear power plants harness radiation energy to make heat for steam generators.

YOU NEED
- miniature 6-volt hobby lamps (bulbs)
- lamp sockets
- hookup wire
- jumper leads with alligator clip ends
- 6-volt lantern battery with spring-top connectors
- modeling clay
- flat sticks (from ice-cream bars) or strong straws
- glue or tape
- toy buildings used for model train layouts
- wire cutters or scissors
- screwdriver

PROCEDURE You can show how energy can be changed from one form to another, transported over a distance, and then changed into another form of energy. The network of electric wiring in your community

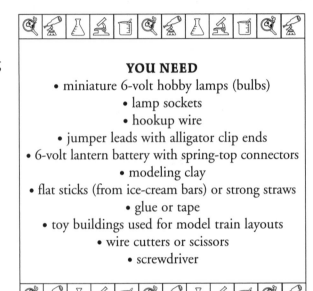

Schematic Diagram

6-volt battery

lamp

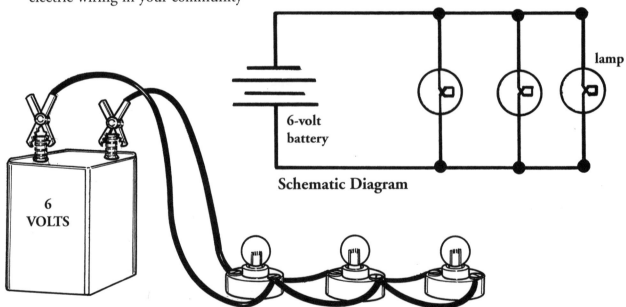

6 VOLTS

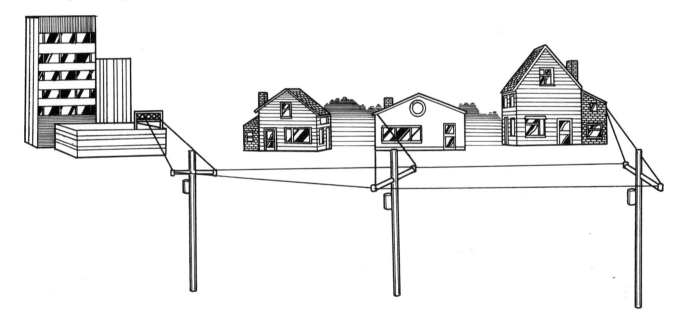

is a perfect example. Build a model town to demonstrate this process. Use a 6-volt lantern battery to represent the electric power plant, where one form of energy is turned into another. (In the case of the battery, chemical energy inside it converts to electrical energy.) With hookup wire, connect three miniature (hobby) lamp sockets together.

Glue or tape flat sticks, or strong straws, together to form a cross or "T" shape These will serve as telephone poles. Make several of these "poles." Push each pole into a lump of modeling clay to hold it upright. Using the appropriate tool, cut a small notch in the top of each telephone pole arm. Place the hookup wire in the notches to hold them in place.

Using houses from a model-train or other set (or making your own out of cardboard), position them to form a small town. Put a lamp in each house to light it. The telephone poles should be positioned to run the wires from the battery and to the lamps in each home.

Energy is changed once again when it reaches each lamp. There, it is converted into light energy to illuminate the model homes, as it is in your own.

RESULTS & CONCLUSION Write down the different forms of energy along the circuit. Research and report on these different forms.

POWER RANGER

MEASURING HOME ELECTRICAL ENERGY USAGE

PURPOSE How much electrical energy does your home use in one day?

YOU NEED
- access to your home's electric meter
- paper and pencil

OVERVIEW Electric power is measured in units called "watts." You've probably heard someone ask for a 40-, or 60-, or 100-watt bulb to change a burned-out light bulb. The number indicates how much electric power the bulb uses to reach full brightness. (Which do you think is brighter, a 60-watt or 100-watt bulb? Which uses more power?)

Every month, the electric company bills people for the amount of electricity they used. Electrical usage is measured in "kilowatt-hours." One kilowatt equals 1,000 watts. One kilowatt-hour is 1,000 watts of electric power being used for one hour. It takes one kilowatt-hour of energy to operate ten 100-watt light bulbs for one hour.

HYPOTHESIS Hypothesize how much electrical usage your home uses in one day.

PROCEDURE Find the electric meter for your home (usually outside, where someone from the power company can find and read it easily). The meter's face has dials on it, marked with numbers. The dials, reading from right to left, show the ones, tens, hundreds, and then the thousands places. When a dial needle is between two numbers, it is the lower number that is read (a needle between 2 and 3 is read as 2).

Before school, read the numbers on the electric meter dials and write them down. The next day, at the same time, read the numbers again and record them. Subtract the second day's numbers from the first reading to find out how many kilowatt-hours of energy your home used over that 24-hour period.

Make a list of the appliances in your home that use electricity from the power company. Saving energy is good for the environment and will save your family money on the monthly electric bill, too. How do you think you can use the appliances on your list more wisely to save energy in your home?

RESULTS & CONCLUSION Write down the results of your experiment. Come to a conclusion as to whether or not your hypothesis was correct.

FOOD ENERGY

THE FUEL OF LIVING THINGS

PURPOSE Where do we get our energy?

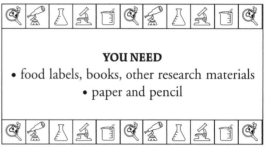

YOU NEED
- food labels, books, other research materials
- paper and pencil

OVERVIEW For the human body to function, it needs energy. The energy for our bodies comes from the food we eat. Energy from foods is measured in units called calories. Our body changes the calories in the food we eat into energy to grow, maintain itself (stay well), and allow us to use our muscles to do work. In cold weather, the body needs more calories to do its work and also keep us warm.

A person who isn't going to drive very far doesn't need much gas in the car. But for a long trip, a car needs plenty of fuel. In the same way, a person who works at a desk and is not very active will not need as many calories as someone who mixes concrete and carries heavy cement blocks around all day. Some people cut down on the number of calories they eat in order to lose weight. When more calories are taken in than the body needs, it stores the rest as fat, causing the body to gain weight. Fat in the body is stored energy, but too much is not a good thing.

HYPOTHESIS Hypothesize that you eat a healthy number of calories in a single day.

PROCEDURE How many calories do you normally consume a day? For one day, list all the foods you eat—don't forget those between-meal snacks!—and how much. Look up how many calories there are in each food and make up a chart. Boxes of cereal and other foods list the number of calories *per serving*—notice the number of servings per box. Books list the calories in different foods, such as: a ¼ lb. hamburger patty, 224 calories; an orange, 50; ½ cup green beans, 15; an 8 ounce glass of milk, 150; a 6 ounce serving of ice cream, 290; one small chocolate chip cookie, 50.

RESULTS & CONCLUSION Total up the number of calories you ate during that one day. Research how many calories a day are healthy for a person of your age and weight. Are you getting too many calories? Are you not eating enough to maintain a healthy body?

SOMETHING MORE How could you change your eating habits to cut down or raise the number of calories in your diet and still enjoy what you like?

WHEN TO SAY WHEN

MEASURING THE ENERGY (CALORIE) VALUE OF FOODS

PURPOSE & OVERVIEW Our bodies convert the food we eat into energy (see the previous project, Food Energy). Food energy is measured in calories. We need a certain number of calories as fuel for our bodies, but taking in more calories than we need causes a person to gain weight.

YOU NEED
• research materials

HYPOTHESIS Hypothesize which foods are high in calories and which you think are low.

PROCEDURE Compare the number of calories in plain foods to the same type of foods that have sugar or something else added to them or are served in a different form. For example, compare the number of calories in a serving of popcorn to a serving of buttered popcorn. Compare the number of calories in a potato to a serving of french fries (or potato chips). Compare the calories in different candy bars that have the same weight. Compare the calories in a serving of peanuts to a serving of honey-roasted peanuts; a serving of whole milk with a serving of chocolate milk. Which foods have more calories?

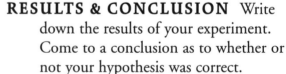

RESULTS & CONCLUSION Write down the results of your experiment. Come to a conclusion as to whether or not your hypothesis was correct.

SOMETHING MORE What ingredients added in the cooking or processing of the foods increase the number of calories in them? By how much—a little, or a lot? According to a published health chart, listing calorie needs for your age and weight, are there some foods you should avoid, or of which you should limit your intake?

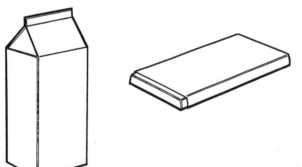

SWEET SEARCH

AN EXAMINATION OF SUGAR,
THE HIGH-ENERGY FOOD

PURPOSE Foods sweetened with sugar do taste good! Unfortunately, too much sugar hurts our body's ability to use certain vitamins. It makes people gain weight, and causes tooth decay. Some children become hyperactive— that is, they can't sit still—when they take in too much sugar.

YOU NEED
- a trip to the supermarket
- paper and pencil

OVERVIEW Sugar comes in many different forms: sucrose, glucose (dextrose), fructose (found in fruits), lactose (found in milk), and maltose.

HYPOTHESIS Hypothesize which cereals you think will be higher in sugar.

PROCEDURE Look at the labels on cereal boxes and compare the number of calories per serving of cereals that are sugar-coated to those that are not. Usually, the ingredient that is contained in the cereal in the biggest proportion is listed first. Is the number-one ingredient usually sugar, or some form of sugar, in those cereals that are sugar-coated? Which cereals, sugar-coated or non-sugar-coated, do you think are better for your body?

RESULTS & CONCLUSION Make a comparison chart showing the cereal's name, the number of calories per serving, and the amount of sugar per serving. Then make a chart comparing calories and sugar per serving of other foods that come in boxes and cans. Come to a conclusion as to whether or not your hypothesis was correct.

SOMETHING MORE Not all labels will list the word "sugar" in the ingredients, even if there is sugar in it, because, as we said, sugar comes in different forms. Research the different kinds of sugar found in our foods. For example, "high fructose corn syrup," a type of sugar, may be one ingredient listed on the label of a can of pork and beans.

THE RIGHT STUFF

SEEDS STORE ENOUGH FOOD ENERGY FOR GERMINATION

PURPOSE If you were traveling on foot for a long period of time, you would carry a backpack. In the backpack you would store all the food you needed to get you to the next camp, where you could replenish your food supply. Now let's see what plants do to store energy.

YOU NEED
- 3 different types of seeds (vegetable or flower)
- potting soil
- a dark place (a closet or basement)
- water
- 3 small containers (plastic drinking cups, etc.)
- masking tape
- paper and pencil

OVERVIEW In the same way, seeds store just enough energy to be able to grow a root and a leaf. Once a seed has formed a root to gather water and nutrients from the soil and a leaf to collect sunlight, it can begin to make food on its own. The process of a plant making its food by gathering the light energy from the sun is called photosynthesis. Also needed in the process are carbon dioxide, water, chlorophyll (which gives leaves their green color), and very small amounts of minerals. The time from when a seed begins to sprout a root and a leaf (using its own stored energy) until it is able to make food on its own is called germination.

HYPOTHESIS Hypothesize that seeds store enough energy to germinate, but then need sunlight to make food in order to continue to grow and live.

PROCEDURE At your local hardware store or garden center, buy three different packages of seeds and a small bag of potting soil. The seeds can be flower or vegetable seeds.

Fill three small containers with potting soil. Plastic drinking cups or short drinking glasses work well. Get three different kinds of seeds; they can be flower seeds (morning glory, marigold, etc.) or vegetable seeds (radish, lima bean, watercress, etc.). Place a piece of masking tape on the side of each container and on each write the name of the

seeds you are going to plant in the container. Then put five of each kind of seed in their proper container (five seeds are planted in case some do not germinate). Push the seeds about ½ inch (about 1.25 cm) down into the soil.

Place the containers in a dark place (a closet, for example) that is at least as warm as room temperature all the time. Water the seeds every day. Keep the soil moist, but not heavily soaked.

Keep a written log of your observations each day. Write down the date and what you see in each container.

Once leaves appear, the stored food energy in the seeds is just about gone, and the plants are ready to begin making their own food. If the plants are kept in the dark and don't get any light to make new food, how long does it take for them to use up their stored energy and begin to die?

If you keep close watch and provide water and light at the right time, the young plants that start withering for lack of food may begin to start getting food from the soil. If not, plant new seeds and give them TLC (tender, loving care), and you may get to see them thrive.

RESULTS & CONCLUSION Write down the results of your experiment. Come to a conclusion as to whether or not your hypothesis was correct.

IN THE PINK

HOME INSULATION KEEPS HEAT IN AND COLD OUT

PURPOSE When the cold winter winds blow, we need to keep the heat energy from our home's heater inside. How?

OVERVIEW Builders use a material called "insulation" to keep warm air inside in the winter and cool, air-conditioned air inside in the summer. Insulation looks like thick blankets of cotton candy, usually pink or yellow in color. It is placed inside walls, ceilings, and sometimes under the floor.

Home insulation is given an "R-rating," which stands for how good a job that particular kind of insulation does. The higher the R-rating number, the better the insulation is at keeping the temperature on one side of the insulation from changing the temperature on the other.

YOU NEED
- 2 shoe boxes
- adhesive tape
- clear plastic food wrap
- scissors
- 2 thermometers
- modeling clay
- a sunny window
- sheets of Styrofoam
(about ½ inch or 1 cm thick)
paper and pencil

HYPOTHESIS Insulating materials do prevent temperatures on one side from affecting the temperatures on the other side.

PROCEDURE Remove the lid from a shoe box, or tear the flaps off of another box about

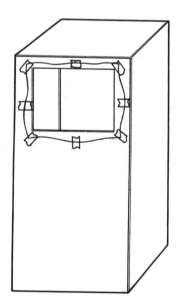
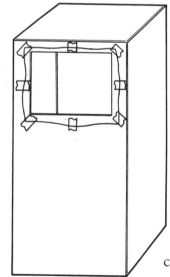

the size of a shoe box. Stand the box upright on one end, so it is tall. With scissors, carefully cut a window in the "front" of the box, as shown. The window should be in the upper ⅓ of the box. Then cover the window by taping a piece of clear plastic food wrap over it. Do the same to a second shoe box.

Turn the boxes around to work on the open "back" side.

Styrofoam is a light, usually white material. It is used for many things, including disposable coffee cups and for packing, so that appliances such as TV sets and microwave ovens are not damaged in shipping. It is also an inexpensive insulating material, which is available in many shapes and sizes at hobby shops and craft stores.

Using adhesive tape or glue, line the bottom half of one shoe box with sections of Styrofoam, covering the three walls and making a "roof."

Inside each shoe box, place a small mound of modeling clay on the bottom. Turn a thermometer upside down and stick it in the clay. Do the same in the other box. The thermometers' bulbs will measure the air temperature inside the boxes.

Cover the open backs of each box with a piece of clear plastic food wrap. Use adhesive tape to make the wrap fit tight.

Place both boxes in a sunny window, with the open "back" side of the boxes facing away from the sunlight. Be sure that the sunlight is not shining directly on the thermometer through the window in the uninsulated box.

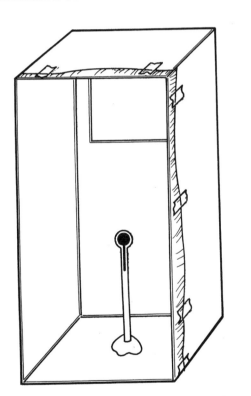
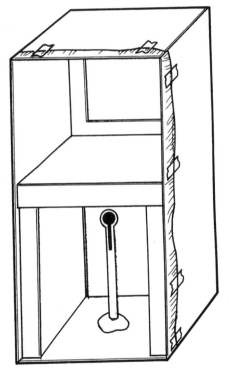

Over a period of one or two hours, take readings and write down the temperature showing on both thermometers every five minutes.

RESULTS & CONCLUSION Write down the results of your experiment. Come to a conclusion as to whether or not your hypothesis was correct. Does the air inside the insulated part of the shoe box stay cooler longer than the air in the uninsulated box?

KEEPING WARM

INSULATING OUR BODIES IN COLD WEATHER

PURPOSE How do our bodies stay warm in the cold?

OVERVIEW In the winter, your body needs more energy to keep you warm. We depend on our clothing to insulate us and keep us from losing our bodily warmth to the cold air when we are outside in bitter weather. What type of clothing material makes a good insulator?

HYPOTHESIS Think about what types of clothing you like to wear in the winter to keep warm. Hypothesize that this type of clothing will insulate you the best.

YOU NEED
- small jar
- several different kinds of material (an old T-shirt, towel, jeans, socks, linen, blanket, sweater)
- clock or watch
- warm tap water
- thermometer
- rubber bands
- scissors
- paper and pencil
- an adult

PROCEDURE Ask an adult to help you gather materials or fabrics to test as insulation. Find as many different kinds as you can. Look through old and worn clothing that are not much use to anyone (ready to be thrown out, not "handed down" or donated). There might already be a bag of rags or scraps stored in a closet. Look over each item for a tag or label that tells what kind of material it is made of. Select several different kinds to test. From each different piece of material, cut a square piece of it large enough to completely wrap around the top, bottom, and sides of a small jar (each piece of material should be the same size).

Turn the hot and cold water faucets on in your kitchen sink, and hold a thermometer in the stream. Adjust the faucets until the water is about body temperature (98.6° Fahrenheit/37° Celsius). Fill the jar with this water. Quickly, stand the thermometer in the jar of water and wrap the jar completely with a piece of material, covering all the sides, bottom, and top. Use rubber bands to hold the material and the thermometer in place—the thermometer sticking up out of the jar.

Every five minutes, read the temperature on the thermometer (pull it up slightly if necessary and then slide it back down). Write the temperature down. Continue to record the temperature until it reaches the temperature of the room.

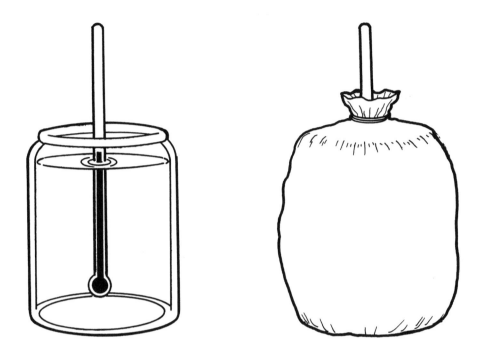

Fill the jar again with body-temperature water, and cover it with a different piece of material. Observe and record the temperature every five minutes until it reaches room temperature. Repeat this procedure for each piece of material you are testing.

(If you have someone to help you, and have more thermometers and same-size jars available, you could test the insulation of several kinds of material simultaneously. Just be sure to keep your records straight when you read the temperatures.)

RESULTS & CONCLUSION Write down the results of your experiment. Come to a conclusion as to whether or not your hypothesis was correct. Which piece of material kept the water warm the longest? Do you know what it is made of? Polyester, rayon, cotton, etc.? Can you find out? Which material do you think would be best for making winter clothes? Which would be the worst?

SHOCK TREATMENT

CAPACITORS AND THE STORAGE OF ELECTRICAL ENERGY

PURPOSE What are capacitors?

OVERVIEW In the field of electronics, capacitors are components that perform many different tasks in an electronic circuit. One thing they do is temporarily store electricity. Unlike a battery, a capacitor must first be "charged up" with electricity.

HYPOTHESIS Hypothesize that you can put together a simple device to show how capacitors work.

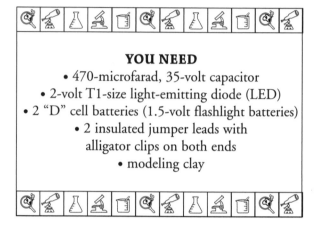

YOU NEED
- 470-microfarad, 35-volt capacitor
- 2-volt T1-size light-emitting diode (LED)
- 2 "D" cell batteries (1.5-volt flashlight batteries)
- 2 insulated jumper leads with alligator clips on both ends
- modeling clay

PROCEDURE Using modeling clay, make a base to hold two 1.5-volt "D" flashlight batteries together. The batteries should be laid down with the positive (+) end of one touching the negative (–) end of the other, just as they would be in a flashlight. The batteries are said to be "in series" with one another. When connected in this way, the total voltage across the two batteries is the sum of each battery: 1.5 volts + 1.5 volts = 3.0 volts.

Connect one end of an insulated jumper lead to one of the leads (wires) coming from a 470-microfarad capacitor. Connect one end of another insulated jumper lead to the other lead coming from the capacitor. Note that batteries have a positive (+) and negative (–) marking on them. Also note that the capacitor has positive and negative markings as well.

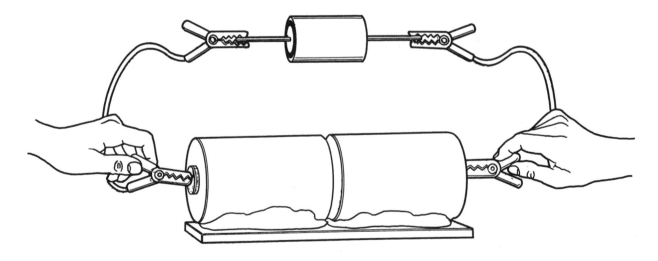

Taking the unconnected ends of the insulated jumper leads, hold the clip connected to the positive terminal on the capacitor to the positive terminal on the battery. Touch the clip connected to the negative terminal on the capacitor to the negative terminal on the battery for about 15 seconds. The capacitor should be charged.

Now touch the leads from the capacitor to the leads of an LED, a light-emitting diode. While the LED does not have + and – markings, it does have + and – leads, and you must match the + lead of the capacitor to the + lead on the LED (and the – lead to the –). You will notice that one side of the LED is a little flatter than the other. The lead that comes from this side is the negative terminal (–).

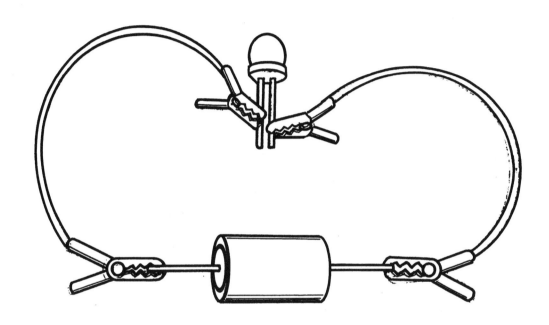

When you touch the capacitor's leads to the LED, the LED will light brightly for about one second. Then, as it quickly uses up the electrical energy stored in the capacitor, you will see the light very quickly grow dimmer.

The ability of a capacitor to store an electrical charge is measured in microfarads, abbreviated UF. Would the LED glow brightly for a longer time if you used a capacitor that was rated at more than 470 microfarads?

RESULTS & CONCLUSION Write down the results of your experiment. Come to a conclusion as to whether or not your hypothesis was correct.

Marble Roll

CONVERTING KINETIC ENERGY INTO POTENTIAL ENERGY

YOU NEED
- marbles
- 2 rulers
- 2 books
- a rug, or carpeted floor
- piece of paper

PURPOSE We can demonstrate the conversion of kinetic energy into potential energy.

OVERVIEW Energy can be transferred from one object to another. "Kinetic energy" is the energy of an object in motion. If an object is moving and it hits another object, its energy is transferred, or handed over to the other object. On a pool table, players hit a ball with a cue stick, giving kinetic (movement) energy to the ball. When the ball rolls into another ball, all or part of this energy is given to the second ball, and the second ball begins to roll. Even though the first ball may stop, the force of kinetic energy continues on in the second ball.

HYPOTHESIS Hypothesize that more energy will be transferred along a non-broken path of balls than a line of balls with gaps.

PROCEDURE Near a rug, or on a floor that has carpeting on it, lay two rulers next to each other, leaving a small space between them. Lay marbles back to back all along the space between the two rulers. Be sure the rulers are close enough together so that the marbles are not touching the floor—but are being held up by the rulers.

At one end of the rulers, open a book to about the middle. Make a ramp out of the open book by propping up the end opposite the rulers with another book.

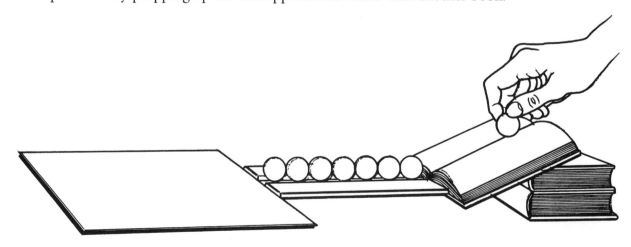

Hold a marble at the top of the ramp. Let go. The force of gravity will give the marble motion energy. When the marble hits the first marble on the rulers, it hands its energy over to that marble. Being up against another marble and unable to move, that marble transfers its energy to the next marble. The energy continues to move from one marble to the next until the last marble is reached. When the energy is given to the last marble, it begins to roll, because there isn't anything blocking it. Is there enough energy to knock the last marble off the rulers? How far does it roll? The rug or carpet offers friction to the marble, and helps slow it down. Mark the spot where the marble comes to rest, or stops, with a tiny piece of paper.

Now, remove a few of the marbles so there are gaps between some of the marbles as shown in the illustration below. Roll the marble down the ramp again. Does the end marble roll as far? If not, why not? Do you think it may be because some of the energy was lost before getting to the last marble?

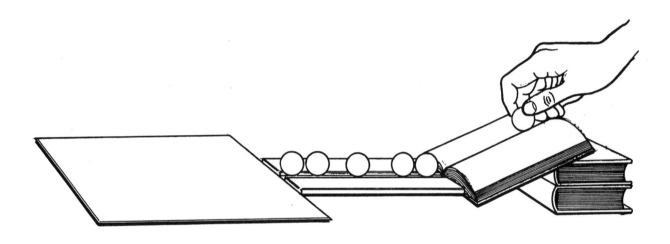

RESULTS & CONCLUSION Write down the results of your experiment. Come to a conclusion as to whether or not your hypothesis was correct.

FROLICKING IN THE WAVE

HOW SOME ENERGY MOVES

PURPOSE Energy can travel in the form of a wave. You are familiar with rolling waves in the ocean. Other types of energy waves, such as sound waves and radio waves, would look similar to ocean waves, if we could see them.

YOU NEED
- jump rope
- a fence
- a friend
- eye dropper
- round cake pan
- water

OVERVIEW A wave has a "crest" or peak, the highest part of the wave, and it has a "trough" or valley, the lowest part. The length from crest to crest (or trough to trough) is called the "wavelength." The wavelength of a tsunami (a tidal wave) can be 100 miles (161 km) long! The wavelength of a 550 Hertz (cycles per second) sound wave, which is a note that is a little higher than "middle C" on a piano, is 2 feet (60 cm).

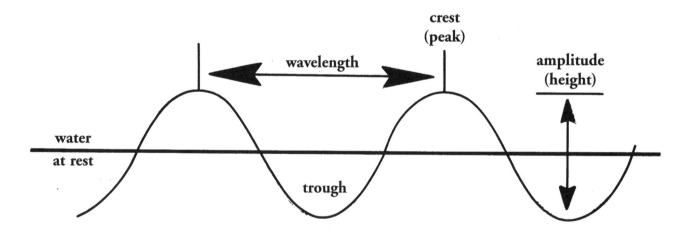

The same thing is true of waves in a lake or an ocean. When you see a rolling wave, it might look like the water is rolling, but very little water is actually moving. The water is only rising and falling as the force of energy passes through it. A boat on the water will bob up and down as the wave energy moves under it. You can demonstrate this by placing a cork or a toothpick in a tub of water and dropping in a stone. The waves created by the stone entering the water will ripple out, and will push the cork or toothpick up and down.

HYPOTHESIS Hypothesize that you can demonstrate the wave pattern in which energy travels.

PROCEDURE Have a friend hold lightly on to one end of a long jump rope as you hold the other end, then quickly whip your end up and down. You will see the rope take the shape of a wave, and travel down the rope toward the other end.

If your friend is holding the rope, when the energy gets to his end, it will yank the rope out of his hand.

Now tie one end of the jump rope to a fence. Quickly whip your end up and down, again and again, and set up a wave pattern. If you want to measure the "amplitude" or height of the wave, have a friend stand along side the rope and hold up a measuring stick, and watch where the lowest point (the trough) and the highest point (the crest) fall.

Fill a round cake pan half full of water. Fill an eye dropper with water. You can find the exact center of the pan by squeezing a drop of water into the pan and causing rippling waves. If you squeeze a drop of water perfectly in the center, the waves will ripple out to the edges of the pan, then back again, and meet exactly at the center point. If the waves didn't meet back together, wait until the water calms; then keep trying it until you find the exact center.

Sound wave energy can also travel through other materials besides air. Put your ear on the metal pipe of a chain link fence and have a friend tap a nail on the pipe at the other end. You will hear the sound travel through the pipe.

RESULTS & CONCLUSION Come to a conclusion as to whether or not your hypothesis was correct.

LITTLE SIR ECHO

MAKING USE OF SOUND WAVES TO MEASURE DISTANCE

YOU NEED
- a large building
- tape measure
- friends

PURPOSE The energy of a sound wave travels through the air at about 1,100 feet, or 335 meters, per second. In previous projects we saw how energy waves travel through a medium (air, water, metal, etc.) but that the molecules of the medium don't actually travel forward with the wave. How does the energy make its way through a medium?

OVERVIEW As a rolling wave moves through the ocean, the wave energy moves forward, but the actual molecules of water only move up and down with the wave's crest and trough. That is why a boat on the water will bob up and down, but not move forward, as a rolling wave goes by. This concept can also be shown by tying a piece of ribbon onto the middle of a jump rope, then tying one end of the rope to a fence, and moving the other end up and down, setting up waves. The ribbon will go up and down, but not forward in the direction of the wave.

The energy of sound waves also travels in the same way. Molecules in the air bump into each other and push the wave along, but the actual molecules travel very little.

Since we know that sound travels at about 1,100 feet per second, we can use it to determine distance. You are probably familiar with counting "one one thousand, two one thousand, three one thousand," to count the seconds between seeing a flash of lightning and hearing the rumble of thunder. Since 1,100 feet is about one-fifth of a mile, a gap of one second between seeing a lightning flash and hearing its thunder indicates that the lighting was about one-fifth of a mile away.

Have you ever gone into an empty room and heard your voice echo off the walls? When your ears hear two sounds that are about one-tenth second or longer apart, your brain interprets those as two distinct sounds . . . an echo, if the two sounds are the same (a loud yell, for example). Traveling at 1,100 feet per second, it takes a sound wave about one-tenth of a second to go 110 feet. If you yell at a large wall, you will hear an echo if the sound travels 110 feet or more to get back to you. That would mean you are 55 feet from the wall, because the sound would have to travel to the wall and back to you ($55 \times 2 = 110$).

HYPOTHESIS Hypothesize that the average distance at which a person will first hear an echo is about 55 feet.

PROCEDURE Find a building that has a broad wall, perhaps your school building. Face the wall and stand about 30 feet away from it. Yell loudly at the wall. Take a step backward and yell again. Continue to move back until you hear your voice echo. Then, using a tape measure, measure the distance from the wall to where you stood when you first heard an echo. Is the distance about 55 feet?

Have your friends try it. Record the distance where each friend first hears his echo. Are the distances close to 55 feet? Add the distances together and divide by the number of friends to find the average distance. How close is the average distance to 55 feet?

RESULTS & CONCLUSION Write down the results of your experiment. Come to a conclusion as to whether or not your hypothesis was correct.

ENERGY UNLEASHED

THE HAZARDS OF FAST-MOVING WATER

PURPOSE Many people have built homes on the beach by the ocean. It's a beautiful place to live . . . until a hurricane comes!

OVERVIEW The kinetic energy of moving water can be very powerful. Water moving normally in a river or stream bed usually stays where it should. But large volumes of fast-moving water can overflow the riverbanks, gouging out huge troughs and, like a bulldozer, pushing over cars, houses, and anything in its path.

HYPOTHESIS Hypothesize that you can demonstrate the erosive force of moving water with a model.

YOU NEED
- sand
- Four 2-liter plastic bottles
- water
- small houses and buildings (scale train-set models, for example)
- large dishpan
- several thick books
- piece of corrugated or stiff cardboard, about 2 by 4 feet (60 × 120 cm)
- plastic food wrap
- adhesive tape
- an area outside

PROCEDURE Set this project up outdoors. Cover an area about 2 by 3 feet (61 × 91 cm) with sand, piling it to a height of about an inch. Make a riverbed in the sand by scooping out a 2 to 3 inch wide (5–7.5 cm) channel from one end to the other of the 3-foot (91 cm) length.

Place some small-scale model buildings along the edge of the "river." Buildings from an electric train set or other small-scale models work well, or you can make your own buildings using cardboard and adhesive tape. Also, place some buildings away from the riverbed, making a town.

Cut a 2 by 4 foot (61 × 122 cm) piece of corrugated cardboard from a box (have an adult help you). Fold the piece of cardboard in half, lengthwise—along the 4-foot (122 cm) length. Then open it up again, but not all the way, making a "V" shape. To keep the top of the cardboard from getting wet, cover it with plastic food wrap or aluminum foil. Use tape to hold it in place. The cardboard "V" will be a slope or ramp that will channel water into the riverbed when water is poured into it.

At one end of the riverbed, place the end of the cardboard ramp. Raise the other end of the ramp to a height of about 6 inches (15 cm) by placing several thick books or blocks of wood under it. To keep it in a "V" shape to make a water chute, stack books on both sides.

Fill four 2-liter plastic soda bottles with water. Very slowly pour water out of each bottle onto the high end of the ramp, allowing the water to trickle through the riverbed in

the model town. After the bottles are empty, look at the river bed and all the buildings in the town. Write down any changes that you see.

Fill the four bottles with water again. Now empty all the bottles into a large dishpan. Dump all the water quickly, at once, down the ramp. The same amount of water now travels through the river as before, but the first release consisted of slow-moving water over a long period of time, and during the second release it is fast-moving water over a very short period of time. Now, when this "flash flood" or hurricane surge of water hits the town, what happens to the riverbed? What happens to the buildings along the river? What happens to the buildings that were not next to the river?

Note: If you have access to a still camera, take "before," "during," and "after" pictures. A camcorder (videotape recorder and camera system) can even capture the live action as it happens.

RESULTS & CONCLUSION Write down the results of your experiment. Come to a conclusion as to whether or not your hypothesis was correct.

SOMETHING MORE Do more research into hurricanes, floods, and erosion.

Sun, You're Too Much!

TAMING SOLAR ENERGY THE NATURAL WAY

PURPOSE Heat energy from the sun is usually thought of in a good way because of the many benefits. But there are times when this heat is unwanted. Have you ever walked on a beach when the sun made the sand so hot that you had to run or put shoes on your feet? Or gotten into a car "baking" in the hot summer sun with the windows closed up?

YOU NEED
- thermometer
- a sunny day
- a large shade tree
- paper and pencil

OVERVIEW In winter, bright warm sunshine streaming through the windows of your home helps keep you comfortable inside. But in summer, this extra heat causes fans and air conditioners to work even harder, as they try to cool down the house.

Trees can provide natural shading for homes. By planting trees along the side of a house where the hot summer sun beats, a home can be kept cooler naturally, and save electrical energy.

HYPOTHESIS Hypothesize that trees lower the temperature of the air in their shade.

PROCEDURE On a hot sunny day, find a large tree and stand in its shade. There, hold a thermometer out at shoulder height, being careful not to touch the bulb. Wait several minutes for the temperature to settle, then read the thermometer and write down the temperature.

Now, stand in the open, in the sun away from any shade. Again, hold out the thermometer and wait for the temperature to settle. Then read and write down the temperature.

Which location had the lower temperature?

RESULTS & CONCLUSION Write down the results of your experiment. Come to a conclusion as to whether or not your hypothesis was correct.

THE GREEN SCREEN

TREES AS NATURAL WIND-ENERGY PROTECTION

PURPOSE Protecting a home from strong, cold winter winds would certainly help to keep heat energy inside the house and lower energy costs. What can help protect a home?

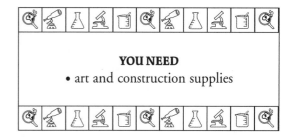

YOU NEED
• art and construction supplies

OVERVIEW Farms often have large open areas in which acres of crops are planted. To slow strong winds down and protect their crops and topsoil from wind damage, and their homes from cold, farmers often plant trees in a row to grow tall and cut the prevailing winds. Long ago, during long, cold winters, such windbreaks were especially important to the families living in farmhouses, when insulating materials and efficient means of heating weren't as good as today.

HYPOTHESIS Hypothesize that you can build a model to show the protective force of trees from wind energy.

PROCEDURE Using art and construction supplies or scale models (the kind used for train sets), construct a model of a farm, showing its open crop-filled fields, the farmhouse, and where rows of trees would be placed to act as windbreaks. Research weather maps in the area of your "farm" for wind direction.

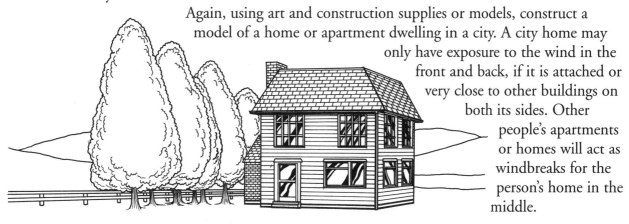

Again, using art and construction supplies or models, construct a model of a home or apartment dwelling in a city. A city home may only have exposure to the wind in the front and back, if it is attached or very close to other buildings on both its sides. Other people's apartments or homes will act as windbreaks for the person's home in the middle.

RESULTS & CONCLUSION Come to a conclusion as to whether or not your hypothesis was correct.

CHOOSE NOT TO LOSE

IDENTIFYING CAUSES OF HOME HEAT-ENERGY LOSS

PURPOSE How does heat escape from our homes?

OVERVIEW The wood in your home or apartment's walls and roof, along with insulation material, does a good job of keeping heat inside in the winter and cool air inside in the summer. Wood is a natural insulator. It has millions of tiny cells, sort of like a honeycomb. These cells are natural pockets that trap air, and air does not conduct heat.

YOU NEED
- your home
- a windy day
- paper and pencil

Home-building experts say that about 75 percent of a door's heat loss occurs around its edges. That is why people sometimes stuff newspaper or old rags around the edges of an unused door, and push a throw rug against its bottom. Heat energy can also be lost around windows, and electrical outlets and switches.

HYPOTHESIS Hypothesize that you will find evidence of heat loss throughout your home.

PROCEDURE Investigate your house for places where drafts can enter and rob your house of heat energy. Draw a floor plan of your house, showing where windows, doors, electrical outlets, and electrical switches are located. Then go to each location and check for the presence of a draft. Pay attention to the sensitive soft cheeks of your face; they are a great way to feel moving air. On your floor plan, write down any locations where you feel a draft.

You might see evidence of a draft by holding something light, such as a very small down feather or tiny piece of lint from a clothes dryer's trap, up to where you suspect air leakage.

RESULTS & CONCLUSION Write down the results of your experiment. Come to a conclusion as to whether or not your hypothesis was correct.

SOMETHING MORE Have your parents or an adult take you to the local hardware or building-supply store and research ways that would help keep heat from leaking from these drafty locations.

NOW YOU HEAR IT . . .

TRACKING RADIO FREQUENCY DIRECTION

PURPOSE & OVERVIEW At radio and television stations, powerful transmitters send radio waves out of the antenna and through the air, on their way to your radio receiver or TV set. Can you use a radio as a direction finder in order to locate the station that a radio wave is coming from?

YOU NEED
- inexpensive AM pocket radio
- aluminum foil
- table

HYPOTHESIS Hypothesize that with an AM radio you can locate the direction of a radio wave.

PROCEDURE Take an inexpensive AM pocket radio and place it on the table. Tune it to a station that is coming in strongly and clearly. Fold a piece of aluminum foil in a shape of a cave or pocket and place it around the top, bottom, and three sides of the radio, leaving only the front of the radio showing in the opening. Place the radio back in position on the table.

Is the station still coming in as strong? Slowly turn your radio, along with its aluminum shield, exposing the open front side to different directions. Is the station still coming in as strong? Continue to turn it around until you have made a complete circle. If the station is strongest when facing one particular direction, then that is the direction that radio waves are coming from.

Do the experiment with several other radio stations. Are the signals coming from the same or different directions? List the stations, by their ID letters or where they are on the radio dial, and write down the direction of their signal transmitter.

RESULTS & CONCLUSION Write down the results of your experiment. Come to a conclusion as to whether or not your hypothesis was correct.

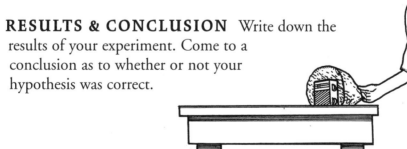

ONCE, TWICE, AGAIN

REUSING PRODUCTS TO SAVE ENERGY

PURPOSE What are some simple ways we can conserve energy?

OVERVIEW It takes energy for a factory to make a product. If that product can be used twice, or used to do more than one job, that reduces the need to make more of the product—saving energy.

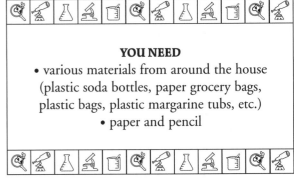

YOU NEED
- various materials from around the house (plastic soda bottles, paper grocery bags, plastic bags, plastic margarine tubs, etc.)
- paper and pencil

HYPOTHESIS Hypothesize that there are many disposable items around the home that can be reused to conserve energy and resources.

PROCEDURE What items around your home or school can be used more than once, or used in a different way after their first use? Plastic products are often handy to keep for other uses. Responses to a consumer poll suggest that 87 percent of Americans had reused a plastic product over the previous six-month period.

Some Added Uses for Manufactured Products

Plastic soda bottles
1. Make into bird feeders.
2. To store cold drinking water in refrigerator.
3. Use as a terrarium.
4. Experiments.
5. A penny bank.
6. Pocket money—return bottles to store for refund.

Can you think of other uses for bottles, and for the other products listed here?

Paper grocery bags

1. Bring to grocery store, when out shopping, to pack order.
2. As covers for school textbooks.
3. To carry things, such as gifts, when visiting relatives.
4. To wrap packages for mailing.
5. For arts and crafts projects, such as masks for plays or Halloween.
6. Spread out to protect work area.
7. Place them in your community's recycling trash pickup.

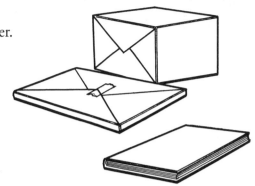

Plastic margarine tubs

1. To store screws or small items.
2. To store food leftovers.
3. As scoop—for dog food, animal feed, fertilizer.
4. To catch water under small flower pots.
5. With puncture holes in bottom to sprinkle water on plants.
6. As beach toys, to hold sand and water, or use as molds for sand castles.

Plastic grocery bags

1. Line small bedroom wastebaskets.
2. To carry school lunches that may be soggy or might leak.
3. To put carried books or packages in when it starts to rain.
4. When packing a wet bathing suit.
5. To hold wet laundry to hang or dry.
6. To keep feet, or shoes, dry in rainstorm.
7. To collect recyclables for pickup.

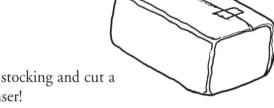

Tip: Stuff each bag, one by one, into the top of an old stocking and cut a hole in the toe to make a handy plastic bag dispenser!

RESULTS & CONCLUSION Come to a conclusion as to whether or not your hypothesis was correct.

UNPLUGGED!

TAKING HOME ELECTRICAL USE FOR GRANTED

PURPOSE To explore the use of electricity in the home.

YOU NEED
- your home
- paper and pencil

OVERVIEW The development of electrical energy has been a wonderful benefit to mankind. But society has become very dependent on electricity. Sometimes the power coming into our homes is interrupted. We take the many things that work by electrical power for granted—until the power is lost! This can happen when there is trouble with the electric utility equipment, lightning strikes a telephone pole, strong storm winds blow down power lines, or too many people simply use too much electricity all at once or for too long. Then, the lights can *go out!*

Losing electric power to a home means that many things we normally do, without giving them much thought, suddenly become inconvenient. Some things are only small inconveniences, such as using candles or flashlights instead of electric lights for a few hours. You may not be able to watch your big-screen TV, but you can still read, play a game, or listen to a battery-operated radio.

However, the loss of electrical power can cause serious problems. If the power fails during the winter and your home is warmed by electric heat, a loss of electricity could make the house uncomfortably cold. If your home has its own water well, an electric water pump cannot work without power. The kitchen sink is not normally thought of as being electrical, but if the water pump is out, you can't bring water into the pipes; so there is no water for drinking, cooking, washing, or for flushing a toilet. No water can be a very serious problem.

HYPOTHESIS Hypothesize that a majority of the electric products in our home would be hard to replace with non-electric products.

PROCEDURE Take a look around your home. What things would stop working if the electric power should go off? What things around your home use energy but are not connected to and dependent on the electric utility company? Examples would be a candle, a wind-up toy, a flashlight, a watch, and a kerosene lamp. Can any of these items be used to replace an item that uses electric power from the power company, and save electricity? A wind-up clock could replace an electric clock; it would require you to wind it up every day, but that would save electrical energy. However, a battery-operated radio would not efficiently replace a radio that runs on house current, because batteries are more expensive.

RESULTS & CONCLUSION Come to a conclusion about your hypothesis.

TREASURE HUNT

YOUR NEIGHBORHOOD WITH/WITHOUT ELECTRICAL POWER

PURPOSE To examine how electric power is immersed in our world.

OVERVIEW When Thomas Edison and his team of scientists perfected the electric light bulb long ago and began building electric stations to generate power, towns and cities took on a whole new look.

YOU NEED
- arts and crafts supplies
- your neighborhood or a nearby town

HYPOTHESIS Hypothesize that electricity is immersed very deeply in our lives.

PROCEDURE Walk down your street or around your neighborhood and imagine what it would look like without electrical energy. What would be missing? Would you see street-lights? Flashing traffic signals? How about those bright, neon signs in storefronts? Television antennas? People lined up at bank ATM machines? A fire box? Satellite dish? Telephone poles? Transmission towers?

Make two drawings, one showing what your street or neighborhood looks like and another of what the same scene would look like if electricity had not been developed.

Compare and contrast the two drawings.

RESULTS & CONCLUSION
Compare the two drawings. Come to a conclusion as to whether or not your hypothesis was correct.

LOOKING UP

MOST OF EARTH'S ENERGY COMES FROM OUR SUN

PURPOSE Let's examine the importance of the sun.

YOU NEED
• arts and craft supplies

OVERVIEW Almost all energy on the earth comes from the sun's energy (geothermal, tidal, and nuclear are the only ones that do not).

Wind is caused by the uneven heating of the earth's surface by the sun. Waves in a large body of water can be the result of winds. Wood, used for many things including firewood to heat homes, comes from trees, which require sunlight to grow. Oil products (coal, gas, oil, kerosene, and propane) are formed by rotting plants and wood, packed down tightly and under great pressure for many centuries.

The energy of moving water in streams is partly caused by the sun's energy. Rivers, streams, and waterfalls are the result of evaporation caused by the sun's energy. The water then falls back to earth as rain, snow, or some other form of precipitation, and gravity moves it from a higher to a lower level.

Electrical energy for our homes is generated at a power plant often by burning a fossil fuel such as coal. Hydroelectric power is generated by water moving through great turbines.

HYPOTHESIS Hypothesize that you can show the different types of energy that result from the sun in a model.

PROCEDURE Construct a model showing objects that represent the types of energy on earth that directly or indirectly are the result of solar energy.

RESULTS & CONCLUSION Come to a conclusion as to whether or not your hypothesis was correct.

NUCLEAR DOMINOS

DEMONSTRATING A CHAIN REACTION

PURPOSE What is nuclear fission?

OVERVIEW One type of energy is released when the nuclei of atoms are either combined (fusion) or split apart (fission). The energy, called "nuclear energy," is released in the form of heat, light, or some other type of radiation. Nuclear energy is used to make electricity by heating water for steam that then drives giant turbine generators.

In the process of nuclear fission, the splitting apart of an atom causes a chain reaction. A radioactive element, such as Uranium-235, is used in the chain reaction. The first fission creates two new neutrons. Each of these neutrons strikes at least two other neutrons, which strike even more, and a chain reaction takes place which continues to grow.

YOU NEED
- dominos
- ruler
- flat table

HYPOTHESIS Hypothesize that dominoes can demonstrate the processes of nuclear fission.

PROCEDURE To demonstrate the concept of nuclear fission, stand dominos in the pattern shown, where one domino is set to start a chain reaction. As it falls, the domino hits two dominos, which each hit two more. The number of dominos hit and falling with each row grows quickly. This chain reaction of falling dominos can be demonstrated easily using only four or five rows; with additional rows the arranged dominos become so packed together that they get in each other's way.

In a nuclear reactor where nuclear fission is taking place, the chain reaction can be slowed down or even stopped by inserting rods made of cadmium or boron. These dampening rods absorb neutrons and slow the process down. Demonstrate this by placing a ruler between two dominos in a row, then push the first domino to start the chain reaction. The reaction stops when it reaches the ruler, which acts like the rods in a nuclear reactor.

RESULTS & CONCLUSION Write down the results of your experiment. Come to a conclusion as to whether or not your hypothesis was correct.

ENERGY STOPPER

FRICTION AND THE REDUCTION OF ENERGY

PURPOSE What affect does friction have on energy?

OVERVIEW Friction is a force that can act on a moving object to slow it down, requiring the use of additional energy if it is to be kept going. Friction is caused by two objects rubbing together. When you are ice skating or riding a sled down a snowy hill, friction tries to reduce your rate of motion. The metal runners on skates and sleds are specially designed to reduce friction so that you are able to go faster.

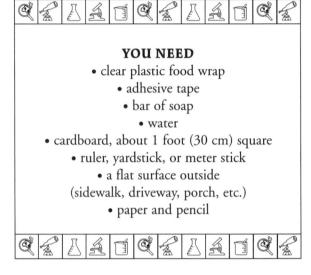

YOU NEED
- clear plastic food wrap
- adhesive tape
- bar of soap
- water
- cardboard, about 1 foot (30 cm) square
- ruler, yardstick, or meter stick
- a flat surface outside
(sidewalk, driveway, porch, etc.)
- paper and pencil

HYPOTHESIS Hypothesize that friction will reduce the amount of energy.

PROCEDURE Cover a piece of cardboard about 1 foot (30 cm) square with clear plastic food wrap. Pull the food wrap tightly across the cardboard and use adhesive tape underneath to keep it tight. Take the cardboard outside and lay it on a flat surface, such as a driveway or sidewalk.

Place a dry bar of soap in the middle of the board. Hold one end and slowly raise it, making a ramp, until the bar of soap begins to slide. At this point, the force of gravity is stronger than the friction. Place the zero-marked end of a ruler or measuring stick on the flat surface and hold its scale markings against the high end of the cardboard ramp. Write down how many inches or centimeters high it had to be to overcome friction.

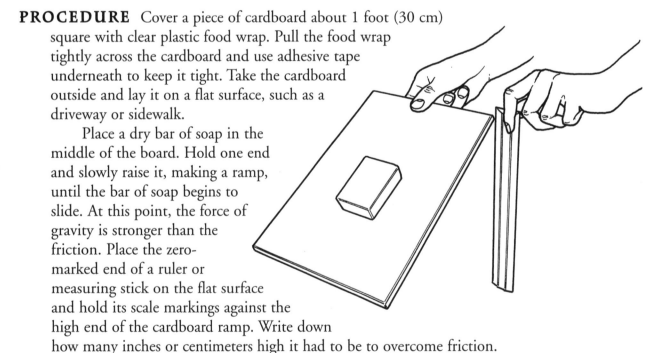

Next, thoroughly wet the bar of soap and pour water onto the cardboard ramp. A watering can would work well for this job. Will water reduce the friction?

Place the bar of soap at the exact spot where it was before, at the middle of the ramp. Lift the end of the ramp until the bar of soap overcomes friction and begins to slide. Measure the height of the ramp. Did the ramp have to be raised as high, before the soap moved the second time?

RESULTS & CONCLUSION Write down the results of your experiment. Come to a conclusion as to whether or not your hypothesis was correct.

SOMETHING MORE Moving through the air causes friction, too. It can increase the energy usage of cars, planes, and other vehicles—which is why they are designed to be as "aerodynamic" as possible. Do more research on how friction can be an energy robber.

CELL MAGIC

CHANGING LIGHT ENERGY TO ELECTRICAL ENERGY

PURPOSE Can light energy be converted to electrical energy?

OVERVIEW The photovoltaic cell, better known as a "solar cell," is a device that turns light directly into electricity. Solar cells are expensive to manufacture, so they are only used when there is no other easier way to get electricity, such as at a remote weather station or in an Earth-orbiting satellite.

A single solar cell does not generate very much electricity, but solar cells can be connected together "in series" and their individual voltages added together.

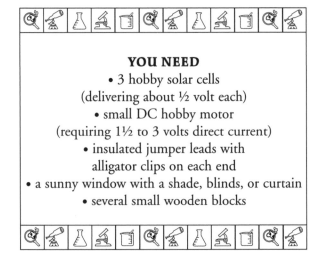

YOU NEED
- 3 hobby solar cells (delivering about ½ volt each)
- small DC hobby motor (requiring 1½ to 3 volts direct current)
- insulated jumper leads with alligator clips on each end
- a sunny window with a shade, blinds, or curtain
- several small wooden blocks

Connecting cells in series means hooking the positive (+) terminal of one cell to the negative (–) terminal of the next. Flashlights have their batteries connected in series, with the negative terminal of one battery touching the positive terminal on the next. When batteries are connected in series, the total voltage available across all of them is the sum of the individual battery voltages as shown. Imagine how much more power you could exert on a rope if the strength of three of your friends were also helping you to pull it.

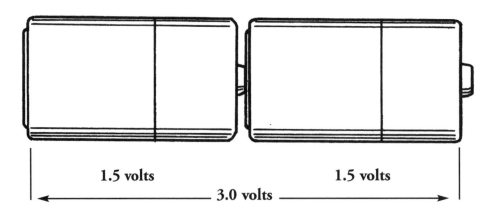

1.5 volts   1.5 volts

3.0 volts

HYPOTHESIS Hypothesize that you can show how clouds affect the amount of solar energy reaching Earth through a solar cell circuit.

PROCEDURE Using insulated jumper leads with alligator clips on each end, connect the positive and negative terminals of a solar cell to a small 1.5-volt hobby motor. Set the arrangement in a sunny place. Use wood blocks behind the cells to tilt them so that they face the sun. You could also use spring-type clothespins clipped onto the sides near the bottoms of the cells to stand them upright. Watch how fast the motor spins. Next, add two more solar cells to the circuit, placing them in series.

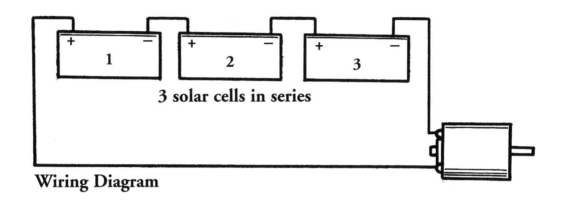

3 solar cells in series

Wiring Diagram

Look at and listen to the motor. Is it spinning faster now that it is getting more voltage? What happens to the motor's speed on a cloudy day?

Create your own "cloudy day" by closing blinds or curtains partway, then all the way. Do you think the voltage produced by the solar cells is less on cloudy days? How do you think that affects the location of where solar cells work best?

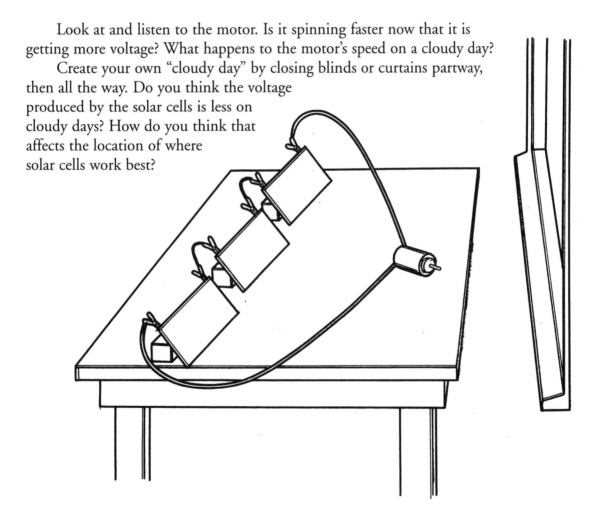

RESULTS & CONCLUSION Write down the results of your experiment. Come to a conclusion as to whether or not your hypothesis was correct.

HEAT LOST?

USING ENERGY TO REMOVE (TRANSFER) HEAT

PURPOSE The invention of the refrigerator has been a tremendous benefit to people, keeping foods from spoiling too quickly. When the refrigerator runs, what happens to the air inside it? Where does the heat go? It doesn't just disappear. The refrigerator actually moves it out into the room.

YOU NEED
- 3 thermometers
- refrigerator
- string

OVERVIEW To cool the air inside a refrigerator, another energy source is needed—electricity. Tubes inside the refrigerator are filled with a fluid called "refrigerant." It absorbs heat. With the help of an electric motor, the heated fluid goes through a "condenser" and the fluid gives up its heat to the surrounding air. The condenser is made up of coils and is found either on the back of your refrigerator or at the bottom. If you don't see the coils behind it, look under the refrigerator.

HYPOTHESIS Hypothesize that units that need to keep cool (a refrigerator or an air conditioner) transfer their heat elsewhere.

PROCEDURE Put a thermometer inside the refrigerator. Place another near the condenser coils, wherever they are on your refrigerator. Tie a piece of string to a third thermometer and hang it on the front door, about in the middle, to measure the room temperature.

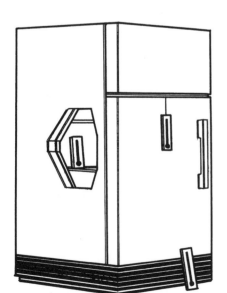

Wait for the refrigerator's condenser motor to turn on, which it will do occasionally when the temperature inside the refrigerator rises above the temperature that its thermostat is set at. Listen for the motor to stop in a few minutes. When it does, read the temperatures on all the thermometers. Is the temperature near the condenser coils warmer than the room temperature shown on the thermometer hanging on the door?

Air conditioners use the same principle. If you have a window air conditioner running, try placing a thermometer inside the window and one on its outside. Is the heat from the room being moved to the outdoors?

RESULTS & CONCLUSION Write down the results of your experiment. Come to a conclusion as to whether or not your hypothesis was correct.

BRIGHT HEAT

UNWANTED HEAT ENERGY FROM INCANDESCENT LIGHT

PURPOSE The most common types of home lighting are incandescent and fluorescent bulbs. In both, electrical energy is turned into light energy.

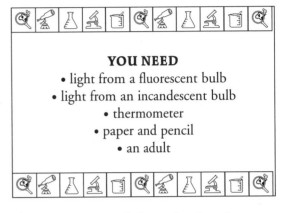

YOU NEED
- light from a fluorescent bulb
- light from an incandescent bulb
- thermometer
- paper and pencil
- an adult

OVERVIEW In an incandescent light bulb, electricity passes through a small wire, called a filament, which glows brightly. In a fluorescent light bulb (usually a long straight or circular tube), the inside of the bulb is filled with a gas. The inside glass of the bulb is coated with materials called phosphors. When electricity is passed through a heating element in the bulb, the gas gives off rays that cause the phosphors to fluoresce (glow).

All we really want from a light bulb is light. However, in the changing of electrical energy into light energy, there is energy loss. Some of that energy is given off as heat, especially unwelcome during hot weather! Which type of light bulb is more energy-efficient (gives off less heat to the surrounding air)?

HYPOTHESIS Hypothesize that either an incandescent bulb or a fluorescent bulb will give off more heat.

PROCEDURE Find a lamp in your home that uses an incandescent bulb; most lamps do. Find a fluorescent lamp. In the home, fluorescent bulbs are often used in kitchens, bathrooms, garages, and workshop areas. Remember, when working around hot light bulbs and electrical fixtures, to have an adult with you. A light bulb may stay quite hot even after it has been turned off, and it can cause a burn—so be careful. Also, do not take bulbs out of their sockets.

Remove the shade from a lamp that has an incandescent bulb. Hold the bulb of a thermometer about one inch (2.5 cm) away from the lit bulb for about three minutes. Record the temperature.

Now hold the thermometer bulb the same distance from a lit fluorescent bulb for three minutes. Record the temperature. Which bulb is more light-efficient?

RESULTS & CONCLUSION Write down the results of your experiment. Come to a conclusion as to whether or not your hypothesis was correct.

UNEQUAL ENERGY

FINDING THE DISTRIBUTION OF HEAT ENERGY IN A ROOM

PURPOSE & OVERVIEW Is the temperature in a room the same everywhere in the room? You might think that it is. But as you do this project, you may be surprised to discover that the air temperature is different in different parts of the room—the heat energy in the room is not equally distributed.

YOU NEED
- a large room in your house
- thermometer
- a clock or watch
- paper and pencil
- an adult

HYPOTHESIS Choose some locations that you believe will be warmer then others. Hypothesize that those locations will have more heat energy than some other locations.

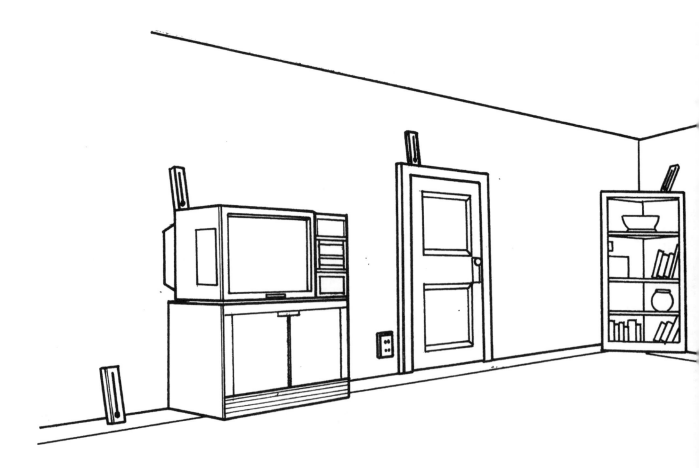

PROCEDURE Pick about ten different locations in a large room in your home. Some locations should be high up, some low near the floor, some on an "inside" wall (a wall with another room behind it), and some on an "outside" wall (with the outdoors on the other side). High locations can be above an inside door (over the open doorway or, with the door ajar, the thermometer lying on top) or on top of a picture frame on a wall. Ask an adult to help you place thermometers in the highest places. One of the locations should be by a window, another by an electric light switch on an outside wall.

Make a chart with two columns and at the head of the first column write "locations"; then list the locations you've selected. At the top of the second column write "temperature."

Put the thermometer at your first location. Wait about three minutes to give the thermometer time to adjust and indicate the correct temperature. Write down the temperature reading for that location. Repeat this procedure for all the locations in your room.

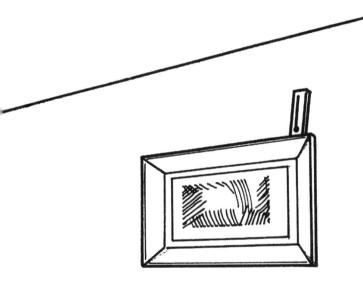

RESULTS & CONCLUSION

Compare the temperatures you have taken around the room. Which location is the warmest? Which is the coolest? Why do you think the temperature may be different at each location? Look up the word "convection" in the dictionary. Do you think poor insulation by a light switch on an outside wall or by a window might be affecting the air temperature at that location?

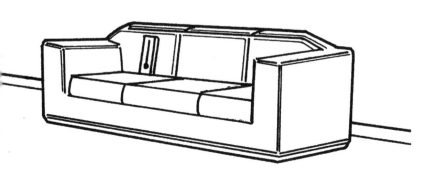

BAND AT TENSION

MEASURING POTENTIAL ENERGY IN A STRETCHED ELASTIC BAND

PURPOSE Have you ever wondered what makes a stretched rubber band fly?

OVERVIEW When you pull the elastic band of a slingshot back as far as it will go and hold it, the elastic band has potential (stored) energy, ready to do work. When you let go, that potential energy is released to do work. This energy in motion is called kinetic energy.

HYPOTHESIS Hypothesize that the more a rubber band is stretched, the more potential energy it has (and the more kinetic energy is released when you let go of the rubber band).

PROCEDURE Let's construct a paper towel

YOU NEED
- Ping-Pong ball
- masking tape
- empty paper towel roll
- thick book
- measuring tape
- rubber band
- board, about 3 to 4 inches (8–10 cm) wide and 1 foot (30 cm) long
- ruler
- 2 nails
- hammer
- paper and pencil

tube "cannon" and use a Ping-Pong ball as a cannonball to measure kinetic energy when it is shot from the cannon. Don't use anything heavier as the cannonball, because flying objects can be dangerous. A Ping-Pong ball is safe to use.

Take two pieces of masking tape about 4 inches (10 cm) long. Lay them on top of each other, with sticky sides touching.

Fold the masking tape over one end of an empty paper towel roll. Position it so that it covers only a part of the paper towel roll opening as shown. Use another piece of masking tape to hold it onto the roll. This tape will act as a "stopper" by making the opening just small enough to keep the ball from falling through, but will let it stick out of the bottom a little. Lay the roll aside for now.

Using masking tape, tape a ruler to a piece of wood about 3 or 4 inches (8–10 cm) wide by 1 foot (30 cm) long. Let about 5 to 6 inches (13–15 cm) of the ruler hang over one end of the board.

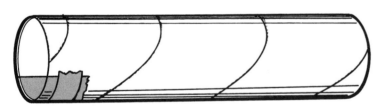

Hammer two nails part of the way into the board, one on each side near the outside edges, about 3 inches (7.5 cm) from the end of the board where the ruler is. Leave the nails sticking up slightly.

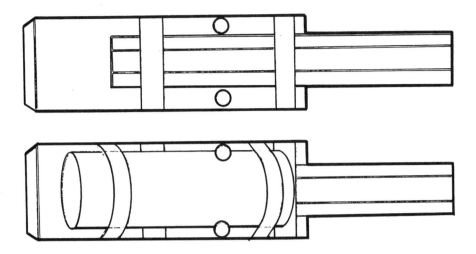

Lay the paper towel roll on top of the ruler and board assembly, between the nails, and fix it in place with masking tape. Set your "cannon" on the floor.

Elevate the front end of the cannon by placing a book under the end opposite the ruler. Put a rubber band across the two nails, stretching it around the bottom of the paper towel tube. Drop your "cannonball" into the tube so it comes to rest at the bottom of the tube, on the masking-tape stopper and the rubber band.

Using the scale on the ruler, pull the rubber band back 1 inch (2.5 cm) and let go. The rubber band will hit the ball and shoot it out of the cannon. Watch where the ball first touches the floor. Use a tape measure to find the distance the ball traveled from the cannon. Make a chart to record how far back the rubber band is pulled and how far the ball travels through the air.

Next, pull the rubber band back 1½ inches (4 cm). Measure and record the distance the ball travels. Repeat this procedure, ½ inch (1.25 cm) at a time, until the rubber band has been stretched back as far as it can.

Look at your chart of data. Does the ball travel farther if the rubber band is pulled farther back? Is there a mathematical relationship (a number pattern) between the distance the rubber band is pulled back and the distance the ball goes? For example, does the ball go 1 foot (30 cm) farther for each inch (2.5 cm) the rubber band is pulled back?

RESULTS & CONCLUSION Write down the results of your experiment. Come to a conclusion as to whether or not your hypothesis was correct.

LESS THAN BRIGHT

BROWNOUTS IN ELECTRIC POWER SERVICE

PURPOSE What is a brownout?

OVERVIEW The demand for electrical energy by those living in our cities and communities changes constantly. For example, on very hot summer days, more people use fans and air conditioners, so the demand for electricity from the power company is higher.

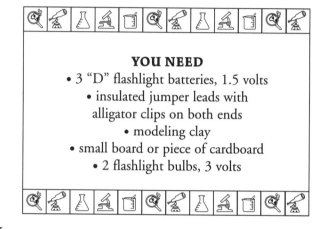

YOU NEED
- 3 "D" flashlight batteries, 1.5 volts
- insulated jumper leads with alligator clips on both ends
- modeling clay
- small board or piece of cardboard
- 2 flashlight bulbs, 3 volts

What happens if a 10-megawatt power plant tries to deliver 10½ megawatts during a time of such high demand? A power company may choose to slightly lower the voltage going out so there is enough to go around to everyone. This is called a "brownout." A power plant representative told us that when demand for electricity goes higher than the plant can produce, the power company can reduce power by 5, 10, or even 15 percent. Most people won't even notice a 5- or 10-percent reduction in power.

In a really bad situation, when more electricity is needed than even a brownout can help with, the power plant may have to turn power off to different areas, each area losing power for 15 minutes at a time. This is called a "rolling blackout." By losing power for only 15 minutes, most people are only slightly inconvenienced.

When a brownout occurs, the normal voltage available to the electrical appliances in your home is reduced. During a brownout, light bulbs in lamps may not shine as brightly as normal.

Although running a light bulb at a lower voltage will not harm it, lower voltages for a long period of time can damage motors. To make up for the voltage drop, a motor will draw more current. The increased flow of electricity through the motor's "windings" (coils of wire inside) makes the wire heat up. This can destroy the motor. Motors can be found in many places around the house: refrigerators, water pumps, air conditioners, swimming pool pumps, fans, and forced hot-air heaters all have motors. If a brownout occurs at your house, alert an adult to turn off appliances until the power returns to normal.

HYPOTHESIS Hypothesize that a simple model can demonstrate a brownout's effects.

PROCEDURE To get a taste of a brownout, in this project we will operate a flashlight bulb at only half the voltage it is designed to take and compare it to a bulb getting full voltage. Using modeling clay, make a base to hold two 1.5-volt "D" flashlight batteries together. The batteries should be laid on a small board or piece of cardboard, with the positive (+) end of one touching the negative (–) end of the other, just as they would be in a flashlight. The batteries are said to be "in series" with one another. When connected in this way, the total voltage across the two batteries is the sum of each battery: 1.5 volts + 1.5 volts = 3.0 volts.

Clip one end of an insulated jumper lead to the small metal tip of a flashlight bulb. Clip one end of another insulated jumper lead to the wide metal base of the bulb. Touch the other two ends of the jumper leads to the batteries as shown.

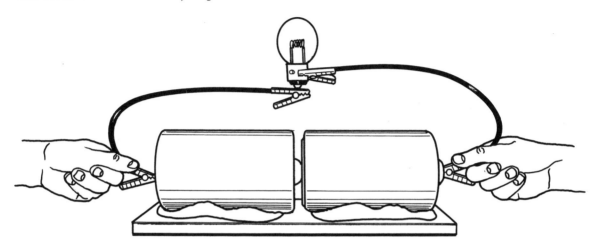

Make another identical setup, but this time only use one battery. Compare the brightness of the two bulbs.

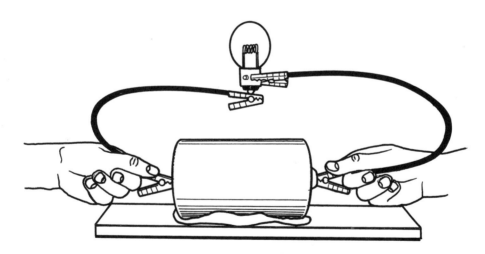

RESULTS & CONCLUSION Write down the results of your experiment. Come to a conclusion as to whether or not your hypothesis was correct.

SOMETHING MORE Call your local electric power company and research more information about brownouts and blackouts.

ENERGY DETECTIVE

HELPING YOUR SCHOOL SAVE ENERGY

PURPOSE & OVERVIEW When energy is used inefficiently by your school, it not only wastes valuable resources, it also costs your family, neighbors, and community money by increasing the school's expenses. Is your school conserving energy? Do an investigative study and give your school a report on its use of energy.

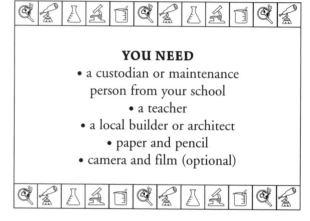

YOU NEED
- a custodian or maintenance person from your school
- a teacher
- a local builder or architect
- paper and pencil
- camera and film (optional)

HYPOTHESIS Hypothesize that your school could improve its usage of energy with some simple steps.

PROCEDURE Start your investigation by talking to one of your school's custodians or maintenance people. Ask about the insulation in the school's walls and ceiling, how old the insulation is, if it is missing or damaged in some areas, and if there is enough insulation. Ask the custodian about the heat and light in classrooms after everyone goes home. Is someone in charge of turning the heat down and making sure unnecessary lights are turned off at night? Are the heating and lighting on timers? Ask if the mechanical and electrical equipment in the school is in good operating condition. Do your own physical inspection of the school building. Ask yourself such questions as:

- Are there a lot of windows in the school? Are they on the side of the building that allows warm solar energy to come in during the winter? Are there shades to keep out the hot summer sun?
- What direction do the prevailing winds come from? Does the school building receive any protection from cold winds, as from other buildings or large trees?
- On windy or cold days, are there drafts around windows and outside doors?
- Are some rooms hotter than they need to be (in winter) or cooler than they need to be (in warm weather)? Use a thermometer to measure the temperature in rooms you feel are too warm or cold.
- Are there dripping or leaky faucets, or long or constantly flushing toilets in the rest rooms? Ask a friend of the opposite sex to help you check for such water waste.
- Is the water coming from the faucets so hot that it might scald someone? If so, the thermostat on the hot water heater may be set too high.
- Do the exhaust fans in the kitchen run unnecessarily?

Interview one or more teachers and ask them what they do to make their classroom more energy efficient. Do they store and use paper, books, and other materials wisely? Do the windows in their classrooms let in enough natural light so that the teacher can turn off some of the electric lights during the day? Are computers, printers, and other electronic equipment turned off when not in use?

Interview a local builder or architect and ask for ideas on improving the energy efficiency of your school building.

Study the data you have collected and compile an energy report for your school. Include suggestions for improvement. Obviously, there will be some things you cannot change, such as the efficiency of the school's boiler. But you can ask teachers to assign a student to see that the lights are turned off when everyone leaves the room for recess or for lunch.

Most trash from schools is paper. Instead of throwing out paper that is only used on one side (old flyers and printed reports), ask teachers about making use of the other sides for scribbling notes or as scrap paper in classes. The school can also set up places where everyone can deposit used white paper for recycling.

RESULTS & CONCLUSION Write down the results of your experiment. Come to a conclusion as to whether or not your hypothesis was correct.

SOMETHING MORE You may want to enhance your report by taking photographs. Show and report on both good and bad points about your school building.

WINDY CORNERS

COMPARING AVAILABLE WIND ENERGY

PURPOSE Are there other forms of energy available to power a home?

OVERVIEW Someday our homes may not need to be connected to electrical power lines for energy. Newly constructed or redesigned housing, with solar cells and efficient windmills, will perhaps in the future be able to gather energy and produce enough power to fill the needs of the families living there.

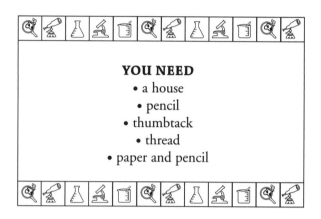

YOU NEED
- a house
- pencil
- thumbtack
- thread
- paper and pencil

If you were thinking of installing a small windmill where you live, where around your house would be the best place to set it up? Usually, windmills are mounted very high up in order to catch the strongest wind. But suppose you had to mount one on the ground. Where, on the ground, do you think the wind is strongest? Is it windier in the middle of the side wall of your house, or at the corners?

HYPOTHESIS Hypothesize about where you think the wind is the strongest.

PROCEDURE To find out, make a device to measure wind strength. Push a thumbtack into the eraser end of a pencil. Tie a piece of thread about 10 inches (25 cm) long onto the thumbtack.

Make a sketch, or rough drawing, of the layout of your house, as it would be seen from overhead. On the drawing, label each side: A, B, C, and so on. Label each corner: 1, 2, 3, in the same way.

Go outside and stand in the middle of each side wall and at each corner of the house. At each position, hold the pencil straight up and at arm's length, to catch whatever wind there is. The windier it is, the greater the angle the thread will be from the

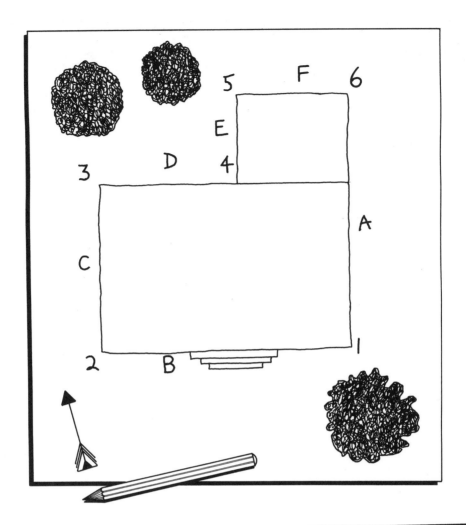

pencil. Is it more windy along the broad sides of your house or at the corners?

Check the effect of the wind every day for a week (some days will be more windy than others). Is it true that the corners (or the sides) are always windier? Why do you think that is?

RESULTS & CONCLUSION Write down the results of your experiment. Come to a conclusion as to whether or not your hypothesis was correct.

ENERGY ATTENDANT

CHANGING ENERGY-WASTEFUL HABITS
IN YOUR HOME

PURPOSE Can you help make saving energy a way of life for the people you live with? Using seat belts has become a good habit for many adults because their children nagged them every time they got into the car—the children having been taught about seat belt safety at school.

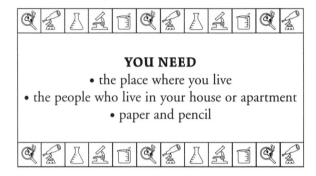

YOU NEED
- the place where you live
- the people who live in your house or apartment
- paper and pencil

OVERVIEW Before saving energy becomes a habit in your house, you will have to be on the alert for times when energy is being wasted and politely point it out to your family. Maybe you can change these energy-wasting patterns for the better, and make energy saving something your family does automatically, as routinely as getting up in the morning, eating breakfast, brushing teeth, and heading out for school or work.

HYPOTHESIS Hypothesize that some simple steps can help your family reduce energy usage.

PROCEDURE Make a list of the ways your family can save energy, and give them a copy to remind them. The whole family should be happy to help, because they can all take part and saving energy will also save them money.

Some Simple Energy-Saving Ideas

• Before opening the refrigerator door, think about what you need. Then open the door, quickly get the items you want, and close the door. Every time a refrigerator door is open, heat from the room goes in, and the refrigerator must work to cool that warm air. It's a good idea to place often-used products (milk, eggs, butter, cheese) in the same place in the refrigerator so they can be found easily and time is not wasted searching.

• Turn off lights when a room is unoccupied.

• Televisions, computers, and radios should be turned off—*if* no one intends to use them within a half-hour. These appliances receive a lot of wear and tear when they are first turned on, so it's better to leave them on, for up to a half-hour, if you or someone will be using them within that time.

• Toast two slices of bread at the same time, instead of first one slice and then another a minute later. Toasters, like other electrical heating devices, use a lot of electricity.

• Encourage the use of a microwave oven to cook, whenever possible. Microwave ovens use about 50 percent less energy than conventional ovens.

RESULTS & CONCLUSION Write down the results of your experiment. Come to a conclusion as to whether or not your hypothesis was correct.

CHECK YOUR GAME

THE ENERGY COST OF ELECTRONIC FUN

PURPOSE How many fun activities do we do which use energy unnecessarily?

OVERVIEW Before electricity was available in every home, families and friends entertained themselves by playing games using cards, boards, dice, "men," marbles, and other objects. With the invention of electricity and new advances in electronics, the world of games has really changed, with all kinds of computer and video games now filling store shelves.

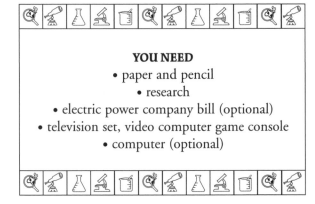

YOU NEED
- paper and pencil
- research
- electric power company bill (optional)
- television set, video computer game console
- computer (optional)

Some games now available on home computers used to be played without using electrical energy. Card games like solitaire and board games like Monopoly, for example, are just two games now popular on computers that can still be played in the "traditional" way, saving energy.

HYPOTHESIS Hypothesize that many electric games we play could be played without using electricity.

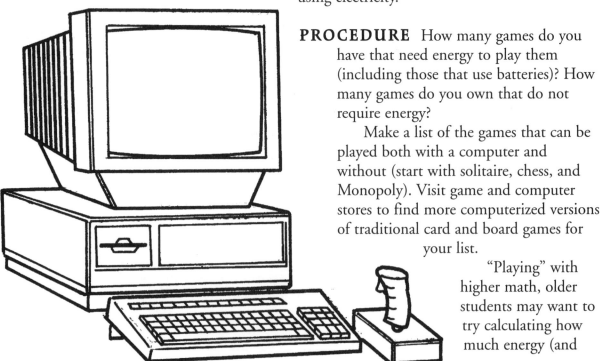

PROCEDURE How many games do you have that need energy to play them (including those that use batteries)? How many games do you own that do not require energy?

Make a list of the games that can be played both with a computer and without (start with solitaire, chess, and Monopoly). Visit game and computer stores to find more computerized versions of traditional card and board games for your list.

"Playing" with higher math, older students may want to try calculating how much energy (and money) can be saved by playing games that do not require electricity. Here's how to do that.

To determine the cost of using an electrical appliance, look for a label or tag on the unit or refer to the owner's manual to find its power consumption. The power consumption figure will be listed in "watts." Electric power companies charge by how many "kilowatt-hours" are used. One kilowatt is equal to 1,000 watts. It takes one kilowatt-hour of energy to operate ten 100-watt light bulbs for one hour (10 × 100 = 1,000).

To find out how much energy it takes to play a TV video game, look on the back of the television set and on the video game console for the power consumption of each, listed in "watts." Add the two numbers together. Let's assume that the video game uses 50 watts and the television set uses 150 watts. That makes a total of 200 watts. To convert this to "kilowatts," a unit the power company uses, divide 200 by 1,000, which equals 0.200 kilowatts. Have an adult search out a recent electric bill and help you determine how much it costs for 1 kilowatt-hour of power. You can get a rough idea by dividing the amount due on the electric bill by the number of kilowatt-hours used that month. This information will be listed on the electric bill.

Suppose your electric bill was $165.13 and the kilowatt-hours used was 1,365. Dividing $165.13 by 1,365 equals 0.12, or 12 cents per kilowatt-hour. So, to play the video game for one hour would cost about 0.200 times 12 cents, or 2.4 cents. It may not sound like much money, but just think of how many hours a year you and your family spend playing that video game! Calculate how much it does cost you for a year!

To find how much energy it takes to play a computer game, remember to add the power consumption of both the CPU (the "central processing unit," or main part of the computer) and the monitor, since both are needed.

RESULTS & CONCLUSION Write down the results of your experiment. Come to a conclusion as to whether or not your hypothesis was correct.

HEAT WAVE

DISCOVERING HOW MICROWAVES GENERATE HEAT

PURPOSE To discover how microwaves create heat.

OVERVIEW Microwaves are a kind of radio frequency energy (electromagnetic waves). Their frequency (the number of times the wave vibrates each second) is much higher than most other types of radio and TV waves.

Microwaves are used for telephone and satellite communications, and for fast cooking. When microwaves pass through food, they cause the molecules in the food to move back and forth very rapidly. This generates heat. Have you ever rubbed your hands together rapidly to warm them? A microwave oven works in a similar way. Microwaves vibrate the molecules of water, sugar and fat in food, but pass right through glass, pottery, paper, wood and plastic. That is why, although food cooks in a microwave oven, the dish doesn't get hot—except for some heat transfer from the food. Metal blocks microwaves, so it should never be used in a microwave oven.

YOU NEED
- use of a microwave oven
- 2 thermometers
- coffee or tea cup (must be "microwave safe")
- water
- an adult

HYPOTHESIS Hypothesize that a microwave oven does not cook by making the air in the oven hot, like a traditional oven does, but by heating up the food from the inside.

PROCEDURE Ask an adult to help, and fill a cup with water. Put it inside a microwave oven and heat it for 60 seconds. Be sure the cup is "microwave safe," that is, made of plastic, glass or pottery without any metal in it or metallic decorations on it.

When the time is up, take the cup out of the oven. Lay a thermometer inside the oven and close the door (but DO NOT turn the oven on). Stick a thermometer into the cup of water. After about two minutes, take the thermometer out of the oven and compare it to the one from the cup of water. Does the thermometer that was in the water read a higher temperature than the one placed in the oven?

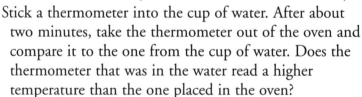

RESULTS & CONCLUSION Write down the results of your experiment. Come to a conclusion as to whether or not your hypothesis was correct.

No Tan Wanted

COLD-BLOODED ANIMALS AND HEAT ENERGY

PURPOSE How do cold-blooded animals stay warm?

YOU NEED
- books, photographs, and other research materials
- arts and crafts supplies

OVERVIEW Animals gather energy from the sun to warm their bodies and maintain their normal life processes. Even turtles, which are cold-blooded animals, sit for hours on rocks along a pond "sunning" themselves. A captive snake is sometimes seen standing straight up. It does this to get more light on its body to warm itself. Iguanas need heat to properly digest their food. Grasshoppers cannot chirp if the temperature falls below 62° Fahrenheit (17° Celsius).

HYPOTHESIS Hypothesize that cold-blooded animals must have sun to keep warm.

PROCEDURE Research cold-blooded animals that must have warming energy from the sun in order to live. Draw or construct a scene showing how these various animals gather warmth from the sun.

RESULTS & CONCLUSION
Write down the results of your research. Come to a conclusion as to whether or not your hypothesis was correct.

STATIC INTERFERENCE

DETECTING SOURCES OF STRAY RADIO FREQUENCY ENERGY

PURPOSE How can we recognize radio frequency energy?

OVERVIEW One kind of energy that we can't see or hear is called radio frequency energy. Radio frequency energy is formed by electro-magnetic waves that travel through the air. Radio frequency energy allows us to communicate with one another. It is used to bring TV pictures and sound to our homes from stations far away. Two-way radios let people talk to each other from remote places (you may even own a pair of "walkie talkies"). Cordless telephones allow people to talk on the phone while walking around the house or going outside without being restricted by a wire connecting the handset to the telephone base. "Cellular phones," both hand-held and car phones, permit communications with people who are not near a regular telephone. All these types of communication are possible because of an invisible kind of energy called radio frequency energy.

Some things may give off radio frequency energy, even when we don't want them to. Things that have electric motors often produce radio frequency energy when they are working. This energy may be unwanted, since it can interfere with other things that use radio frequencies, such as TVs, radios, and cordless telephones.

What things around your home do you think might be radiating (giving off) radio frequency energy? How about an electric shaver, a fluorescent light, an electric blanket, an electric hair dryer, an AM radio, a personal computer, or a television?

YOU NEED
- electric shaver
- cordless telephone
- fluorescent light
- electric blanket
- electric hair dryer
- AM radio
- personal computer
- television
- paper and pencil

HYPOTHESIS Hypothesize that since we cannot see or hear radio frequency energy, we can use a radio as a detector to help us find things around the house that are producing radio frequency energy.

PROCEDURE Tune a portable AM radio to a spot on the dial where no station is heard. Bring the radio close to each of these objects:
- an electric shaver
- a fluorescent light (often found in the kitchen or bathroom)
- an electric blanket

- an electric hair dryer
- a personal computer
- a television (turn the volume down on the TV set)

Write down your observations about each appliance. Did you hear a sound in the radio? If so, describe the sound; was it a crackling sound or a humming sound?

Call a friend on a cordless telephone. Ask your friend to be quiet and listen. Then hold your phone close to each of the appliances listed above, asking your friend each time what she or he hears, if anything. If your friend has a cordless phone, it's your turn to listen. What do you hear?

What other things around your home or school can you check out as radio frequency producers? What do you think—which makes the better radio frequency detector, an AM radio, or a cordless telephone?

RESULTS & CONCLUSION Write down the results of your experiment. Come to a conclusion as to whether or not your hypothesis was correct.

GREAT BARRIER ICE

MAGNETISM VS. WATER AND ICE

PURPOSE & OVERVIEW Magnetism, an invisible form of energy, can go through air. Can it go through water? What if the water is in the form of ice, where the molecules are in a more orderly and structured form. Does it affect magnetism?

HYPOTHESIS Hypothesize that water and ice will affect magnetic attraction.

PROCEDURE Fill a long, cylindrically shaped balloon with water. Don't inflate the balloon, just fill it with water in its uninflated shape. Tie the balloon to the middle of a pencil. Lay the pencil across two cups or glasses to let the balloon hang down.

> **YOU NEED**
> • strong magnet
> • staple, from stapler
> • 2 cups or glasses
> • 2 books
> • pencil
> • cylindrically-shaped balloon
> • use of a freezer
> • ruler

Lay a book on either side of the cups, so that they are separated by the balloon. On one book place a staple, and on the other, a strong magnet.

With the water-filled balloon between the staple and magnet, move the staple and/or the magnet until they are just close enough to each other that the staple is captured by the magnetic force of the magnet. Note the spot where the staple first showed signs of being attracted by the magnet. Measure the distance between the magnet and this spot.

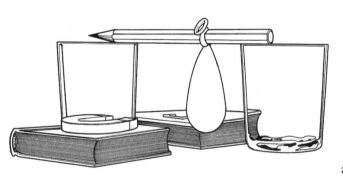

Without disturbing the books or the magnet, move the cups, with the pencil and balloon in place, to the freezer. Keep the setup the same, so the balloon will have the same shape as when the ice was water. When the water in the balloon has frozen, remove the setup from the freezer and put it back by the books.

Place the staple back on the book opposite the magnet at the spot where it was first attracted to the magnet. Does the force of magnetism go through the ice and move the staple? If it does, is there any difference in the distance between the staple and the magnet before the magnetic attraction affects the staple?

RESULTS & CONCLUSION Write down the results of your experiment. Come to a conclusion as to whether or not your hypothesis was correct.

ONWARD AND UPWARD

TRANSFERRING ENERGY UPHILL

PURPOSE & OVERVIEW Can a wave of energy travel uphill? We learned, in the Marble Roll and Frolicking in the Wave experiments, that energy travels in the form of a wave, and that it moves forward even though the objects passing the energy along do not. (They may move, but only a short distance compared to that of the energy transferred.) But uphill . . . ?

YOU NEED
- ruler
- dominos

HYPOTHESIS Hypothesize that either a wave of energy can travel uphill or it cannot.

PROCEDURE Place two dominos under a ruler to make a sloping ramp. Stand a domino on the ruler with its broad sides facing the ends. If the standing domino falls over, remove a domino under the ruler. If it stays standing, try to add another domino to make the ramp even steeper. Add dominos under the ruler until the ramp is as steep as possible without the upright standing dominos on top falling over. When you have made the ramp as steep as you can, stand a line of dominos along the ramp. Space them about 1 inch (2 cm) apart.

Push on the top half of the first domino, on the lowest part of the ramp, and tip it forward into the next-higher one. Does a chain reaction occur and knock the top domino off the ruler? If so, a wave of energy, which came from your "push," traveled uphill, even though the actual domino you pushed only moved a little bit.

To do more experimenting with this project, you may want to try making a wave of energy go even more steeply uphill. You can do this by building steps with building blocks, or other materials, and again using dominos to try to transfer the energy uphill. With steps, the dominos can stand on a level surface; but remember that to make the next domino in line fall forward, it must be hit on its top half. If it is struck near the middle or its lower half, it could fall backward instead of forward.

RESULTS & CONCLUSION Write down the results of your experiment. Come to a conclusion as to whether or not your hypothesis was correct.

INVISIBLE BEAMS

LOCATING LIGHT IN THE DARKNESS

PURPOSE & OVERVIEW Some kinds of energy are invisible. A beam of light energy itself is invisible. We see light only when the light energy directly enters the eye, or reflects off an object and bounces into the eye.

Normally, we can't see the light rays that are coming from the sun (*never look directly at the sun*), but we see only the things the sunlight shines on. At dusk, after the sun has set where you are, you may have noticed the sun's light shining brightly on an airplane flying overhead. High in the sky, the sun's light energy rays are still hitting the airplane, even though you can no longer see the sun from Earth's surface.

YOU NEED
- flashlight
- small cardboard box
- scissors
- talcum powder
- a dark room
- an adult

You may also have seen sunbeams, when the sun's light streams through a break in the clouds. Because there are billions of tiny dust particles in the air, it's possible to see the sun's light energy bouncing off them against a dark sky beyond. Other times, after a

rainstorm, the water droplets in the atmosphere behind us, away from the setting sun, will reflect the sun's light at different angles and show you a rainbow. Sunlight also contains other types of invisible energy rays that we cannot see. In the summer, you cannot see the ultraviolet rays coming from the sun, but too much of this kind of energy will give you a sunburn!

HYPOTHESIS Hypothesize that light rays can be seen with the help of some household products.

PROCEDURE To make light rays visible, have an adult help you cut a small hole about the size of a large coin in a small cardboard box (a shoebox would work well). Turn a flashlight on and place it inside the box so that its light shines out through the hole. Close up the box so that the hole is the only place where light can escape from inside.

   Place the box on a table or dresser in a very dark room. Standing several feet in front of the box, gently shake or squeeze some talcum powder from its container into range of the light energy coming out of the box. The light from the flashlight in the box can now be seen bouncing from the powdery talcum particles.

   A light beam can also be a useful tool, helping us to see particles in the air that are normally too small for us to notice or see well. Instead of using talcum powder, if you have them try clapping two chalkboard erasers together. You can also shake a fresh facial tissue, right from a box, into the beam. Try different brands of facial tissue. Do some give off more lint particles than others?

RESULTS & CONCLUSION Write down the results of your experiment. Come to a conclusion as to whether or not your hypothesis was correct.

PENNY SHOOT

NEWTON'S LAW AND THE TRANSFER OF ENERGY

PURPOSE What is Newton's First Law of Motion?

OVERVIEW Sir Isaac Newton, an early scientist born in England in 1642, discovered some important principles of natural science, including the Laws of Motion in physics. His First Law of Motion states that "an object at rest tends to stay at rest, and an object in motion tends to stay in motion." A famous trick demonstrates this law. A playing card is placed over a drinking cup and a coin is laid on top of the card, directly over the mouth of the cup. Then the edge of the card is given a sharp tap with a finger or pencil. The blow knocks the card off the cup, but the coin on the card, being at rest, stays in position. Then gravity pulls down on the coin and it drops into the cup.

YOU NEED
- section of wood, 3 to 4 inches (8–10 cm) wide by about 2 feet (60 cm) long
- five coins
- a smaller coin
- two nails
- hammer
- small rubber band
- stapler
- thin cardboard
- scissors
- smooth paper

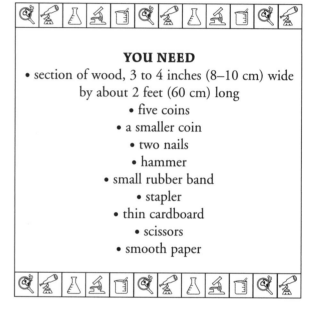

HYPOTHESIS Hypothesize that we can build a device that will not only demonstrate this law of Newton's, but also show a transfer of energy (energy from one object being handed off to another object).

PROCEDURE Cut a strip of smooth paper to fit on the wooden board. Lay it on top of the wooden board. Towards one end of the board, hammer two small nails, spaced about 3 inches (7.5 cm) apart, partway into the wood. The nails should be sticking up out of the wood about an inch (2.5 cm), looking like goal posts at a football field.

Stretch a small rubber band between the two "goal post" nails. Cut a small strip of thin cardboard, about one inch (2.5 cm) wide by two inches (5 cm) long. Fold it in half around the rubber band (in the middle) and staple the cardboard ends together. Push the rubber band down on the goal posts, so it rests almost against the wood.

About 1 inch (2.5 cm) in front of the goal posts, place one of the medium coins face up. Then stack four more coins on top, but with tails up.

Grab the stapled piece of folded cardboard between your thumb and index finger and pull back. A stretched rubber band is said to have "potential energy," energy that is stored up and ready to do work.

While the rubber band is stretched, place the smaller coin between the goal posts. Release the cardboard so that it strikes this coin and shoots it towards the stack. The idea is to knock the bottom coin out from under, leaving the other four stacked coins at rest (although they will drop straight down due to gravity).

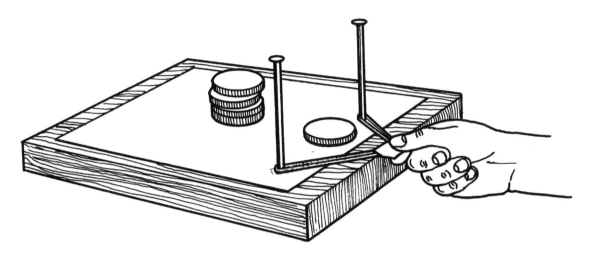

You may have to try this several times. Your aim may be off, and sometimes the smaller coin may fly slightly upwards and miss hitting the bottom coin. If a coin does move from the stack, it may happen too fast for you to see. To be sure it was the *bottom* coin that really was knocked out, see if the coin that was moved has heads or tails up. If it's heads, then you successfully shot out the bottom coin.

This project also shows two examples of the transfer of energy. When the stretched rubber band (potential energy) is released (kinetic energy), energy from the rubber band is transferred to the smaller coin, giving it motion. Energy is then transferred again when this coin hits the stacked coins. The force must be great enough for this struck coin to overcome the friction of the coins on top of it, and the surface under it, which is why we placed a piece of smooth paper under the stack.

The "momentum" of the moving coin will determine just how far it will travel after it has been shot out from under the pile. Remember, "objects in motion tend to stay in motion," so once the coin is moving, it will *naturally* try to keep going; friction eventually slows it down enough to make it stop.

RESULTS & CONCLUSION Write down the results of your experiment. Come to a conclusion as to whether or not your hypothesis was correct.

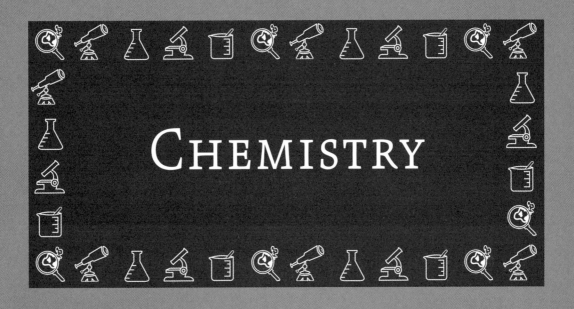

CHEMISTRY

INTRODUCTION TO
CHEMISTRY

Welcome to the world of chemistry! This section explores projects in this fascinating field. Chemistry is the study of what substances are made of, how they can be changed, and how they can be combined with other substances to make new substances. When substances are changed or combined, their old properties are changed, and new ones are taken on. Plastic is an example of a new substance made from other substances.

Chemistry is a branch of physical science. It is one of the most interesting and motivating topics in science. It's important to understand chemistry because so many of its principles are found in other science disciplines, including astronomy, geology, mathematics, environmental science, botany, health and medicine, electronics, physics, and even the arts. Some of its basic principles are safety, measurement, the scientific method of procedures and evaluation, cause and effect, written reporting of results, and problem recognition.

Chemistry is at work all around us, and is a part of our daily lives. Medicines, garden fertilizers, food preservatives, synthetics, energy from batteries and the burning of coal to make electricity, glass made from limestone and sand, explosives, disinfectants for cleaning, and even the baking of yeast to cause bread to rise are all examples of chemistry at work. Read the label on packaged foods and cleaning supplies and you will often see listed the names of chemicals that are contained in it.

Energy can be given off from chemical changes: electricity, light, and heat. When something burns, a chemical reaction is taking place, with light and heat given off. Chemical changes can occur when elements come in contact with each other, when they decompose, or when temperature or pressure are changed.

UNDER PRESSURE

HOW HANDLING AFFECTS SUBSTANCES

PURPOSE Studying the effects of squeezing on liquid, a solid, some gel, and a colloidal substance.

OVERVIEW Pressure sometimes causes a change in matter. Great underground pressure is what creates diamonds. But even squeezing by hand can cause change in certain substances. Cornstarch, made from corn and used in cooking as a thickening agent (as in gravy), is what is called a colloidal substance. It is made up of small particles that don't dissolve but stay suspended in a fluid. Mixed with water, when cornstarch is at rest, it forms a substance that somewhat resembles a liquid, but the substance changes its property to be more like a solid when pressure is applied.

YOU NEED
- cornstarch
- teaspoon
- water
- gelatin dessert
- piece of ice

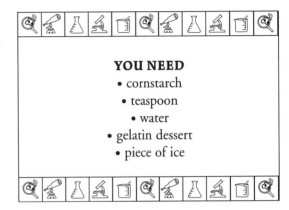

HYPOTHESIS Of four sample materials, only the colloidal substance will undergo physical change (other than breaking up) when hand pressure is applied.

PROCEDURE Take some gelatin dessert from the refrigerator, place it into the palm of your hand and use the forefinger and thumb of your other hand to apply pressure. The *constant* is the application of this pinching pressure. The *variables* are the materials being tested. Now, apply pressure to an ice chip or cube, and to some water.

   Next, shake about a teaspoon of cornstarch into your palm. Add a few drops of water to the cornstarch, and stir it around to mix it in. Slowly add a few more drops, a little at a time. When the mixture is slightly watery, it's ready. Now, squeeze the colloidal substance between your forefinger and thumb and the pressure causes it to become putty-like. Stop, and it becomes more liquid, with a little water seeping into your palm. Do it again. Doesn't it have a strange feel? What a great natural toy!

RESULTS & CONCLUSION Write down the results of your experiment. Come to a conclusion as to whether or not your hypothesis was correct.

SOMETHING MORE Does a flour-and-water mixture become a colloidal substance?

LEMONY LINEUP

REAL LEMON OR FAKE FOOD FLAVORING?

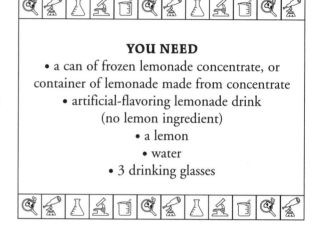

PURPOSE Can the natural flavor of a fresh-squeezed lemon in water be recognized in a lineup when compared to a drink made from frozen or lemon drink "concentrate" or an artificially flavored lemonade?

YOU NEED

- a can of frozen lemonade concentrate, or container of lemonade made from concentrate
- artificial-flavoring lemonade drink (no lemon ingredient)
- a lemon
- water
- 3 drinking glasses

OVERVIEW Through chemical research, substances have been created that smell or taste like other natural substances—and even more so! Often, it's these substances, rather than the actual items, that are used in manufactured and food products to make the products more appealing to the consumer.

If you have ever been in the kind of store that sells leather goods such as pocket books, attaché cases, travel luggage, or saddles, you may have noticed a strong scent of leather. It could be the real smell of the leather or it could be a case of chemical trickery, where the products, real leather or not, have been chemically treated to make them smell more "leathery." Maybe the leather scent was even just sprayed into the air! Is that great smell of apples and cinnamon in your local bakery real? Is baking actually done on the premises?

People tend to associate the smell of lemon with cleanliness and freshness. That's why, on supermarket shelves, you will find dish detergents, laundry detergents, and liquid bathroom cleaners that have a lemon scent. Although the products smell like lemon, they very likely don't really have lemon juice in them at all.

In the same way, manufacturers will sometimes place flavoring additives in their products, to make them taste even more like the fruit they are supposed to contain, "even fruitier" than the fruit would be by itself. Are you surprised to think that a drink that has been artificially flavored may taste more "real" than a drink made from the real fruit? Read the ingredients listed on your favorite drinks. Does the grape drink really have grape juice listed as an ingredient? Is it mostly water (the higher-quantity substances are listed first) or other less flavorful juices? Has grape or other flavoring been added? Look at the ingredients listed on powdered drink mixes, too.

HYPOTHESIS A drink made with a lemon concentrate and/or artificially flavored lemonade mix will taste more "lemony" than one made with the juice of fresh-squeezed lemon.

PROCEDURE For the project, prepare three "lemonades." First, using a can of frozen lemonade concentrate, add water and mix according to the instructions . . . or simply pour some from a container of "made from concentrate" lemon drink.

Next, pour some artificially flavored lemon drink from a container, or mix up a serving from a packet of artificial lemonade mix that needs water added to it. Read the labels on the containers, cans, or packets, to be sure you are using the right thing. Here, look for the phrase "artificial flavoring." Pour some into a drinking glass.

Carefully cut a lemon in half, squeeze some of the juice into a drinking glass and add a little water to it. (You might want to add a tiny bit of sugar, too.) Stir.

Do a taste test. If the real lemon drink tastes weak, too watery, squeeze out more lemon juice. You want to taste the lemon. The *constant* is your body's taste system. The *variable* is the source of the lemon flavor.

Which drink tastes more lemony to you: the juice from a fresh lemon, lemonade made from concentrate, or artificially flavored lemonade?

RESULTS & CONCLUSION Write down the results of your experiment. Come to a conclusion as to whether or not your hypothesis was correct.

SOMETHING MORE
1. Have your friends and family members taste each of the three drinks, without them knowing the source of each juice. Do they come to the same conclusion that you did?
2. Would the results be any different if other juices were compared? Try orange or lime.

NOTHING TO SNIFF AT

SMELL AND THE SECRET OF "WAFTING"

PURPOSE How to smell a strong substance safely.

OVERVIEW Smells come from in-air particles in the form of gases and vapors. The chemical solution and nerve cells that line our noses interact with the vapors, and the brain interprets the smell.

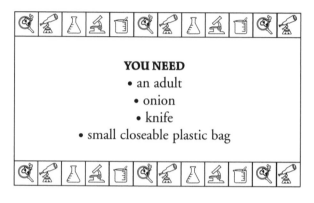

YOU NEED
- an adult
- onion
- knife
- small closeable plastic bag

Although some scents, like flowers, cinnamon, and coffee, are nice, others are unpleasant and can even be hazardous. Breathing gas, for example, given off by powdered chlorine granules used in swimming pools when even a little water is spilled on them, can make you deathly ill. *Never* inhale, or take a deep breath, of any substance that you are not perfectly sure is completely safe!

A safety practice in chemistry of just "sampling" a scent, which should be used throughout your life, is called wafting. It's a way to get just a "whiff" of the odor a substance gives off. A very small amount is mixed, with a wave of your hand, into a puff of air—then you quickly "sniff."

HYPOTHESIS You can "sample" an odor in a way that avoids physical discomfort.

PROCEDURE This science project demonstrates the seriousness, and danger, of breathing in substances. The *constant* is the human olfactory system—the nose. The *variable* is the method used to introduce the onion odor to your nose.

First, have an adult chop up a strong fresh onion and close it in a plastic bag. Open the bag near your face. Quickly wave your hand over the opening, fanning some of the onion vapors past your nose. Sniff, and close the bag. Did you smell the onion? Now open the bag and take in a good deep breath. You'll probably cough and your eyes will tear up. Which do you think is the safer way to smell the vapor?

RESULTS & CONCLUSION Write down the results of your experiment. Come to a conclusion as to whether or not your hypothesis was correct.

SOMETHING MORE Try wafting other unpleasant-smelling, safe (food) substances.

IT'S LITMUS!

MAKING pH (ACID/BASE) TESTING STRIPS

PURPOSE Learning the best way to make homemade litmus testing papers for experimenting.

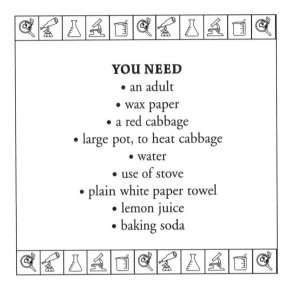

YOU NEED
- an adult
- wax paper
- a red cabbage
- large pot, to heat cabbage
- water
- use of stove
- plain white paper towel
- lemon juice
- baking soda

OVERVIEW One characteristic of chemical substances is the amount of acid or base they contain. Foods that contain weak acids, for example, lemon or lime juice and pickles, taste sour. On the pH scale, the opposite of acid is base, also called alkali. Bases have a slippery feel and taste bitter. Examples of base substances are milk of magnesia, baking soda, soap, ammonia, and many cleaners. Both strong acids and bases may be very hazardous; they can burn and hurt you. Powerful cleaning products, especially those that unclog household drains, contain very strong bases that can be hazardous if they get on your skin or are breathed in.

In the way a ruler is used to measure how long something is and a thermometer is used to show how hot something is, chemists use the pH scale as a measurement of the amount of acid or base a substance contains. The technical term pH comes from "the **p**otential of power + **H**ydrogen." Chemists have a meter that can measure the pH electronically, but that is not how pH was measured long ago, and we can still do it this original, easier way.

The pH scale goes from 0 to 14, 0 being the strongest acid, 7 being neutral (in the middle), and 14 the strongest base, or alkali. Pure water has a pH of 7. If you have a swimming pool, you may have used pH testing, where a sample of water is collected and a few drops of a special chemical are added and mixed together. The resulting color of the water is matched against a color comparison chart to find the exact pH.

One way to measure pH is by using litmus paper. Litmus paper comes in different colors to measure different ranges of pH. Red litmus paper turns blue in a base solution. Blue litmus paper turns red in an acid solution. A color chart is used to compare the color that the litmus paper turns to a pH number.

Note: The information in this project serves as a background for the following few projects, which also work with pH, acids, and bases.

HYPOTHESIS Hypothesize that homemade litmus paper can be made from the juice of a red cabbage, and for best results the juice should be concentrated.

PROCEDURE Litmus paper is inexpensive and can be purchased at a science shop or through a science catalog, but you can also make your own. Have an adult help you boil a red cabbage (the kind of cabbage that is purple in color). It should be cut into quarters, placed in a pot with a cupful of water, and boiled. After about fifteen to twenty minutes, turn off the stove.

Cut some plain white paper toweling into small strips. When the pot's contents have cooled, transfer the cabbage water to a glass and dip several strips into it. Place them on wax paper to dry.

Now we want to make a second batch of strips by dipping them into cabbage water that is more concentrated to see if the stronger liquid will make the litmus strips react and change color more clearly. The paper toweling and the evaluation materials (the lemon juice and baking soda) are the *constants*. The *variable* is the concentration of the cabbage water.

For the second batch of strips, let the cabbage water sit in the glass for several days in a warm, sunny spot in your home until a lot of the water has evaporated. This will mean the cabbage water that remains is more concentrated. Dip strips of paper towel into this concentrated solution and lay them on wax paper to dry.

Use your homemade litmus paper to test lemon juice (an acid) and baking soda mixed in water (a base). What color does your homemade litmus paper turn when a few drops of lemon juice are placed on it? What color does the litmus paper turn when a few drops of baking soda mixed in water are placed on it? Do strips from the second batch of litmus paper change color more clearly than those from the first, and so make a better indicator?

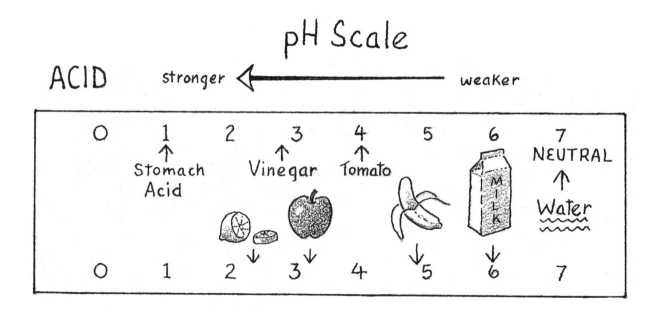

RESULTS & CONCLUSION Write down the results of your experiment. Come to a conclusion as to whether or not your hypothesis was correct.

SOMETHING MORE

1. In addition to making litmus paper, simply pour ¼ cup of the cabbage water into three glasses. Add a little baking soda to one glass and some lemon juice to another. Watch the color changes. Compare the two colors to the original color.

2. Make your own color comparison chart for use with your homemade litmus paper. See the pH scale chart shown at the bottom of these pages. The pH numbers are given for different items such as vinegar, bananas, and milk of magnesia.

weaker ⟶ stronger   BASE

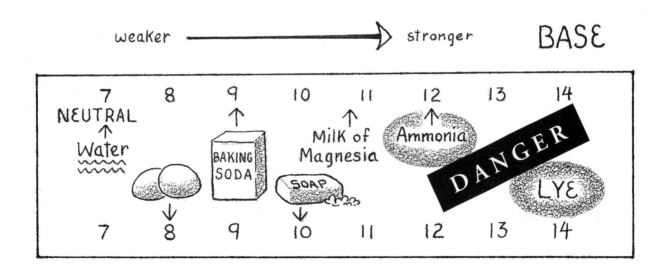

ACUTE CUKE

THE CHEMICAL CHANGE CALLED PICKLING

PURPOSE Some like sweet pickles, some like sour ones, some prefer regular cucumbers. What's the difference in their pH readings?

YOU NEED
- dill pickle
- fresh cucumber
- litmus paper
- color comparison chart for litmus paper
- 2 spoons

OVERVIEW Pickling is a chemical process used to preserve food. Fruits, vegetables, and even meats can be pickled. The food to be preserved is soaked in vinegar and brine (brine is very salty water). Sometimes sugar and spices are added to change the flavor.

The most common food that is processed that way is the cucumber, which is then called a "pickle." Dill pickles are the most common type of sour-tasting pickles. Small pickled cucumbers, called gherkins, are known for their sweet taste.

Does a food that tastes sour have a low pH, meaning it is an acid? (Refer to the detailed explanations of pH and litmus paper in the glossary and in the previous project, It's Litmus!)

HYPOTHESIS Hypothesize that a sour-tasting pickle will have a low pH.

PROCEDURE Squeeze some cucumber juice onto a spoon and some pickle juice onto another spoon. Use a strip of litmus paper to test the pH of the cucumber juice, then the juice of the dill pickle. Which is more acidic? Which tastes more sour? The *constants* are your taste buds and the litmus paper pH indicators. The *variable* is the state of the cucumber—fresh or dilled.

RESULTS & CONCLUSION Write down the results of your experiment. Come to a conclusion as to whether or not your hypothesis was correct.

SOMETHING MORE Do sweeter pickles, such as gherkins, have low pH? Test several kinds of pickle after hypothesizing which will have lower pH. Then eat them.

BAD COW?

A NON-TASTE TEST FOR SOUR MILK

PURPOSE Milk may smell okay, but is it? We need a way to see if milk is bad without tasting it.

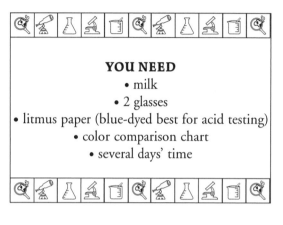

YOU NEED
- milk
- 2 glasses
- litmus paper (blue-dyed best for acid testing)
- color comparison chart
- several days' time

OVERVIEW Milk is kept in the refrigerator so it will keep fresh longer. When it sours, an acid is formed. Since no one likes to get a mouthful of sour milk, can we find out if milk is still good by testing instead of tasting it? (Smelling the milk sometimes works—but not always.) Since an acid forms in sour milk, how about checking its pH?

HYPOTHESIS Hypothesize that you can tell if milk is sour by using pH testing.

PROCEDURE Pour some fresh milk into a glass. Use litmus paper to check its pH and write it down. Now let the milk sit at room temperature for a few days. Once a day, use litmus paper to check the pH of the left-out milk. The *constant* is the litmus paper used as a pH indicator. The *variable* is the milk.

   After a number of days, pour some fresh milk into another glass and test them both. Compare the pH of the fresh glass of milk to the original pH test on the first glass. Is it the same . . . or nearly? (The refrigerated milk may also not be as fresh as it was some days ago.) Observe the condition of the milk that had been left out and compare it to the newly poured milk. Does it look different? Smell different? If you are not sure you see a difference, leave the "old" milk out another day or two. Does milk that has spoiled measure as more acid?

RESULTS & CONCLUSION Write down the results of your experiment. Come to a conclusion as to whether or not your hypothesis was correct.

SOMETHING MORE Do foods like hot pepper sauce and horseradish taste "hot" because they have a low pH?

LESS IS MORE

FOR GREATER CONCENTRATION, EVAPORATE!

PURPOSE To find out if an acidic liquid increases in acidity from concentration due to evaporation.

OVERVIEW When water in a solution evaporates, what is left in the liquid becomes more concentrated. A pool of salt water becomes saltier; the amount of salt stays the same but is less diluted. During a hot dry spell, the sodium, calcium, and pollutants in the waters of ponds, lakes, and tide pools can become more concentrated, where no new water is added. This may put a strain on the plant and animal life that live there.

As evaporation takes place and the water remaining becomes more concentrated, is there a change in pH?

YOU NEED
- litmus paper
- color comparison chart
- drinking glass
- lemon juice
- water
- spoon
- a sunny window
- several days' time

HYPOTHESIS Hypothesize that pH change is measurable as liquid evaporates.

PROCEDURE Pour several spoonfuls of lemon juice into a drinking glass. Fill the rest of the glass with water. Stir. Using litmus paper and a color comparison chart, determine the pH of the solution. Is this solution an acid or a base?

Place the glass in a sunny window until only about a third of the solution is left. Check the pH again. Has it changed? Has the solution become stronger, that is, more acidic (a lower pH number)? The *constant* is the room environment and the litmus paper test strips. The *variable* is the liquid as it becomes more concentrated.

RESULTS & CONCLUSION Write down the results of your experiment. Come to a conclusion as to whether or not your hypothesis was correct.

SOMETHING MORE
1. Would the lemon juice itself, composed mostly of water, evaporate and become more concentrated? Could this be measured by a change in pH?
2. Compare the pH difference of fresh-squeezed lemon juice and bottled concentrate.

COOKING pHACTS

THE EFFECT OF COOKING ON pH

PURPOSE To find out if the process of cooking changes a food's pH.

OVERVIEW Foods can change quite a bit when they are cooked. Some taste differently than when they are raw. (A friend who likes to eat bell peppers that are cooked, such as "stuffed pepper" for dinner, can't stand to eat them raw, in a salad.)

Sometimes cooking removes vitamins from a food. This is especially true of water-soluble vitamins (vitamin C, for example). Does cooking also change the pH of foods?

YOU NEED
- an adult
- onion
- litmus paper
- color comparison chart
- a bowl
- garlic press
- cooking pot
- use of stove

HYPOTHESIS Hypothesize that the pH of onion juice is changed by cooking.

PROCEDURE Peel an onion. Using a garlic press, squeeze some pieces of onion and catch the juice in a bowl. Determine the pH of the onion juice with litmus paper and a color comparison chart.

Pour the juice into a small cooking pot and slowly bring it to a boil. Be careful working around a hot stove. Be sure to have an adult present for safety. As soon as the juice boils, turn the stove burner off and let the pot and juice cool. When cool, measure the pH again. Has it changed? The litmus paper used as a pH indicator is the *constant*. The onion is the *variable*, cooked or raw.

RESULTS & CONCLUSION Write down the results of your experiment. Come to a conclusion as to whether or not your hypothesis was correct.

SOMETHING MORE Try checking the pH of other liquids and then bringing them to a boil to see if cooking affects pH. Use a solution of baking soda and water (which is a base) and then test lemon juice (which is an acid).

Getting Ahead

REACTION BETWEEN A BASE AND AN ACID

PURPOSE Can lemon juice replace vinegar in the traditional "volcano eruption" project?

YOU NEED
- baking soda
- lemon juice
- vinegar
- 2 same-size drinking glasses
- teaspoon
- a sink

OVERVIEW When baking soda and vinegar come together, a chemical reaction takes place. (Baking soda is a "base" and vinegar is an "acid.") Carbon dioxide gas, known as CO_2, is quickly released. Bubbles foam up and spill out of the container in a violent eruption that's impressive but an all-too-common project. But, is there something special about vinegar that causes this reaction, or is it simply the fact that vinegar is an acid?

HYPOTHESIS Because vinegar and lemon juice are both acids, their reactions to baking soda will be similar.

PROCEDURE Pour some vinegar into one glass and the same amount of lemon juice into the other. Holding the glass with vinegar over a sink, add a teaspoonful of baking soda. A chemical reaction takes place, releasing CO_2—like opening a soda can that has been shaken. Notice the size of the bubble "head."

Then, hold the glass with the lemon juice—an acid, too—over the sink. Add the teaspoonful of baking soda. The baking soda is the *constant*. The *variable* is the type of acids used, vinegar and lemon juice. Does the lemon juice solution bubble?

RESULTS & CONCLUSION Write down the results of your experiment. Come to a conclusion as to whether or not your hypothesis was correct.

SOMETHING MORE
1. Try other substances with acid pH: orange, grapefruit, other citrus juices. Check their pHs first. Is the reaction bigger with lower pH juices (more/less acidic)?
2. Does temperature affect the reaction of acid and baking soda? To test, put some pH acid in the refrigerator and an equal amount in a warm, sunny window. Once temperatures have adjusted, add an equal amount of baking soda and observe the reactions.

WE SALUTE SOLUTION

UNDERSTANDING BASIC CHEMICAL TERMS

PURPOSE "Solutes" and "solvents" can chemically combine, other substances don't. True?

OVERVIEW A "mixture" is two or more substances mixed together which do not chemically combine but remain the same as before. In a solution, a substance (called a solute) dissolves, becoming evenly distributed throughout another substance (called a solvent).

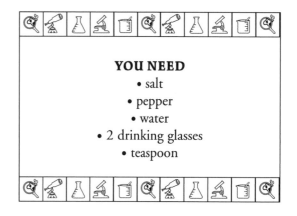

YOU NEED
- salt
- pepper
- water
- 2 drinking glasses
- teaspoon

HYPOTHESIS Hypothesize that pepper, which is not a solute, does not chemically combine with water. Salt, however, will combine with water.

PROCEDURE Add a teaspoon of salt to a drinking glass filled with water. Stir. The salt dissolves into the water and can no longer be seen nor easily removed. The water and salt have chemically combined to form a "solution."

Add a teaspoon of pepper to another glass filled with water. Stir. Has the pepper dissolved in the water, or is it floating on top or rising slowly within it? Has the pepper stayed essentially the way it was before it was added to the water? Pepper and water make a "mixture." The water and the amount of material added to the water are *constant*. The type of material added to the water is *varied* (salt, then pepper).

RESULTS & CONCLUSION Write down the results of your experiment. Come to a conclusion as to whether or not your hypothesis was correct.

SOMETHING MORE
1. Can you add salt to a glass of water until so much is added that no more will dissolve into the water, and the salt instead settles to the bottom of the glass?
2. You can separate pepper from water by skimming it off the surface. Is it possible to recover salt from water? What if the water were evaporated?
3. Adding powdered chocolate to warm milk to make hot cocoa is a solution. Does adding sugar to iced tea make a solution or a mixture?

Go, Old Mold!

FOOD ADDITIVES KEEP BREAD GOOD LONGER

PURPOSE Determine which brands and types of bread you buy have chemical mold inhibitors added to them.

OVERVIEW A science experiment traditionally done in elementary school grades involves growing mold on a slice of moist bread. Molds are microscopic plants. Molds grow from tiny particles called spores, which travel through the air. A moist slice of bread is an excellent "home" for mold to grow.

However, in recent years teachers are finding that growing mold on bread isn't always easy! The reason is that many breads today have some kind of special chemical added to them to stop mold. It is called a mold inhibitor.

Food additives are substances added to foods during processing to either help preserve them, improve color or flavor, or make their texture more appealing. Chemists have also devised food additives that inhibit (slow down) the growth of molds, and some of those additives are commonly placed in packaged bread. These food additives have passed many tests and have been approved by the United States Food and Drug Administration as being safe to eat before manufacturers were permitted to add them to their food products.

By adding such mold-inhibitor chemicals to breads, today's baked loaves will not go moldy and will remain edible for a longer period of time.

> ### YOU NEED
> - packaged white bread
> - fresh white bread (home-baked or local bakery)
> - rye bread
> - wheat bread
> - water
> - four plates
> - teaspoon
> - pencil
> - paper

Does fresh-baked bread from a local bakery provide a better medium (place) for growing mold than mass-processed, packaged bread from a supermarket, which may contain food additives as preservatives?

HYPOTHESIS Hypothesize that some breads are made with mold inhibitors added, so mold will not grow on them as quickly as on other breads.

PROCEDURE Select four slices of bread and place each on a plate. Each slice should be a different kind of bread. One slice should be from a fresh-baked loaf from a local bakery. One should be a packaged white bread, another a slice of rye bread, and another a slice of wheat bread. You may also wish to test oat-nut bread, a multigrain bread, or any other interesting bread you find at the store or is home-baked.

Set the plates in an out-of-the-way place. Every day, sprinkle three drops of water on each slice of bread to keep them moist. Write down your observations about each slice of bread every day. How long is it before you see mold forming? Which bread is the first to begin growing mold? Which is the last?

For your report, ask your local bakery if it uses any preservative or mold-inhibitor food additives in the bread you used in your project. Compare the lists of ingredients of each loaf of packaged bread you tested.

RESULTS & CONCLUSION Write down the results of your experiment. Come to a conclusion as to whether or not your hypothesis was correct.

SOMETHING MORE
1. Hypothesize that keeping bread cooler will also help preserve it. Repeat the above experiment, but place an additional slice of each bread in the refrigerator. Check all the breads once a day and write down your observations.
2. One possible variable in the "something more" experiment above that wasn't controlled was light. The slice of bread *in the refrigerator* did not have light. Was it the temperature or the absence of light that affected the mold test results?
3. If spores get onto the bread from the air, would placing a fresh slice of bread of the type that gets moldy quickly inside a piece of clear plastic wrap keep it from getting moldy?

CAPTURED CARBON

THE CHEMICAL REACTION OF BURNING

PURPOSE Is it possible to detect and display the carbon given off from a burning candle?

OVERVIEW Oxidation is a process that occurs when oxygen combines chemically with other substances and changes them. Oxidation can happen quickly: wax oxidizes rapidly on a burning candle. Oxidation can happen slowly: an iron object oxidizes as it turns to rust.

When oxidation occurs fast, heat is given off quickly and sometimes light is given off, too. When a wooden log burns in a fireplace, the log is oxidizing rapidly, giving off heat and light.

Carbon is also a result of burning. Carbon is one of the basic elements of matter. It combines with many other substances to take on different forms. Diamonds are carbon. Gasoline and even beets contain carbon. Carbon can combine with oxygen to form carbon dioxide, which is a gas that plants absorb to make food for the plant.

HYPOTHESIS Hypothesize that light and heat are not the only things given off by a burning candle; that carbon is given off, too, as a result of the rapid oxidation taking place.

PROCEDURE We can prove the hypothesis by capturing some of the carbon being produced as a candle burns.

YOU NEED
- an adult
- candle
- candleholder
- matches
- dinner plate
- piece of paper toweling

Place a candle securely in a candleholder on a high table. Have an adult light a candle and stand by to help. Then, grasp a china dinner plate or bowl by its edge. Be sure that the dish is made of china, ceramic, or a similar material that does not burn (do not use a paper or plastic plate). Use caution around the lit candle.

Looking at the candle flame, hold the dish so the center of it is just about 1 inch (2.5 cm) above the flame tip. Hold it there for only

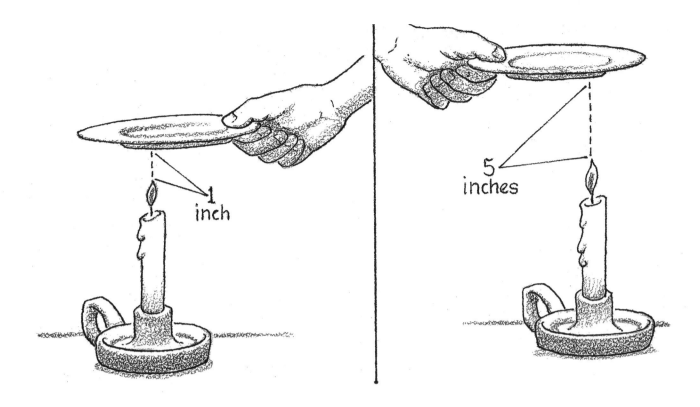

several seconds. Do not hold the plate over the flame too long or it might become too hot to hold.

Observe the bottom of the dish. Is it turning black as carbon is collected? Hold the dish away from the candle until it cools and can be touched. Rub your finger across the black carbon that has been captured on the plate. Notice how it easily wipes off the plate and onto your finger. Use a paper towel to clean your hand, and be sure to wash the plate.

Hold the plate over the candle again, this time keeping it about 5 inches (12 cm) from the tip of the flame. Does carbon build up as quickly? Carbon builds up, laying on itself. Can you collect more carbon by holding the plate close to the tip of the flame, or farther away? The *constant* is the burning candle. The *variable* is the distance of the dish from the flame.

Extinguish the candle flame when you are done.

RESULTS & CONCLUSION Write down the results of your experiment. Come to a conclusion as to whether or not your hypothesis was correct.

SOMETHING MORE Could you use the collected carbon for face painting at a party or for doing artwork?

TICK TOCK TACK

TESTING THE OXIDATION TIME OF METALS

PURPOSE To determine what materials become oxidized.

OVERVIEW Oxidation is a process that occurs when oxygen combines with various substances. As explained in the previous project, oxidation can occur rapidly, as when a candle burns; or take a long time, as when iron rusts.

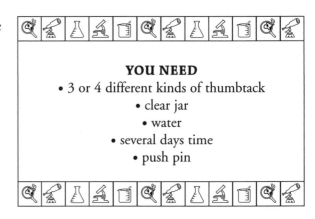

YOU NEED
- 3 or 4 different kinds of thumbtack
- clear jar
- water
- several days time
- push pin

If you wished to tack up posters or hang holiday decorations outdoors, you'd want to be sure the thumbtacks or push pins would hold up well in the weather.

HYPOTHESIS Hypothesize which items in water will rust.

PROCEDURE Find several kinds of thumbtacks. Some may be coated, some may be brass. Place the tacks along with a push pin in a clear jar filled with water. An empty mayonnaise, peanut butter, or pickle jar will work well. The jar may be plastic or glass.

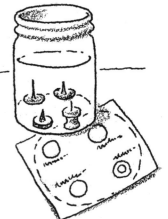

Draw a diagram on a piece of paper showing the location of each thumbtack and the name of its brand. Set the jar in an out-of-the-way place. Once a day, look at the objects in the jar and write down your observations. The water and the period of time under test is the *constant*. The *variable* is the different materials being tested.

After one week, examine your notes on the observations you made. Which one started to rust first? Are there any that did not rust? Why do you think some did not rust as much as others?

RESULTS & CONCLUSION Write down the results of your experiment. Come to a conclusion as to whether or not your hypothesis was correct.

SOMETHING MORE Try using other types of metal objects, such as staples and brass fasteners. Make daily observations and note any changes.

A PATCH OF WHITE

GREEN PLANTS AND PHOTOSYNTHESIS

PURPOSE Will chlorophyll return to grass that has been deprived of light? Let's figure it out.

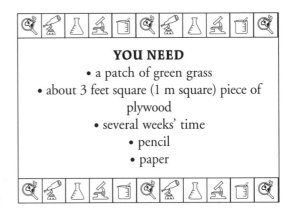

YOU NEED
- a patch of green grass
- about 3 feet square (1 m square) piece of plywood
- several weeks' time
- pencil
- paper

OVERVIEW Chlorophyll is a chemical in plants that makes them green. With the help of light energy, a plant's chlorophyll turns carbon dioxide and water into sugars it uses for food (the process of photosynthesis) and causes oxygen to be released. If a plant doesn't get the light it needs, photosynthesis can't take place and the plant loses its green coloring. If such a patch of grass is later opened to sunlight again, will the blades of white grass recover . . . turn green again?

HYPOTHESIS Decide whether you think white blades of grass do recover and turn green again, or if they wither and die and new green grass grows from the roots.

PROCEDURE To test your hypothesis, lay a piece of plywood over a section of green grass in a sunny area. Every day, lift up the plywood for a moment and observe the color of the grass underneath. Write down your observations. Is the green color becoming paler? Compare it to the color of the surrounding grass. The patch of grass remains *constant*. The *variable* is the light reaching the grass.

When the patch of grass has become white-looking, remove the plywood and leave it off. Every day, look at the grass patch and write down your observations. Does photosynthesis begin again in the blades of grass once the light has returned?

RESULTS & CONCLUSION Write down the results of your experiment. Come to a conclusion as to whether or not your hypothesis was correct.

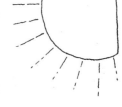

SOMETHING MORE If blades of grass do not recover once they turn white, would they start photosynthesis again if the length of time sunlight was kept from them was reduced? How can you test and show this?

POP GOES THE SODA

REDUCING CARBONATION IN SOFT DRINKS

PURPOSE How can we minimize the amount of carbon dioxide ingested from drinking a carbonated soda?

YOU NEED
- 2 twenty-ounce plastic bottles of soda
- 2 gallon-size sealable clear plastic food bags
- a sunny window
- use of freezer
- clock or watch

OVERVIEW In 1772 in England, Joseph Priestly was trying to discover how to imitate the natural bubbling waters of some mineral springs. That was the beginning of what is done today in many popular drinks. The ingredient that gives soda, sparkling water, and other such drinks their bubbly taste is carbon dioxide (chemical symbol CO_2). It makes a soda tickle your mouth and nose when you drink it.

When you breathe out, carbon dioxide is exhaled. Carbon dioxide gas is also formed by burning things that have the element carbon in them, which includes wood, coal, and oil (In the project Captured Carbon, carbon was collected from the gas of a burning candle.) Trees and plants take in carbon dioxide and release oxygen. This cycle is nature's way of providing clean air for people and animals to breathe, as well as carbon dioxide for trees and plants.

Carbon dioxide can be put under pressure and added to drinks to give them a pleasant biting taste and bubbly appearance. When carbon dioxide is added to water it is called soda water. Soft drinks (often called soda pop, or simply soda or pop) have become a big part of our society. They are called soft drinks to distinguish them from beverages containing alcohol (hard drinks). Can you imagine having a barbecue without soda to drink?

Although the carbon dioxide in our drinks is not harmful, the bubbles may cause gas in your stomach, which could cause some discomfort. If you wanted to minimize the

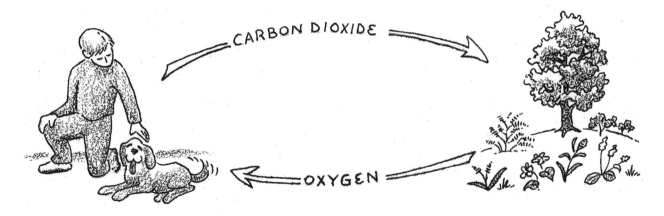

amount of carbon dioxide that you ingest, would it be better to drink your soda cold or warm it up, open the cap, then cool it before drinking?

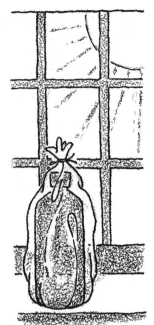

An interesting historical note: Soft drinks are also called "pop" because the bottle caps used prior to the 1890s made a popping noise when removed from the bottle.

HYPOTHESIS Hypothesize which of two bottles of soda will give off more carbon dioxide when opened, as detected by the sound of escaping gas when their caps are finally unsealed.

PROCEDURE Place a 20-ounce bottle of soda in a clear plastic food bag, one that can be sealed. Similarly, place another 20-ounce bottle of the same kind of soda in a plastic bag. Set one soda in the freezer section of a refrigerator. Set the other soda in a sunny window. Wait one hour (*no longer!*—we do *not* want the soda in the freezer to freeze).

Place the two sodas on a table, keeping them in the sealed bags. Unscrew the cap from each by grasping the cap through the sealed bag. The *constants* are the type and amount of soda. The temperature is the *variable*.

Which soda made the loudest hissing sound as gas escaped when the cap was opened? Which one spilled out the most gas and soda? The soda which made the loudest hiss and pushed out the most liquid now has less carbonated gas in it. If you drank that one, there would be less gas in your stomach. If it was the warm soda, you could now pour it in a glass, add ice to make it more desirable to drink, and it would put less gas in your stomach.

RESULTS & CONCLUSION Write down the results of your experiment. Come to a conclusion as to whether or not your hypothesis was correct.

SOMETHING MORE
1. Would the color of soda affect results? Repeat the experiment using a clear-colored soda (or use a dark-colored soda if you did the experiment first with a clear-colored soda).
2. Does shaking a bottle before opening it cause it to release more gas when the cap is unsealed? (Do this outside or in a container, so as not to splatter soda on your clothing or other objects around you.)

HOW ELECTRIFYING!

EXAMINING THE CONDUCTION OF SUBSTANCES

PURPOSE Learning what common materials are good conductors of electricity.

OVERVIEW Substances are described by color, texture, smell, feel, and hardness. Another characteristic might be an ability to conduct electricity.

Gather some common items (see "needs" list): metal coins made of basic elements like copper, gold and silver jewelry, and a plastic comb (or other item made from a chemical process using oil).

A battery is used to store electricity (a chemical reaction takes place within the battery). Electricity flows from the negative terminal on one battery to the positive one of another following a path, such as a piece of wire. The material used for the path is called a conductor. An electrical conductor is any material that allows an electric current to flow through it easily. Metal is a good conductor. Copper is used as a conductor in some phone wires, computers, and other electronic appliances.

When a conductor provides a path between the negative terminal on a battery and the positive terminal, electricity flows through the conductor. Think of the flow of electricity as if it were flowing water. A metal wire carries the electric flow, just as pipes carry water flow. If we put something in the path of the electric current, the current will try to flow through the object. If that substance is a conductor, the current will flow through. If it is not a good conductor, little or no current will flow through. By placing a light bulb in the path, we can see when current is flowing in the wire, since the current will light the bulb as it flows through it.

HYPOTHESIS Hypothesize which gathered materials are good electrical conductors.

PROCEDURE The battery and light bulb conductivity tester we will construct is the *constant*. The *variables* are the types of material being tested.

YOU NEED
- brass fastener
- coins (penny, nickel, dime, quarter)
- plant stem
- twig from a tree
- teabag
- water
- gold ring or necklace
- piece of silver jewelry
- nail
- plastic comb
- insulated jumper leads with alligator clips at each end
- dual "D" cell battery holder
- 2 batteries, 1.5 volt "D" size
- flashlight bulb
- bulb socket

At your local electronic parts store, you should have been able to find two "D" cell flashlight batteries, a dual "D" cell battery holder, a flashlight bulb, a socket for the bulb and a set of insulated jumper leads with alligator clips on each end. The alligator-clip leads make it quick and easy to connect all the components together, and to clip onto the different materials we want to test as conductors. Using those alligator clip leads, connect the components together as shown below. Be sure to place the batteries in the holder correctly, each one facing a different direction. The two batteries used together make 3 volts (each is 1.5 volts and 1.5 + 1.5 = 3).

The battery holder must be one with a wire running from positive terminal (raised "+" end) on one battery to the negative terminal (flat "−" end) on the other to form an electrical path. This connection is made at the opposite end of the battery holder from where the alligator clips are attached. If the holder you have doesn't have this connection, a 3-inch-long (7.5 cm) strip of aluminum foil ½ inch (1.25 cm) wide can be placed inside the battery holder, touching the positive end of one battery terminal to the negative end of the other.

The path is completed by clipping a coin between the two alligator clips. Does the bulb light up? Now unclip the coin and, in turn, clip on the other things you've collected (coins, a twig, nail, plastic comb). Make two piles, one of electrical conductors and one of nonconductors.

Note: In a science fair, avoid possible theft from an unattended display by leaving expensive jewelry or coins at home.

RESULTS & CONCLUSION Write down the results of your experiment. Come to a conclusion as to whether or not your hypothesis was correct.

SOMETHING MORE It's interesting to note that many household items that do not conduct electricity (called insulators) can build up static electricity—a balloon, wool sweater, comb made from plastic, and glass stirring-rod, for example. Static electricity is a buildup of electrons. Try to build up a static charge on these items. Hold a balloon against the screen of a television set. Take a wool sweater out of a clothes dryer. Run a plastic comb through your hair when it's very dry. Check the items on the conductor tester you constructed in the above experiment and prove that these items do not conduct electric current, even though they can hold a static electrical charge.

WE DEPLORE POLLUTION

WATER DILUTES, BUT POLLUTION REMAINS

PURPOSE A trace (an extremely small amount) of a solute in a solvent may not be detectable by taste.

YOU NEED
- sugar
- gallon container
- drinking glasses
- water
- teaspoon
- hand towel

OVERVIEW Just a few drops of an unwanted substance can ruin another substance. A little pollution in pure water can make it undrinkable. Just imagine how few molecules of a substance are necessary for air to carry and spread them. When a batch of cookies or a cake is baking in the oven, you can smell it all through the house. Yet, such a small amount of cake is lost to the air that it isn't measurable by us.

For a while, some people thought that unclean water could be cleaned by diluting it (making it weaker). The popular saying was, "The solution to pollution is dilution." Environmentalists now know that just isn't true. That is why everyone must be responsible, so as not to pollute our environment. It may be difficult or even impossible to make water clean and drinkable once certain substances have been mixed into it.

Even if something is diluted, it can still remain contaminated. Even if we cannot taste or see something in the water, that doesn't mean that it is not there. Prove this by using sugar and water.

HYPOTHESIS Hypothesize you can't detect a trace amount of sugar when it is heavily diluted in water. Being aware of this shows the importance for us to be environmentally wise and keep water from becoming polluted.

PROCEDURE Fill a clean, empty one-gallon jug with tap water. The jug may originally have held milk or mineral water. Then fill a drinking glass with the same water.

Add a very, very small amount of sugar to the water in the jug, only about ⅛ of a teaspoon. Put the cap on the jug and shake it. Wipe the mouth of the jug with a towel to be sure there are no granules of sugar on it. Pour a little into a new glass and take a sip.

Do you taste any sweetness from the sugar you put in? Take a drink of the glass of plain water and compare the taste. The water is *constant*. The *variable* is the water which contains a trace amount of sugar.

Even though you may not taste any sweetness, the sugar is still present in the water. The sugar is very diluted (weak), but it is there, making the water not completely pure. You know the sugar is in there, because you put it in.

This shows that even though we may not be able to detect the presence of a substance because it is not there in sufficiently large amount, some of the substance could still be present.

Water may meet all of the government regulations for drinkable water, but that water may still have some contaminants in it that may not be healthy for us to drink.

RESULTS & CONCLUSION Write down the results of your experiment. Come to a conclusion as to whether or not your hypothesis was correct.

SOMETHING MORE Add another ⅛ of a teaspoon of sugar to the jug, shake it and taste it. Continue adding sugar until you can finally taste its presence. How much do you have to add before you can taste the sweetness of sugar?

No Syrup

THE CONCEPT OF VISCOSITY

PURPOSE You may like thick pancakes, while your friend prefers thin ones. Is it possible to control the thickness of pancakes? Let's study the viscosity of pancake batter.

OVERVIEW One of the properties of fluids is viscosity. Viscosity is the ability of a fluid to resist flowing quickly. A fluid that flows slowly is said to have a high viscosity; it is "thick." Honey, for example, has a higher viscosity than milk.

Temperature can also be a factor in the viscosity of a fluid (hence the old phrase "as slow as molasses in January"). Gravy that is placed in a refrigerator overnight becomes so viscous that it turns gel-like.

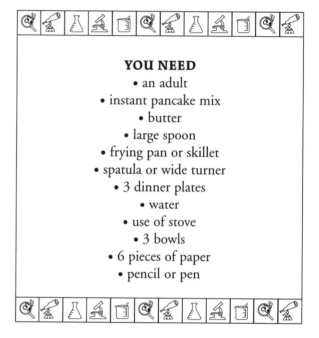

YOU NEED
- an adult
- instant pancake mix
- butter
- large spoon
- frying pan or skillet
- spatula or wide turner
- 3 dinner plates
- water
- use of stove
- 3 bowls
- 6 pieces of paper
- pencil or pen

HYPOTHESIS Hypothesize that the more viscous the batter, the thicker the pancake will be when cooked.

PROCEDURE Use some instant pancake mix to make pancake batter. Follow the directions for adding water (or milk) and mix or stir as instructed.

Pour the batter into three bowls. Add some water to one bowl to make the batter more watery (lowering its viscosity) and stir.

To the second bowl of batter, add more of the mix powder and stir.

Do not add anything to the batter in the third bowl. Place each bowl on top of a separate piece of paper and write on each paper the contents of the bowl: "standard mix," "more water," "more powder."

With an adult standing by to help, place some butter in a skillet or frying pan, turn the stove burner on to medium heat and spread the butter to grease the pan.

Pour one large spoonful of batter from the standard-mix bowl onto a skillet and cook until golden brown. When done, place the pancake on a plate and lay a piece of paper next to it indicating "standard mix."

In the same way, pour one large spoonful of batter from the "more water" mix on the pan, and cook until golden brown. Lay the finished pancake on a plate and label it "more water." Each pancake should contain the same amount of batter. The heat applied to the pancakes will remain *constant*. The viscosity of the batter is the *variable*.

Repeat the procedure for the "more powder" batter.

When done cooking, examine each of the three pancakes. Write down your observations. Did one take longer to cook than the others?

Next, taste each one. Is there any difference in taste? Even if they all taste the same, which one is more appetizing to you, a thinner pancake or a thicker one?

If you make pancakes in the future, which will you prefer: making the batter exactly as the instructions recommend on the package, making the batter more viscous, or making it less viscous?

RESULTS & CONCLUSION Write down the results of your experiment. Come to a conclusion as to whether or not your hypothesis was correct.

SOMETHING MORE
1. How does the amount of time the pancake is cooked affect its thickness, if at all?
2. Does a thicker pancake absorb more syrup than a thinner pancake, making it sweeter when eaten?

EGG HEAD

MEASURING ENDOTHERMIC REACTIONS IN EGGS

PURPOSE Boiling an egg causes a chemical reaction to take place inside the egg. This is an endothermic reaction.

OVERVIEW There is a change in energy when a chemical reaction takes place. Sometimes energy is needed to make a chemical reaction happen. A chemical reaction that absorbs energy is called an endothermic reaction. Cooking and baking are endothermic reactions. Breads and cakes rise in the oven because of the heat.

> **YOU NEED**
> - an adult
> - 6 same-size eggs
> - water
> - cooking pot
> - use of stove
> - large spoon
> - clock or watch
> - 5 bowls
> - paper
> - pencil

When an egg is boiled, heat is absorbed and a chemical reaction takes place inside the eggshell. You cannot see any difference from the outside between a raw egg and one that was boiled just by looking at them. (Many people "mark" eggs they have boiled before putting them back in the refrigerator.) Yet, the heat energy absorbed has caused the egg substance inside the shell to change.

HYPOTHESIS Hypothesize that you can tell how long an egg was boiled—subjected to endothermic reaction—by making a five-egg comparison.

PROCEDURE Place five eggs in a pot of water. Have an adult set it on a stove and bring the water to a slow boil, so as not to have the water splatter and to prevent the eggshells from cracking. Use caution when working around a stove and hot water!

Have an adult lower an egg on a large spoon carefully into the pot of boiling water. Note the time on a watch or a clock. After one minute, have the adult remove the egg. Place the egg in a bowl on a piece of paper marked "1 minute."

Repeat the procedure of boiling each egg, but boil the next one for two minutes, and the one after that for three minutes, and each additional egg for one minute longer. Lay each one in a bowl and the bowl on a piece of paper labeled with the number of minutes it sat in the boiling water. Be sure to let the eggs cool before handling them. Remember, a hot egg will not look hot. Turn off the stove when all five have been removed.

When the eggs have cooled, open each one. Keep them over their bowls, so as not to spill any contents from the eggs onto the table.

Examine each one. How has the heat affected the contents of each egg?

The temperature of boiling water is a *constant*, and it's assumed that all the eggs sold in a carton (marked large, extra-large, jumbo) are also *constant*. The amount of time each egg is boiled is the only *variable*.

If someone boiled another egg between one and five minutes and gave it to you, could you tell how long it had been boiled by using your five eggs as a comparison? Have a friend or family member boil an egg and, without being told how long they dipped it in boiling water, take on the role of investigator to determine about how long it was cooked, using your five eggs to make comparisons.

RESULTS & CONCLUSION Write down the results of your experiment. Come to a conclusion as to whether or not your hypothesis was correct.

SOMETHING MORE How would this work with other foods, such as fried eggs or chocolate chip cookies?

ONE CANDLE-POWER

UNDERSTANDING EXOTHERMIC REACTION

PURPOSE Burning causes a chemical reaction called an exothermic reaction.

OVERVIEW The previous project explained that there is a change in energy when a chemical reaction takes place. Sometimes energy must be used to make a chemical reaction happen, and sometimes energy is given off as a chemical reaction takes place. When energy is released during a chemical reaction, it is called an exothermic reaction.

    Anything that is burning is an example of exothermic reaction. When a candle is lit, the wick and wax are made to burn, causing a chemical change. This chemical reaction is invisible, in that we can't actually see the wax as it is as it is undergoing the change. It's only after the candle has been burning for a while that we see that change has actually taken place. Carbon, gas, and energy in the form of heat and light are given off from a burning candle.

> **YOU NEED**
> - an adult
> - candle with straight sides (not tapered)
> - gram-weight kitchen food scale
> - match
> - pencil
> - paper
> - ashtray
> - butter knife
> - ruler

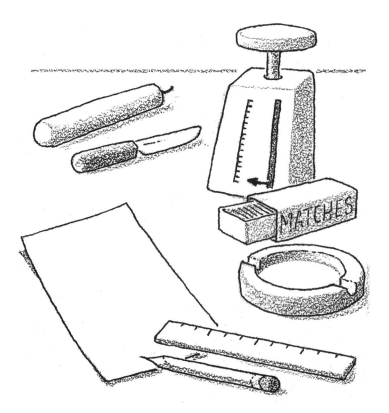

HYPOTHESIS Hypothesize that if half the length of a candle is burned, a chemical reaction takes place that will cause the candle to have half its original mass (half its weight).

PROCEDURE Using a gram-weight kitchen food scale, weigh a candle. Write its weight down, then use a ruler to measure the length of the candle. (*Note:* The candle used must have straight sides, not tapered sides.) Only measure the wax; do not include the length of wick that sticks out of the candle's top. Divide the length by two to find the middle. With a pencil, make a slight mark or indentation at the point on the candle marking the middle.

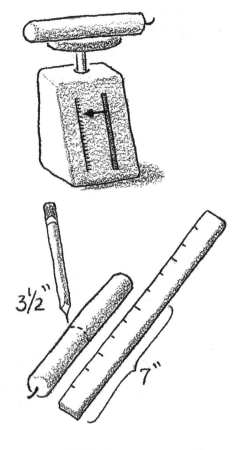

Have an adult light the candle and burn it until it is half gone, and reaches the marking. Let the adult extinguish the flame, then wait a few seconds for the wick to cool. The candle is the *constant*. The *variable* is the length and mass of the candle before burning compared to after burning.

Again, weigh the candle. How much of the candle's weight was chemically changed? Into what was it changed?

RESULTS & CONCLUSION Write down the results of your experiment. Come to a conclusion as to whether or not your hypothesis was correct.

SOMETHING MORE
1. Does the size of the candle have anything to do with the size of the flame?
2. A unit of measurement of light is "candle power," being the amount of light that is given off by one candle. But do all candles give off the same amount of light? Obviously, a bigger candle will burn longer, but is it brighter or less bright than a small candle? Can you think of a way to check this?

FADE NOT

NATURAL DYES AND SUNLIGHT

PURPOSE What is the effect of sunlight on various naturally staining chemical substances, such as those that come from fruits?

OVERVIEW Your parents may have been upset when you or someone in your home spilled a certain drink or fruit juice on a good carpet. Some drinks and juices stain. Have you noticed that certain foods even stain your lips and tongue when you eat them? Could fruit or vegetable juices be used as natural dyes for clothing? If so, how do they hold up in sunlight, which often fades the synthetic dyes in carpets and upholstered chairs that are near sunny windows?

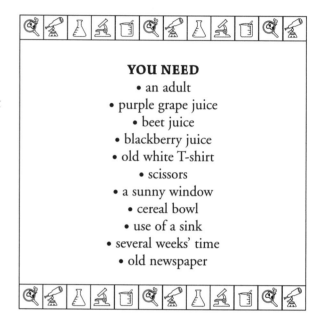

YOU NEED
- an adult
- purple grape juice
- beet juice
- blackberry juice
- old white T-shirt
- scissors
- a sunny window
- cereal bowl
- use of a sink
- several weeks' time
- old newspaper

HYPOTHESIS Which of the staining liquids in the experiment do you think will resist fading the most? Hypothesize that grape juice (or whichever juice you chose) will resist fading better than the others.

PROCEDURE Take an old white T-shirt, pillowcase, or bedsheet. Check a "rag bag" if you have one, where worn or torn clothing and bedding are kept for use in cleaning or painting jobs. Cut 6 small squares (about 3 inches [7.5 centimeters] square) of white material.

Place a cereal bowl in a sink. Working in the sink will keep any juice from spilling on the floor. Pour a little blackberry juice into the bowl. Dip two white cloth squares in the blackberry juice. Lay the squares on an old piece of newspaper to dry.

Rinse the bowl with clear water. Pour in a little beet juice. Dip two white cloth squares into the beet juice and then lay them on the newspaper.

Again, rinse the bowl. Pour in a little purple grape juice. Dip two more pieces of cloth in the grape juice and lay the pieces on the newspaper to dry.

When dry, place one of each colored square in a sunny window (one blackberry, one beet, and one grape juice colored squares). Place the remaining three squares in an area away from any direct sunlight. A dresser drawer or on top of the refrigerator would be good places. Can you guess which ones will fade more? Write down your guess to later check and see if you were correct.

After a week or two, compare the colors of the squares that have been in direct sunlight and also the squares that were not exposed to sunlight. Are there noticeable color changes?

The different staining juices are the *variables*. The sunlight in the experiment is the *constant*, but also in this case a *variable* since two pieces of cloth are stained the same—one kept in the dark (the control) and one exposed to sunlight.

Interestingly, some fluorescent-colored bathing suits come with a label attached, warning "Do not expose to direct sunlight for long periods of time!" Does the manufacturer expect people to swim only at night or indoors? Of course, too much direct sunlight isn't good for your skin either!

RESULTS & CONCLUSION Write down the results of your experiment. Come to a conclusion as to whether or not your hypothesis was correct.

SOMETHING MORE Do your naturally dyed pieces of material lose their color when they are washed?

Look around your house and see if you can find discoloration caused by sunlight in the dyes in carpet and upholstered chairs and sofas. Move small furnishings a little or ask an adult to move something if the object is heavier, and look at parts of a carpet that have been covered (protected from sunlight) for many years. Is the color of the carpet the same on parts that have been largely "in the dark" as on the parts that were in direct sunlight?

STICKY-GOO!

EMULSION, THE "CHEM-MAGICAL" CLEANER

PURPOSE Have you found that water alone cannot really clean an object covered with oil? Let's study the releasing property of soapy water.

OVERVIEW Remember the last time you ate some delicious fried chicken? Finger-licking good, maybe; but what happened when you tried to finish cleaning your hands by simply wiping them on a paper napkin? Did napkin shreds stick to the your fingers? Did you then try rinsing off your fingers with plain water but could still feel grease on your hands? That's when you finally gave up and grabbed the soap, right?

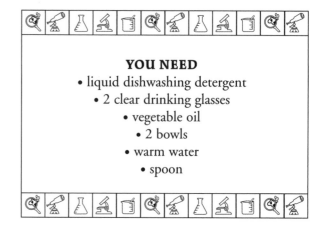

YOU NEED
- liquid dishwashing detergent
- 2 clear drinking glasses
- vegetable oil
- 2 bowls
- warm water
- spoon

Soapy water is an emulsifier, meaning it has the ability to cut through fat and grease, turning them into tiny droplets that can be washed away. Normally, water does not mix with oil, fat, dirt and grease. The surfaces of these substances will normally resist water. Soapy water breaks through to the substances themselves so that they, with a little rubbing, are carried off into the soapy water and can be rinsed away.

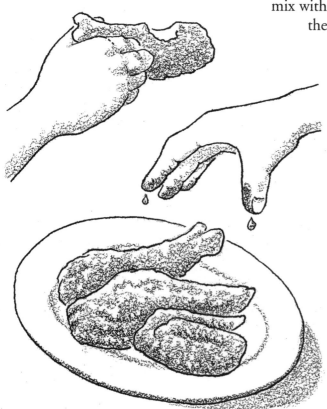

HYPOTHESIS Hypothesize that when soap is added to water its ability to remove cooking oil is improved.

PROCEDURE Hold a clear drinking glass or mug. Tilt it a little and let some vegetable oil flow down along the inside of the glass. Do this to a second glass, also. Let the glasses dry for about a half hour.

Fill two bowls with warm water. Add liquid dish detergent to one and stir.

Dip the side of the glass that has the streak of oil into the bowl of water, then remove it. Dip the other glass in the bowl of soapy water, then take it out. Hold the glasses up to the light or in sunlight and look at the side of the glasses where the oil had flowed. Does the glass that was dipped in plain water still have vegetable oil on the side? Does the glass that was dipped in soapy water look different?

The *constant*s are the warm water, the surfaces of the drinking glasses and the vegetable oil. The *variable* is the addition of soap to one of the bowls of water.

RESULTS & CONCLUSION Write down the results of your experiment. Come to a conclusion as to whether or not your hypothesis was correct.

SOMETHING MORE Does the temperature of the water have an effect on soapy water's ability to clean grease and oil? Fill a bowl with water and place it in a refrigerator for an hour. Fill another bowl with hot water from the kitchen faucet. (Don't make the water so hot that it might burn you.) Add an equal amount of liquid dish detergent to each bowl and stir. Pour an equal amount of vegetable oil along the inside of two glasses. Use the two batches of soapy water to clean the glasses. Does soapy hot water remove the oil more easily and thoroughly than the soapy cold water?

WORTH THE WAIT

UNRIPE FRUIT TO SUGARY TREAT

PURPOSE Stores often sell fruit that doesn't taste especially good, so why keep it? Well, there's this little thing called ripening that makes all the difference.

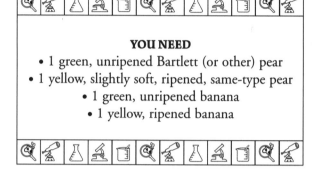

YOU NEED
- 1 green, unripened Bartlett (or other) pear
- 1 yellow, slightly soft, ripened, same-type pear
- 1 green, unripened banana
- 1 yellow, ripened banana

OVERVIEW Produce that is sold by corner groceries and supermarkets is often shipped and trucked over long distances. In order for fruits and vegetables to reach those stores in good condition, they are often picked and gathered before they are ripe. This produce then ripens in transit, on the way to the grocer's bins, or soon after reaching the stores.

It is important to buy and consume fruits because they contain vitamins and minerals important to a healthy diet. Mature, or ripe, fruits also contain sugar that makes them sweet and good to eat. When fruits are not fully ripe, they don't taste as sweet as they should. This is because, as a fruit ripens, a chemical process that goes on inside the fruit changes a good part of the fruit to sugar.

Unripened fruit is usually green and hard. A green banana or pear will not taste as sweet as a ripe yellow banana or pear. Unripened fruit is also sometimes hard to digest, so may cause a stomachache. On the other hand, when fruit is overripe, it usually turns brown. Have you ever eaten a banana that has a brown spots on it? Some people don't like the mushy texture and avoid eating brown spots in fruit, but those over-ripe spots are very sweet (brown spots can also be caused by bruising).

HYPOTHESIS Hypothesize that a ripe banana will taste sweeter than an unripe one, and that a ripe pear will taste sweeter than an unripe one of the same type.

PROCEDURE First, always wash off with water any produce you buy before you eat it. This will remove dirt, or any chemicals that may have been sprayed on it to protect it from insects while it was growing or during shipment.

Take a small bite of a green, hard, unripened pear (just to get a taste, you don't want that stomachache). Then take a bite of a yellow, slightly soft, ripened pear. Does one taste sweeter than the other? Which one tastes sweeter? Which one do you think contains more sugar? For fun, weigh a pear when it is not ripe, then weigh it again after it ripens. Is there a difference in its weight?

Now conduct the taste comparison using a green banana and a yellow banana. The reaction of your own taste buds to the different fruits is a *constant*. Also, the type of fruit remains *constant* (we are comparing pears to pears and bananas to bananas). The *variable* is the condition of the fruit, ripe or unripe.

RESULTS & CONCLUSION Write down the results of your experiment. Come to a conclusion as to whether or not your hypothesis was correct.

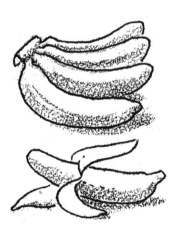

SOMETHING MORE
1. How does the sweetness of ripened and unripened fruit compare to the sweetness of the same kind of fruit when it is dried? Dried banana chips, papaya, pear, and pineapple are available at most supermarkets.
2. Compare the taste of an unripe, ripened, and overripened banana. (You must eat the brown spots on the overripened banana. Many people do not like the thought of eating this mushy part, while some people love the sweetness of it.)

SWEETER SWEET

NATURAL SUGAR OR CHEMICAL SUBSTITUTE

PURPOSE Do people generally prefer the taste of natural sugar food products to the taste of products made with chemical sweetener substitutes?

OVERVIEW Most people love sweet-tasting foods. Even ancient peoples used sweeteners such as honey to make other foods taste better.

"Natural" table sugar is concentrated and causes health problems, including tooth decay, hyperactivity, hypertension, and obesity. It is high in calories, too, so concerned people try to cut down on sugar when they diet. In response, food chemists have created sugar substitutes, to make things taste "sweet" but with fewer calories. That's why so many "low calorie" products are on the market.

"Aspartame" is one chemical often used as a sugar substitute. You may have seen the word—or NutraSweet, the name it is marketed under—on low-calorie food labels.

> **YOU NEED**
> - an adult
> - 1 box of sugar-based gelatin dessert powder (any flavor)
> - 1 box of sugar-free gelatin dessert powder (same flavor and brand as sugar-based)
> - kitchen measuring cup
> - 20 plastic disposable spoons
> - 20 paper cups
> - 2 large bowls
> - water
> - pencils (or pens)
> - 10 small notepad-size pieces of paper
> - a cooking pot
> - use of a stove top burner
> - use of a refrigerator
> - masking tape

Although the ingredients making up aspartame (phenylalanine, aspartic acid and methanol) occur naturally in foods, aspartame itself does not, so there is still some controversy regarding how healthful it is for us.

Aside from the health questions, how does the taste compare? Are your friends, neighbors, and family members willing to drink and eat foods that use sugar substitute chemicals to benefit from the lower calories, even if they don't like the taste as much? Or, do they prefer the taste of sugar-free foods over sugar-based versions?

HYPOTHESIS Hypothesize that more people prefer the taste of natural-sugar gelatin dessert over a sugar-substitute, aspartame, version.

PROCEDURE At the supermarket, find a company that makes both sugar-based and sugar-free gelatin dessert products. Purchase one box of each, choosing the same flavor for both. With the help of an adult, follow the instructions on the packages and make a batch of each dessert: sugar-based and sugar-free. In this experiment, the gelatin flavor of the dessert is held *constant* and the sweetener is the *variable*.

On the bottom of a large bowl, place a piece of masking tape. Write "sugar-based" on it. Pour the sugar-based gelatin into the bowl. Place a piece of masking tape on the side and write "Sample #1" on it.

Place a piece of masking tape on the bottom of another bowl and write "sugar-free" on it. Pour the sugar-free gelatin into the bowl. Place a piece of masking tape on the side and write "Sample #2" on it. Place the two bowls in the refrigerator for cooling and hardening.

Survey 10 people by placing a spoonful of gelatin from bowl #1 into a paper cup and a spoonful of gelatin from bowl #2 into another cup. Have each person taste the gelatin from bowl #1 and #2 and write down on a piece of paper which one they liked better. Do not tell them which is which. Use a clean spoon and cups for each person you survey. Do not let anyone see the number being written down, to avoid influencing some else's opinion. Test your friends, family members, or classmates.

We are assuming that 10 people will be a large enough "sample size" to give us an approximation of what people prefer. We are using a few people to estimate how the total population may respond to the test. A sample size is a small group that is tested which, if large enough, will hopefully give a true picture of the large group.

Count how many people surveyed preferred gelatin sample #1 and how many preferred gelatin sample #2. Which taste did they like most?

RESULTS & CONCLUSION Write down the results of your experiment. Come to a conclusion as to whether or not your hypothesis was correct.

SOMETHING MORE
1. Chemists use the word "sugar" to refer to the group of related carbohydrate compounds, including dextrose (corn sugar), fructose (sugar occurring naturally in fruits), lactose (milk sugar) and maltose (malt sugar). Learn more about these and other sugars. Learn about mannitol and sorbitol.
2. Test 100 people to see how accurate the results of the smaller sample group (of 10 people) was in predicting the results of the larger group.

CHEMICAL TEARS

OVERCOMING AN ONION'S NATURAL GAS

PURPOSE "I like onions but they make me cry." Can something be done to help the problem?

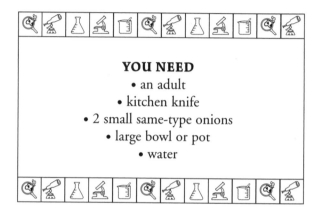

OVERVIEW Onions add their own special flavor to many of the foods we eat, from tunafish sandwiches to meat loaf. People who have backyard gardens usually grow onions, although they are not particularly high in vitamins, because of their wide use in preparing so many different dishes.

The problem for the food preparer is peeling and slicing them.

Onions contain a chemical in the form of an oil which easily turns into a gas whenever the onion is chopped or squeezed. The vapors given off are invisible, but affect the nose and the eyes, making tears flow and the eyes burn . . . sometimes so much that it's hard to see.

YOU NEED
- an adult
- kitchen knife
- 2 small same-type onions
- large bowl or pot
- water

HYPOTHESIS It's possible to trap an onion's vapors by cutting it under water and so prevent the tearing and burning of the eyes.

PROCEDURE First, *does* the chemical vapor of an onion carry through the air? Ask an adult to help peel, slice, and squeeze a strong onion. (Be very careful working with knives. They can be very sharp.) Does the onion make your eyes burn and tear?

When your eyes are back to normal, peel, slice and squeeze another onion while it's submerged in a large bowl or pot of water. What happens? Does the water keep the vapor from escaping into the air? The onions are the *constant*. The *variable* is the environment in which the onion is cut, either in the air or in water.

RESULTS & CONCLUSION Write down the results of your experiment. Come to a conclusion as to whether or not your hypothesis was correct.

SOMETHING MORE
1. Test several kinds of onions. Which give off the strongest vapors?
2. Do onion vapors disperse evenly throughout the air or do they only rise, from chopping (waist) level to nose? How could you find out?

SAUCY CLEANER

A NATURAL TARNISH REMOVER

PURPOSE Is it spaghetti's low pH that removes tarnish from copper, or is it something else?

OVERVIEW Compare a shiny new copper penny (current or recent year) to an old tarnished one. Tarnish is the result of a chemical reaction over time between copper and air. Have you ever noticed a shiny spot on the tarnished copper bottom of a washed pot after a spaghetti dinner? Could spaghetti sauce be a copper cleaner?

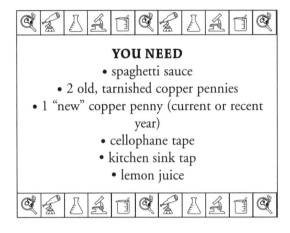

YOU NEED
- spaghetti sauce
- 2 old, tarnished copper pennies
- 1 "new" copper penny (current or recent year)
- cellophane tape
- kitchen sink tap
- lemon juice

HYPOTHESIS Tarnish is removed by spaghetti sauce that has a low pH, but low pH is not the only factor in its removing that tarnish.

PROCEDURE Take an old, tarnished penny. Cover half with some tomato sauce. After a half hour, rinse the penny in water. Is the tarnish gone? Now try removing the tarnish with something other than tomato sauce, but still acidic (with low pH). We'll use lemon juice. The tarnished pennies we are testing are the *constant*. The *variable* is the substance (tomato sauce or lemon juice) applied to the coins.

Carefully place a drop of concentrated lemon juice on one half of an old, tarnished copper penny. Cover half of the penny with cellophane or masking tape to protect it. This way we can easily make a before-and-after visual comparison. After about a half hour, wash the coin in water. Did the lemon juice remove the tarnish, too?

RESULTS & CONCLUSION Write down the results of your experiment. Come to a conclusion as to whether or not your hypothesis was correct.

SOMETHING MORE Gather three similarly tarnished copper coins (compare the shades of tarnish). From three brands of prepared spaghetti sauce, place a bit of sauce onto each penny. Which brand removes the tarnish best? Read the labels on the sauces and compare their ingredients. Do any of the sauces contain acidic ingredients (for example, citric acid)?

THE YEAST BEAST

FERMENTATION PROVES YEAST IS ALIVE!

PURPOSE When yeast is used in baking, many recipes also call for sugar as an ingredient. The yeast uses the sugar to make carbon dioxide and give the item to be baked a light and "airy" consistency. But can a sugar substitute be used instead, to activate yeast in baking and have the yeast produce carbon dioxide?

YOU NEED
- active dry yeast (available at the grocery store)
- 3 clear drinking glasses
- warm tap water
- measuring cup
- natural white sugar
- brown sugar
- sugar substitute (saccharin)

OVERVIEW For many hundreds of years, people baked bread, using yeast as an ingredient, without knowing just why it makes bread dough bubble and rise. They thought it was simply some sort of chemical reaction. It took Louis Pasteur and other scientists doing experiments in the 1850s to prove that the yeast ingredient was actually a living organism. It is this organism that causes the chemical change in bread dough.

Yeast digests sugar and starch and turns them into alcohol and carbon dioxide gas. This breaking down of sugar and starch is called fermentation. The carbon dioxide gas bubbles up through the bread dough, making the bread rise higher and become more porous (full of tiny holes). Although the fermentation process is also used in making alcohol, we don't taste alcohol when we eat bread with yeast, because any alcohol that is produced evaporates while the bread is being baked.

Does fermentation also take place when a sugar-substitute product is used in baking with yeast? This is an especially important question if someone wants or needs to bake sugar-free foods and is considering using a sugar substitute in a recipe.

HYPOTHESIS More gas is released when yeast is mixed with water and sugar than if it is mixed with water and a sugar substitute.

PROCEDURE Pour a little active dry yeast into each of three clear drinking glasses. Pour just enough to cover the bottom of each glass completely.

Add one level teaspoon of natural white sugar to one glass, one level teaspoon of brown sugar to another glass and one level teaspoon of an artificial sweetener (such as saccharin) to the third glass.

Measure and pour ¼ cup of warm tap water into each glass and swish the glass around, making a circular motion with your hand, to gently stir the contents. The amount of yeast and water is kept *constant*. The *variable* is the type of sweetener that is used.

Set each glass on a sheet of paper and write on the paper the type of sugar that the glass contains. When doing science experiments, it's important to label or identify each container as you do your experiments, in order to avoid confusion later.

Observe the glasses for a little while, watching for a foam of bubbles to appear, indicating the presence of carbon dioxide gas. Which one foams up the most and thus has the most response to the yeast?

RESULTS & CONCLUSION Write down the results of your experiment. Come to a conclusion as to whether or not your hypothesis was correct.

SOMETHING MORE Experiment to check the reaction of yeast to other types of substances that contain sugar (honey or pancake syrup, for example).

BETTER BUBBLES

SAFE AND NATURAL MONSTER-BUBBLE SOLUTIONS

PURPOSE Everybody likes to make bubbles— the bigger, the better. But is your bubble solution toxic or entirely safe?

OVERVIEW Bubbles form in water when air is trapped. But bubbles made of water alone cannot be very large or survive in air. Something must be added to water to chemically change it so that water molecules will hold more tightly together (called surface tension).

When you buy "bubble stuff" in a toy store, an ingredient may have been added to make larger and longer-lasting bubbles (possibly glycerin) but the solution can be toxic, or poisonous, if swallowed.

YOU NEED
- confectioners' sugar with cornstarch
- warm water
- measuring cup
- liquid dish soap
- tablespoon
- a bottle of "bubble stuff" from the toy store
- a bubble wand (from store or homemade)
- bowl

HYPOTHESIS Hypothesize that it is possible to make a monster-bubble solution that is safer, so that even little kids can enjoy making big bubbles.

PROCEDURE Pour ¾ cup of warm water into a bowl. Add 4 tablespoons of dishwashing liquid. This liquid soap is an "emulsifier" that will help the molecules of water hold together. Stir in 2 level tablespoons of confectioners' sugar (which contains cornstarch).

Now make bubbles with the store-bought "bubble stuff," using the wand that comes with the bottle. Then, rinse off the wand and use it to make bubbles with your homemade bubble solution. The wand used to create the bubbles is the *constant*. The bubble solution is the *variable*. (You can use a pipe cleaner or some other wire bent in the shape of a wand, too, but you must use it the same way for both bubble solutions because it must remain constant for the project.)

Does your homemade bubble solution make as many bubbles and as large bubbles as the store-bought bubble liquid? If so, you have made a safe bubble toy. Of course, you still don't want to swallow your homemade soapy liquid, but it would not harm you if you did.

RESULTS & CONCLUSION Write down the results of your experiment. Come to a conclusion as to whether or not your hypothesis was correct.

SOMETHING MORE
1. How big can you make a bubble using your bubble solution before the water molecules can't hold together? How long will a bubble last before it pops? Why does it pop (could it be due to evaporation)? Will a bubble last longer in higher humidity (in a steamy shower, for example)?
2. Is there any difference in using warm water or cold water in making your homemade bubble solution?
3. Will the kind of water matter—for example, tap water, distilled water, or spring water? Does the "softness" or "hardness" of water make a difference? "Hard" water has more minerals, which usually makes it more difficult to make suds.
4. Experiment by substituting other safe ingredients. Instead of using confectioners' sugar, try honey or maple syrup as a thickening agent, but only use a very small amount.

ONION SWITCH

CHANGING THE TASTE OF ONIONS BY COOKING

PURPOSE Onions usually have a very strong taste. Some people don't like the strong flavor, so they avoid eating onions. Can the taste of an onion be changed to make it more palatable?

OVERVIEW Heat (cooking) can affect the chemical makeup of foods and make them taste different. In onions, this chemical change makes them taste much sweeter than when the onions are raw. Test your taste buds and see if you can detect this change in sweetness, once a cooked onion cools down.

YOU NEED
- an adult with knife
- onion
- water
- saucepan or container
- use of stove or microwave

HYPOTHESIS Hypothesize that cooking an onion will reduce its strong taste and give it a sweeter flavor.

PROCEDURE Have an adult help by removing the onion ends and cutting it in half. For the *constant*, we need to use pieces from the same onion. Your taste buds will also remain the same. In this project, the onion is also the *variable*, because half will be left raw and half will be cooked.

Peel the onion. Ask an adult to cook half the onion (sliced or not) in a little water on top of a stove or in a microwave. Once it has cooled, take out the cooked onion. Taste a bit of the raw onion and then some of the cooked onion. Compare them. Does the cooked onion taste sweeter?

RESULTS & CONCLUSION Write down the results of your experiment. Come to a conclusion as to whether or not your hypothesis was correct.

SOMETHING MORE Make the cooked onion even tastier by making a simple white sauce to have with it. While the onion pieces are boiling in enough water to cover them, add some margarine, a sprinkle of salt, two teaspoons of cornstarch and simmer for 20 minutes. The sauce ingredients should not add sweetness, but will make the onion even more presentable, chemically, to your taste buds.

EATERS' DIGEST

DISSOLVING FOODS WITH ACIDS

PURPOSE We can't see what happens in our stomachs, or can we? We do know that some common foods (such as lemon juice and vinegar) can break down other foods, so . . .

OVERVIEW The organ called the stomach is very important in digestion, breaking down the foods we eat. Inside the stomach are strong acids, given off by glands, which dissolve and break down foods for energy the body needs. Do acidic foods like tea (contains tannic acid) dissolve other foods faster than plain water?

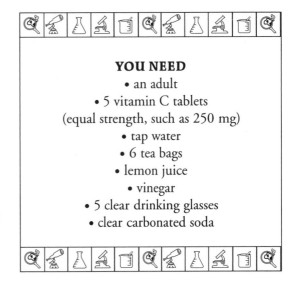

YOU NEED
- an adult
- 5 vitamin C tablets
(equal strength, such as 250 mg)
- tap water
- 6 tea bags
- lemon juice
- vinegar
- 5 clear drinking glasses
- clear carbonated soda

HYPOTHESIS Hypothesize that a vitamin C tablet will dissolve more quickly in a liquid that is acidic as opposed to plain water, which has a neutral pH.

PROCEDURE Fill five glasses with equal amounts of liquid, a quarter to half the height of the glass: put tap water in one glass, vinegar in another, lemon juice in the third, and clear carbonated soda in the fourth. In the fifth, place six tea bags and hot tap water.

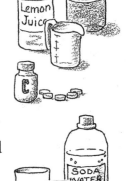

Let the glasses sit for an hour or until they are all at room temperature. Squeeze the tea out of the tea bags and into the glass as you remove them. The amount of liquid, the tablet strength (mg), the time of wait, and the temperature are held *constant*. The *variable* is the liquid used to try to dissolve the vitamin C tablets.

When all the liquids are at room temperature, drop a vitamin C tablet into each of the five glasses. Let the experiment sit for several hours, without disturbing the glasses. Watch the vitamin C tablet in each glass. Do the vitamin tablets dissolve faster in the acidic liquids than in the one with plain water?

RESULTS & CONCLUSION Write down the results of your experiment. Come to a conclusion as to whether or not your hypothesis was correct.

SOMETHING MORE Would other vitamin forms (capsules or caplets) dissolve faster?

LEFT BEHIND

IT'S IN YOUR WATER

PURPOSE It's possible to show that, over time, the presence of water can leave something behind from the "invisible" materials that are in it.

YOU NEED
- an adult
- toilet with a tank
- sinks
- tea kettle or coffeemaker
- garden hose

OVERVIEW When you look at a glass of water that you've filled from the kitchen tap, the water looks perfectly clear—like ordinary, plain water. That may be, but there are often chemicals and other substances in our tap water, or any water, that we don't see. Fluoridation of water is commonly used in fighting dental cavities. Minerals such as calcium, magnesium and iron are very often found in drinking water. Homes that have copper water pipes will sometimes have some copper in their water, too. The minerals in the water are in amounts too small to see. However, deposited and built up over time on sinks and the insides of toilet tanks, they become visible as residue.

You can get some idea of how impurities that are dissolved in a liquid can be detected by the residue (buildup of materials remaining when the liquid is gone) left behind by adding powdered chocolate to a glass of milk. Stir it with a spoon to dissolve the powder and enjoy a tasty glass of chocolate milk. When you have finished, examine the inside of the glass. Do you see a residue of chocolate on the inside of the glass, even though the milk is gone?

HYPOTHESIS Hypothesize that, on investigation, you will be able to find residue in many places where water is often present.

PROCEDURE Have an adult help by lifting the covering (it's heavy!) off your toilet's tank. The water inside is clear (the same water you drink from the tap), but is the inside jacket of the tank discolored and stained from mineral residue? Rub your finger along the inside. Does the chemical and mineral residue come off onto your finger? What color is it? What substance do you think is causing it?

Using your powers of observation, check the sinks around your home, school, and public library to see if there are any stains or residue buildup caused by minerals in the water, and possibly a leaky faucet that causes a steady drip.

Examine the inside of a tea kettle or water tank of a coffeemaker looking for the telltale stains of residue. Look for places where water drips constantly or runs past, such

as the nozzle of a garden hose. The *constant* is the passage of water on or past the surface being examined. The *variable* is the item being examined.

RESULTS & CONCLUSION Write down the results of your experiment. Come to a conclusion as to whether or not your hypothesis was correct.

SOMETHING MORE
1. In the supermarket you can buy automatic toilet bowl cleaners which hang in your toilet tank and are activated every time you flush. Some make the water in the bowl turn blue. How do these work? Are they adding a chemical to the water?
2. Distilled water is pure water, free of minerals. It is available at supermarkets and pharmacies. Car manufacturers advise using distilled water in a car's radiator, rather than water from a home faucet. The makers of steam irons, which smooth wrinkles out of clothes, also recommend using distilled water in their irons. Why do you think these manufacturers want this especially pure water to be used in their products?
3. Can you examine the deposits taken from the inside of your toilet tank under a microscope? Can you match them to other deposits you may find around the house or school?

REPEAT, THREEPEAT

EXACT DATA ALLOWS REPEATABLE RESULTS

PURPOSE Accurate measurement is very important in science, and also in making cookies! Like scientists with a project, cooks need to follow a recipe exactly to get the kinds of result they did before: the same tasty, crunchy or chewy cookies.

OVERVIEW Sometimes a cooking or a baking recipe will call for "just a pinch" of an ingredient, or says to "season to taste." Such amounts are not precise (not "quantified," or exactly measured). In science, however, and especially in chemistry, it is important that measurements be exact and accurate so that results can be replicated (done again and again with the same result by others).

We can show the importance of quantified measurement by using a recipe for baking old-fashioned sugar cookies. To do this we'll need three batches of cookies. For one batch, we'll follow the instructions using the exact measurements of the basic recipe. For the second batch, we'll use much less flour than the recipe calls for, and we'll make the third batch using far too much flour. Ask an adult to help you measure the ingredients accurately. For safety, always have an adult present when working around an oven or stove.

YOU NEED
- an adult
- deep bowls, spoons, mixer, measuring cups, baking tin
- sugar
- butter
- flour
- salt
- 3 eggs
- vanilla
- baking powder
- baking soda
- milk
- use of oven

HYPOTHESIS Hypothesize that cookies from each batch will taste differently, because of a different amount of flour in each batch.

PROCEDURE We need to mix three batches of cookie dough. All the ingredients and their proportions will be *constant*, except for the flour. The amount of flour used in each batch of cookies is the *variable*.

Place three rows of cookies on a baking sheet. Make one row from the first batch, one from the second, and one from the third. By baking samples of all the batches at the same time, we are sure that the oven temperature and baking time are variables that, for this experiment, are kept constant. This is another important point when doing a science experiment.

We must hold everything constant except for the one thing we want to change, which in this case is the amount of flour used. To do this, we'll use the basic two-mix recipe below as a guide to making three cookie batches.

Old-Fashioned Sugar Cookies

In mixture #1 bowl:
- 1 cup sugar
- ½ cup butter, softened
- ½ egg
- ½ teaspoon vanilla

Mix these ingredients together.

In mixture #2 bowl:
- 2½ cups flour (2 cups for batch two, 3 for batch three)
- ½ teaspoon salt
- ½ teaspoon baking powder
- ½ teaspoon baking soda

Mix these ingredients together.

Alternately add mixture #2 and ½ cup of milk to mixture #1. Mix it until the batter is as soft it can be, then drop a full tablespoon of batter onto a baking sheet. Flatten it slightly with lightly floured fingers. Drop a spoonful of cookie dough at a time onto the sheet, until you have a long row of cookies. (Remember, we'll make three rows, one row of each batch of dough. Be sure to mark somehow which row is made from which mixture.) Set any extra batter in the bowl aside.

Now make another batch of cookies using the same basic recipe, except use only 2 cups of flour in mixture #2 (instead of 2½ cups as in the first batch). You can reuse the same bowls as you did for the first batch. When the dough is all mixed together, make a second row of cookies on the baking sheet and set aside extra batter.

Finally, make a third batch of cookie dough, this time using 3 cups of flour for mixture #2 (instead of 2½ or 2 cups). When mixed, make a third row of cookies on the baking tin.

Have an adult help by placing the cookie sheet in the oven and baking the cookies at 400° F for 10 to 12 minutes, or until their edges are slightly brown. When done, after the cookies have cooled, taste a sample from each row—that is, one from each cookie mix. Does altering the recipe by the amount of flour have an effect on the results?

Put the extra batters together and bake more cookies to enjoy with milk!

RESULTS & CONCLUSION Write down the results of your experiment. Come to a conclusion as to whether or not your hypothesis was correct.

SOMETHING MORE Make a batch of chocolate chip cookies, but change the quantity of chocolate chips in a second batch. How has the cookie flavor changed?

PAINT BY SUGARS

COMBINING DYES

PURPOSE Create new food colors by combining the four common colors, usually available in packages of food coloring sets at grocery stores.

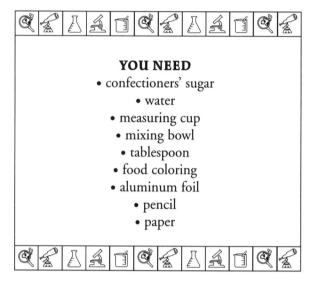

YOU NEED
- confectioners' sugar
- water
- measuring cup
- mixing bowl
- tablespoon
- food coloring
- aluminum foil
- pencil
- paper

OVERVIEW Dyes are substances that combine with other substances to change their color. Dyes have been used for thousands of years. Beautifully colored dyed clothing was even found in the ancient Egyptian pyramids. Natural dyes are made from plant, animal, and mineral substances. Chemists have learned to make synthetic dyes. William Perkin, a chemist, discovered a new color, "mauve," in 1856.

Think of all the things around your home that have probably been colored by dyes to make them more attractive: clothing, bath towels, bedsheets, carpeting, upholstered chairs and sofas, and curtains.

Colored dyes can be combined in different amounts to make many different colors. Food coloring sets found in the supermarket usually consist of a package of four small bottles of red, green, yellow, and blue coloring. These dyes can be used separately or mixed in different combinations and amounts to create a wide variety of colors.

HYPOTHESIS Select a "mixed" color you especially like, for example, purple and hypothesize how many drops of which colors will be needed to create that color.

PROCEDURE In a bowl, mix confectioners' sugar and water until a paste is formed. On a piece of aluminum foil, drop a dozen spoonfuls of the paste, making small mounds. Use the back side of the spoon to press a concave depression, a dent, into the top of each mound. Add different colors and amounts to each mound to create new colors. Can you predict what will happen when you add one color to another? Keep a record of how each color was formed; for example, 3 drops of red and 6 drops of yellow. The *constants* are the four basic dye colors, used to form all the other colors. The *variable* is the amount of each color used which, when combined, creates the new color.

Mix the colors into each mound and use the colored pasty mounds to create an artistic design or shape (heart, diamond), creature (bird shape), or to make letters on a cake. When they harden, eat them. Enjoy!

RESULTS & CONCLUSION Write down the results of your experiment. Come to a conclusion as to whether or not your hypothesis was correct.

SOMETHING MORE
1. Create more unusual colors by combining three or even four colors in varying amounts (use a toothpick to pick up a very small drop of a color). Be sure to write down exactly how you got each new color, so that color can be made again by repeating the same quantities of each color.
2. Use your knowledge of coloring to create a rainbow. Be sure the colors are in the correct order as a natural rainbow.
3. Select simple color art from a magazine or book and try matching the colors to use as "paint" to reproduce the picture.

COLORFUL DISGUISE

SMELL AND TASTE: TEAM PLAYERS

PURPOSE How important is the sight of a food in its identification, compared to smell and taste?

OVERVIEW Our senses of smell and taste are chemical processes that our bodies use as a team to help us evaluate foods. But do you think it is easy to identify a food from taste only, or in combination with smell, without the aid of the sense of sight?

YOU NEED
- an adult
- several friends
- apple
- pear
- cucumber or squash
- cantaloupe or other melon
- knife
- 4 bowls or containers
- aluminum foil
- blue food coloring
- eyedropper
- paper and pencil

To test this, we want to prepare pieces of several fruits and vegetables for various friends and others to sample a taste. And since they may be able to identify even a small piece of fruit or vegetable by sight (and we'd rather not subject them to being blindfolded), we will disguise each food sample so it cannot easily be identified.

To carry out the experiment, we'll need to use fruits and vegetables with similar textures. Then we'll cut the pieces into very small cubes and change the normal "look" of the food with food coloring, so its color will not be a help in guessing a food's identity.

HYPOTHESIS Your friends will make more incorrect (or correct) guesses than correct (or incorrect) guesses based on taste alone . . . or based on both taste and smell.

PROCEDURE Have an adult help you cut the *fleshy* part of an apple, a pear, a melon such as a cantaloupe or honeydew, and a cucumber into a number of small cubes. Be sure not to include any seeds or skins, which might be a help in identifying the food.

Place apple pieces in one bowl, melon in another, pear in a third and cucumber in a fourth bowl. Write the name of each test fruit or vegetable onto a piece of masking tape and stick it onto the bottom of the proper bowl of test samples.

Now take a single piece of each fruit or vegetable and place it in a small section of aluminum foil and close it up loosely. Place it alongside the bowl of fruit samples. Disguise the remaining cubes of food in the bowl with *blue* food coloring (except for berries, blue is not a common fruit or vegetable coloring).

Place the sampling bowls at least a few feet apart and, one by one, have a few of your friends approach a bowl. While holding their nose tightly, have them take a cube of food,

taste it and guess what they think it is . . . by *taste alone*. Then let them sniff the bowl of colored fruit pieces, thereby adding the sense of smell, and allow them to change their taste-only guess if they wish to. Once each friend finishes the test, let him or her see the normal-colored fruit pieces that you placed in each foil packet. Are your friends now able to recognize the fruit? Keep track of all their guesses. You can use the information to make up a chart for your project display.

The senses used by each individual taking the test and the fruits used remain *constant*. The color of the fruits are the *variable* from their natural color. Tally how many guesses were right after tasting and after smelling (and seeing with normal coloring) and how many were wrong.

RESULTS & CONCLUSION Write down the results of your experiment. Come to a conclusion as to whether or not your hypothesis was correct.

SOMETHING MORE
1. Do the above experiment, first testing five children your age and then five adults. Do you think adults will have more correct guesses than your friends?
2. Select other fruits and vegetables that have similarly fleshy parts so they could be used in this type of taste test. How about squash and tomato? What about the strength (sweet, sour, bitterness) of the flavors?
3. In addition to fruits and vegetables, do a similar experiment using cubes of lunch meat, for example, bologna and turkey breast, or different cheeses.

You've Changed!

IDENTIFYING CHEMICAL AND PHYSICAL CHANGES

PURPOSE Understanding the difference between a physical change and a chemical change.

OVERVIEW Some changes which take place in substances are "physical changes" and some are "chemical changes." What is the difference?

When a chemical change takes place, the substance often takes on new properties. Glass is made from sand and limestone, but has properties unlike either sand or limestone. Carbon, hydrogen, and oxygen can be combined to form table sugar, a compound that is nothing like the elements that make it up. Hydrogen and oxygen by themselves burn, but when two atoms of hydrogen combine with one atom of oxygen it forms a molecule of water, which not only doesn't burn, but can be used to put out fires!

YOU NEED
- drinking glasses
- water
- ice cubes
- 2 slices of bread
- use of a toaster
- pepper
- fruit (for fruit salad)
- fresh milk
- sour milk
- unbaked cookie dough
- baked cookies

It is often difficult or impossible to "undo" the results of a chemical reaction. However, a physical change can usually be reversed.

For example, heat may cause a chemical change. Compare a slice of bread to one that has been toasted. The heat has caused a chemical change in the bread, and we cannot restore the bread to the way it was before it was toasted. A log burning in a fireplace is having its chemical composition changed to carbon, heat, light, sound, and gases. It would be impossible to combine carbon, gases, and remove heat to restore the log to its former state.

Water can be changed by temperature to take the form of a gas, a liquid, or a solid (ice). This is not a chemical change; it is a physical change. Ice can easily be turned back into a liquid, and the liquid retains all of the same properties it had when it was previously a liquid. This is a case where heat causes a physical change but not a chemical change.

HYPOTHESIS By gathering together some common everyday materials, it is possible to clarify and display the results of three physical changes and three chemical changes.

PROCEDURE Set up the following examples of change and explain the differences:

Physical change:
1. a glass of water and ice cubes
2. a glass of plain water and a mixture of water and black pepper (pepper does not combine with water, and can be easily removed)
3. cut-up fruits and a fruit salad (even though fruit pieces are mixed together, you can still pull out individual slices to separate them again)

Chemical change:
1. a slice of bread and a slice of toasted bread
2. unbaked cookie dough and a baked cookie
3. fresh milk and sour milk

The foods you start with, before any changes are made to them, are the *constant*. The physical *variable* with water and water containing pepper is the addition of pepper; with water and ice cubes the *variable* is temperature; with cut-up fruit and fruit salad the *variable* is the mixing.

The chemical *variable* with bread and toasted bread and with unbaked and baked cookie dough is the addition of heat; with fresh and sour milk is the *variable* the souring.

RESULTS & CONCLUSION Write down the results of your experiment. Come to a conclusion as to whether or not your hypothesis was correct.

SOMETHING MORE
1. Can you name some physical changes that, at first, appear to be chemical changes? For example, adding powdered drink mix to water. It is physical, because the water can be separated from the mix by evaporation (leaving the mix behind). Baking cookies is a chemical change. Breaking the finished cookie in half to share with a friend is a physical change.
2. If newspaper is placed in a sunny window for several days, it changes color. Is that a physical or a chemical change? Can it be easily reversed?
3. Is rotting fruit a chemical or a physical change?

SCENT IN A CUBE

RELEASING FRAGRANCE WITH HEAT

PURPOSE You know that flowers outside give off fragrances and will do so in your home if you bring them inside. But how can you make something in your home give off more of its scent?

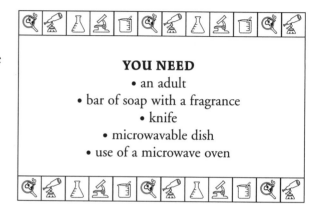

YOU NEED
- an adult
- bar of soap with a fragrance
- knife
- microwavable dish
- use of a microwave oven

OVERVIEW Smell is a chemical process that takes place as tiny invisible molecules leave an object and travel through the air to reach our nose, where a chemical solution and nerve cells line the inside of the nose to detect the smell.

Smells can remind us of special times and events. The smell of cedar may make you think of a cedar chest someone in your family uses to store clothing. If you decorate a live tree at Christmas time, you may get the feeling of that season when you smell that particular kind of tree. Think about what odors remind you of a happy time at home during a holiday, or a visit to grandma's house. Many people like the smell of peppermint, apple, pine, and cinnamon. They buy candles that are scented which give off their aroma when lit. They buy incense burners to spread an aroma throughout their room. There are small potpourri pots where water and pieces of fragrance are heated with a small candle underneath.

Heat can cause a material to release molecules into the air and be diffused (going from an area of more concentration to an area of lesser concentration). Then we can detect the airborne molecules with our nose. That is why a scented candle can be in a room, but

you won't smell it until it is lit, and the potpourri pot does not release its scent until it is warmed.

HYPOTHESIS Hypothesize that heat will cause the fragrance in a perfumed soap to be released and fill the air in a room with an aroma.

PROCEDURE Have an adult carefully cut a small cube from a bar of soap that is perfumed or has a fragrance. Notice that you probably do not notice the scent very much unless you place the soap fairly close to your nose. The soap is *constant*. The *variable* is the heat that is applied to the soap.

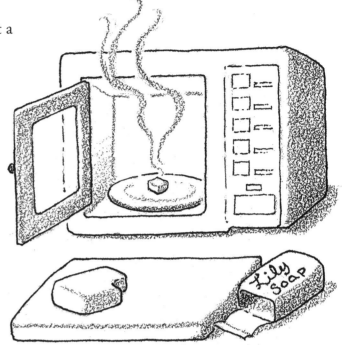

Place the soap on a microwavable dish and place it in a microwave oven. Heat it for several seconds. Microwave ovens have different powers, so you may have to experiment with the amount of time. Start with about five seconds.

Open the door of the microwave, but *don't touch the soap*; it may not *look* hot to you, but it might still be hot enough to burn. After a few minutes, walk around the room and sniff the air. Can you detect the soap's smell in all areas of the room? How about in the next room?

RESULTS & CONCLUSION Write down the results of your experiment. Come to a conclusion as to whether or not your hypothesis was correct.

SOMETHING MORE
1. Can the same piece of soap be reheated again and again to release even more fragrance?
2. Purchase two identical car fresheners, the small decorative fresheners made to hang from the rearview mirror. Put one in a sealable plastic bag and place it in a refrigerator freezer. Place the other in a sunny window. Later, remove the one from the refrigerator and open the bag. Is its smell as strong as the freshener in the sunny window? If the freshener in the sunny window has a stronger smell, does this mean that car fresheners give off more scent in the summertime than they do in winter?

STAYING ON TOP

REDUCE A SOAP'S DENSITY . . . AND IT FLOATS!

PURPOSE Soap normally sinks—but can it be changed in some way so it will float in water?

OVERVIEW The "density" of a material refers to how closely packed together the matter is that makes it up. The density of an object determines its weight, or mass, but not its size. A piece of metal that is exactly the same size as a piece of cork will be denser than the cork. Objects that are less dense than water will be supported by the water and so will float.

Look at a sponge used for cleaning and compare it to a block of wood the same size. The sponge is less dense; it contains less material than the wood, yet it is the same size. The sponge weighs less than the wood.

One feature of a popular brand of soap is that it floats. That's because it's less dense than water. Is it possible to decrease the density of a soap that normally doesn't float, so it will? One way to make a substance less dense is to expand its size and add air into it, making it less compact. We will use heat to expand the soap.

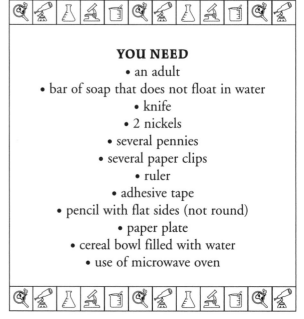

YOU NEED
- an adult
- bar of soap that does not float in water
- knife
- 2 nickels
- several pennies
- several paper clips
- ruler
- adhesive tape
- pencil with flat sides (not round)
- paper plate
- cereal bowl filled with water
- use of microwave oven

HYPOTHESIS Hypothesize that you can change the shape and density of a piece of soap but its weight will not change.

PROCEDURE Lay a pencil on a flat table. The pencil should have flat surfaces on it, not round. Set a ruler across the pencil, at about the middle of the ruler, so that it looks like a seesaw. Use adhesive tape to fix a nickel near each end of the ruler.

Have an adult cut two small chunks out of a bar of soap. Place one chunk in a small bowl filled with water. Be sure the soap sinks. This ensures that we are using soap that will normally sink when placed in water. Set the other chunk on one of the nickels at the end of the ruler. Lay pennies and paper clips on the other end of the ruler until the ruler balances as best as possible on the pencil.

Lift the chunk of soap off the ruler, being careful not to disturb the pennies and paper clips. Lay the soap on a paper plate and place it in a microwave oven. Because microwave ovens differ in the amount of power they have, you will have to experiment with time. Start by running the oven for 10 seconds. Watch the soap. We are watching for it to expand and look more like whipped cream than a solid chunk. Try running the oven for another 5 seconds if you haven't observed much change in the soap.

When the soap seems to have expanded, foaming up like whipped cream, remove the plate from the oven, but *don't touch* the soap for a few minutes until it cools.

Carefully lay the puffed-out soap back on top of the nickel on the ruler. The balance scale system, used to weigh the soap before and after being exposed to the microwave oven, is the *constant*. The *variable* is the addition of heat from a microwave being applied to the piece of soap.

We are using the nickel because now the soap has changed to a bigger shape and we want to be sure we place the soap at the same point on the ruler that it was before. The soap should rest completely on the nickel and not touch the ruler.

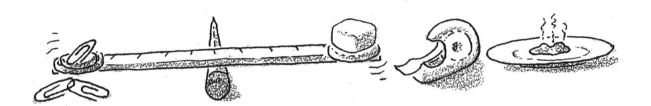

Does the soap still balance? We increased the "volume," or size, of the soap and decreased its density (it is now more spread out), but we haven't changed its weight significantly. Most of the material that was present before it was heated is still there, so it weighs the same.

Place the puffed soap in the bowl of water. Have we reduced the density enough so that it now floats?

RESULTS & CONCLUSION Write down the results of your experiment. Come to a conclusion as to whether or not your hypothesis was correct.

SOMETHING MORE

1. Do you think soap that has been expanded and made less dense will be used up more quickly in the shower? The surface area of the expanded soap is greater, so more of it will be exposed to the water and the washcloth when you're washing.
2. Take a lump of clay and place it in water. It will sink. Mold it into the shape of a row boat and place it in the water again. Does the clay still sink or does it now float?

BASIC BUILDING BLOCKS

GETTING TO KNOW THE PERIODIC TABLE

PURPOSE There are natural rules on how elements will or will not combine with each other.

OVERVIEW Everything in the world is made up of basic "elements." In chemistry, an "element" is matter than cannot be separated into simpler parts by either chemical or physical means.

Some things are made of two or more elements that have combined. Metals, wood, plants, bodily tissues, and even the air we breathe are combinations of elements.

Elements are made up of tiny, invisible particles called atoms. Atoms are made up of even smaller parts, and some atoms have more parts than others. One atom part is called a "proton." Every element has been given a number, called its "atomic number," which is the number of protons one atom of that element contains.

Chemists learned that the elements could be arranged, based on their atomic number, in rows and columns to form a helpful table. This table is called the periodic table because it displays a regular pattern of properties among the elements. Some elements have similar properties and features, and we say these elements make up a "family."

28	29	30
Ni	Cu	Zn
Nickel	Copper	Zinc
58.71	63.54	65.37
46	47	48
Pd	Ag	Cd
Palladium	Silver	Cadmium
106.4	107.87	112.40

Atomic Number

Symbol for the Element

Name of the Element

Average Atomic Mass

IRON

COPPER

SILVER

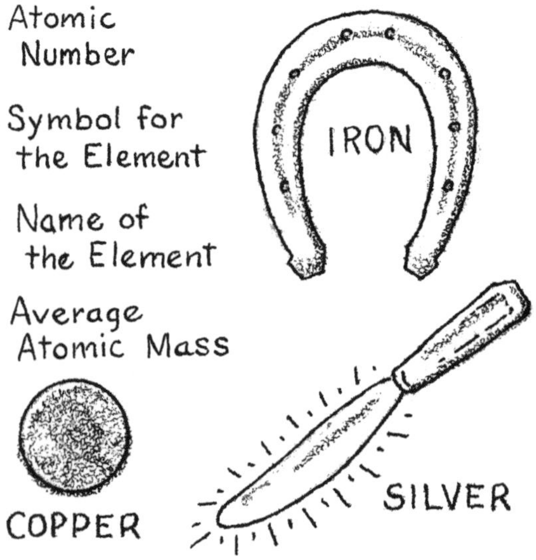

Chemists have given elements one or more letter symbols to represent their name: Zn for zinc, Cu for copper, Ag for silver, etc. The first letter is always capitalized, and if there are additional letters, they are written in lower-case letters. The symbols are used on the periodic table, and are also used when equations are written, showing the combining of elements and their results.

HYPOTHESIS   Hypothesize that toy construction pieces will easily fit together if they are from the same "family" or type of toy, but pieces from different sets will not work well together.

PROCEDURE   Using different sets of children's building toys, show how the building pieces from the same "family" fit together, but they do not fit together with pieces from other building toys. The construction pieces within a given set are *constant*. The construction pieces from different sets when tried to be combined are *variable*.

This is similar to elements on the periodic table; some elements combine more easily. In fact, when sodium combines with water, it explodes!

RESULTS & CONCLUSION   Write down the results of your research and come to a conclusion as to whether or not your hypothesis was correct.

SOMETHING MORE
1. Which element do you think is the most abundant on Earth? Research "Periodic Table" under "Elements" in an encyclopedia volume or computer CD-ROM. Look on the Internet for the very latest information, because new elements, mostly synthetic radioactives, are still being discovered. (Recently, 109 Unnilennium and 111 Unununium were created in laboratories—but lasted for only a fraction of a second).
2. Zn is the symbol for zinc. O is the symbol for oxygen. You can easily see how these symbols were chosen to represent their elements. But the symbol for iron is Fe; sodium is Na; potassium is K. Research how these symbols were derived.

STRESSED OUT

THE EFFECTS OF WEATHERING ON ELASTICITY

PURPOSE Rubber bands are elastic . . . until something happens. Let's examine how stress and weather conditions affect elastic bands.

OVERVIEW Signs of deterioration in a rubber band are discoloring, cracking and splitting, and the loss of elasticity (it doesn't return completely to its original shape). This is what happens when you see a rubber band that has been left outside for even a few days. Yet, rubber bands left in a drawer in your home can stay there, sometimes for years, without showing signs of deterioration.

What is it about the outdoors that might affect the rubber material? Perhaps ozone or other gases in the air attack rubber. There may be acids in rain. Sunlight contains ultraviolet and infrared rays which may alter rubber material. Temperature and humidity changes may also be a factor.

> **YOU NEED**
> • 3 equal-size small rubber bands
> • 3 paper clips
> • 3 empty soda cans (with pull tabs)
> • water
> • magnifying glass
> • index card
> • hanging area outside
> • hanging area inside

HYPOTHESIS Hypothesize that a rubber band that is stressed (stretched) and exposed to outside elements will show definite signs of deterioration within a few days, while one under the same stress but kept indoors, will show little or no deterioration in that short time.

PROCEDURE In addition to comparing two stressed rubber bands, one indoors and one outdoors, let's also try to narrow down the possible cause of deterioration. The rubber bands are the *constant*. The stretching and exposure to outdoor elements are the *variables*.

Bend the metal opener tab on a soda can upward so that, while still attached to the can, the tab is at a 90-degree angle to the can top. Push a small rubber band halfway through the hole in the tab.

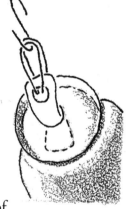

Bend a paper clip to form an "S"-shaped hook and hang the two loop ends of the rubber band onto one paper-clip hook. Bend the hook closed to keep the rubber band from slipping out. In the same way, put rubber bands and hooks on two more cans.

Fill all three cans half-full of water. Using the other end of the paper-clip hooks, hang two cans outdoors on a clothesline that is in full sunlight. Find an out-of-the-way spot indoors to hang the third can. You can hang it on a bedroom door jam (the molding around the door). Be sure the indoor can is not in direct sunlight, as it would be if you hung it on a window curtain rod.

You can add more water or remove some to make the rubber bands you have stretch, but not stretched to their maximum.

Let the cans hang from their stretched rubber bands for five to seven days. If rain is coming, move one of the two outdoor cans indoors and hang it from the door jam. When the rain stops, take the can back outside and hang it on the clothesline again. Be sure to mark this can so you can identify it as being the one that is usually outdoors but is not exposed to rain.

Now you have three stressed rubber bands: one kept indoors away from the elements of weather and sunlight; one outdoors that is fully exposed to sunlight, air, temperature changes, and rain; and one that is exposed to sunlight, temperature changes, and air, but not rain.

Check your rubber bands daily. One or both of the outdoor rubber bands may deteriorate so much as to break before a week has passed. At that time, end your experiment and examine all three rubber bands.

Examine them by looking at each one under a magnifying glass. Has there been a change in color? Do you see cracks or splits developing? Cracks can also be detected by holding a rubber band in the stretched position and running the edge of an index card up and down the length of it. You will hear a noise if cracks have developed.

Check the elasticity of the rubber bands. Do they snap back to their original shape when stretched?

RESULTS & CONCLUSION Write down the results of your experiment. Come to a conclusion as to whether or not your hypothesis was correct.

SOMETHING MORE
1. Try this experiment using rubber bands of different sizes, thicknesses and colors.
2. Try this experiment using other elastic materials, for example, party balloons.

HEAVY GAS, MAN

RELEASING TRAPPED GAS TO EXTINGUISH FLAME

PURPOSE To learn about an important characteristic of carbon dioxide, that it is heavier than air—and how that characteristic can be used.

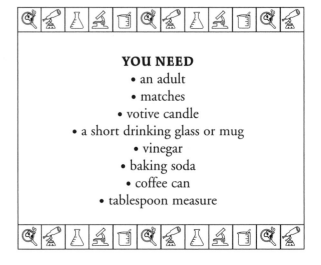

YOU NEED
- an adult
- matches
- votive candle
- a short drinking glass or mug
- vinegar
- baking soda
- coffee can
- tablespoon measure

OVERVIEW Does the chemical term "sodium bicarbonate" sound familiar to you? Actually, you probably have a box of it in your home. Maybe you will recognize it more by its common name, "baking soda."

Baking soda is a white powder that has many uses. In the kitchen it is often called for in baking recipes. In the bathroom, it is used as a tooth cleaner . . . for brushing teeth. Added to a laundry load, it enhances the action of liquid chlorine bleach, to make clothes whiter. When placed in the refrigerator, it absorbs food odors. As an antacid, it helps relieve heartburn and sour stomach. It can even be used in a bowl of warm water to soothe aching feet. Sodium bicarbonate is truly a useful household chemical.

Baking soda can also be used in the kitchen for putting out small fires; for example, a grease fire in a frying pan. When baking soda is thrown on a fire, the powder helps cover whatever is fueling the fire and cuts it off, like a blanket, from exposure to air. But its real fire-fighting ability comes from its release of carbon dioxide gas, caused by the heat of the fire. Carbon dioxide gas actually puts out fires.

Carbon dioxide gas can also be released from baking soda by mixing the soda with vinegar. Since carbon dioxide gas is also heavier than air, it stays near the ground if free or, if in a container, it will stay in the bottom until it's released.

HYPOTHESIS Hypothesize that you can put out the flame of a candle by releasing carbon dioxide gas from baking soda and "pouring it" onto the flame.

PROCEDURE Set a votive candle in a short glass or coffee mug. Have an adult light the candle.

Take an empty coffee can filled only with air. Carefully, tilt the can over the glass containing the candle, as if you are "pouring" air into the glass. (Always be alert and careful working around open flame or anything hot.) Observe that there is no change in the lit candle when you "pour" the air.

Next, scoop 2 tablespoons of baking soda and dump them into the empty coffee can. Pour 3 tablespoons of vinegar into a small glass or container. Pour the vinegar quickly, all at once, into the coffee can containing the baking soda. A violent reaction will take place and carbon dioxide gas will be released, causing bubbles to foam up. When the fizzing has settled down after two or three seconds, quickly tilt the coffee can and pour the "invisible" carbon dioxide gas in the can onto the lit candle. Be careful not to tilt the can so much that the baking soda mixture itself spills out and makes a mess. Does the flame on the candle go out?

The flame and the candle are the *constant*s. The *variable* is the addition of carbon dioxide gas.

Although the carbon dioxide gas that is poured out can't be seen, you can detect its presence by its effect on the lit candle.

RESULTS & CONCLUSION Write down the results of your experiment. Come to a conclusion as to whether or not your hypothesis was correct.

SOMETHING MORE Is there enough carbon dioxide generated to put the candle out even if it is not sitting in a small cup? Can you possibly measure the amount of a gas you cannot see?

HAVE A TASTE, BUD

SUGAR SWEETNESS A MATTER OF CHEMISTRY

PURPOSE We experience the sense of taste when we eat or otherwise put things in our mouths. What do we taste and why do we taste it? Let's find out.

OVERVIEW The sense of taste is a chemical action that takes place on our tongues. Test that taste is a chemical process by laying a dry cornflake on your tongue. It won't have any taste at all until your saliva begins dissolving it. Do the same with a dry cracker.

YOU NEED
- corn flakes
- crackers
- peppermint stick hard candy
- piece of licorice
- cherry lollipop
- grape lollipop
- lemon lollipop
- glass of water

Because food must be dissolved before it can be tasted is proof that taste is a chemical process. It is only possible for us to taste foods that are in a liquid state. If they're not, the saliva in our mouth dissolves the food, turning it into a liquid.

Small organs, called "taste buds," on our tongues then evaluate the dissolved food and give us the sensation of taste. Four sets of taste buds are used to detect the sweet, sour, salty, and bitter taste groups. As shown, these four kinds of taste buds are located at different areas on top of the tongue.

You can easily test this; open your mouth wide and briefly rub a piece of peppermint stick against the back part of your tongue, being careful not to touch the front part. Don't place the candy too far back on your tongue or it might make you gag. After a brief rubbing, notice any taste in your mouth. Now rub the peppermint on the front area of your tongue. Can you taste the sweetness of the candy better?

HYPOTHESIS Hypothesize that the organs that cause you to be able to taste and isolate flavors are grouped on top of the tongue.

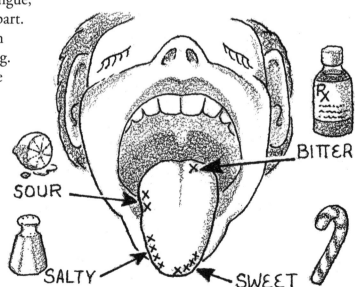

SOUR
BITTER
SALTY
SWEET

PROCEDURE Place a hard candy peppermint stick under your tongue and a small piece of licorice on top of your tongue. Wait a few moments for your saliva to dissolve some of the candies. Which candy do you taste?

Take a sip of water to clear the taste from your mouth (official tasters call it "clearing the palate"). Now reverse the candies, placing a licorice piece under your tongue and touching the peppermint stick to its top. Which candy do you taste now?

Experiment further by placing various flavors of lollipop under your tongue and onto areas of its surface; try cherry, grape, lemon, lime, and other flavors that you know and are easy to identify. Your tongue with its taste buds is the *constant*. It's the different *areas* of the tongue undergoing testing that are the *variables*, as are the different lollipop flavors.

RESULTS & CONCLUSION Write down the results of your experiment. Come to a conclusion as to whether or not your hypothesis was correct.

SOMETHING MORE Prepare small pieces of fruit: orange, apple, grape, peach, and others. Have friends close their eyes while you lay a piece of fruit on their tongues. Can they identify the fruit? Can they tell the difference between sweet, sour, salty and bitter?

SETTLE UP

OIL AND WATER DON'T MIX . . . USUALLY

PURPOSE To determine if an oil spill would clean up more quickly in freshwater than in saltwater.

OVERVIEW When huge ships carrying oil (oil tankers) have an accident that causes a breach (a hole) in their hull, thousands of gallons of oil can leak into the water. Oil spills are terrible environmental problems. The oil pollutes the water and often harms fish and wildlife.

You may have heard the old saying, "Oil and water don't mix." It is true that oil, including cooking oil found in your kitchen, does not mix easily with water. It has a tendency to float on top of water. Have you ever watched someone cooking spaghetti and seen them add a little vegetable oil to the pot of boiling water? Did you notice that the oil stayed on top of the water?

The fact that oil floats on water certainly helps environmental crews who are assigned the task of cleaning up oil spills from oil tankers. In the open sea, it would be nearly impossible to contain oil if it immediately mixed with water and was carried down to all depths by currents, as well as spreading out from the ship.

Does oil float better in saltwater than freshwater? If so, then would an oil spill in saltwater be easier to clean up than one in freshwater? If the oil and water are slightly mixed, as they would be by waves in the ocean, does the oil settle up quicker in one type of water than the other? That would make oil cleanup quicker, although not necessarily easier.

YOU NEED
- 2 clear jars with screw-top lids
- water
- vegetable oil
- salt
- tablespoon measure
- kitchen measuring cup
- spoon
- clock or watch
- masking tape
- pen or pencil

HYPOTHESIS Form a hypothesis as to whether you think oil mixed with water settles up (floats) quicker in saltwater or freshwater. Or, you may hypothesize that there is no noticeable difference.

PROCEDURE Gather two clear jars with lids that screw on tight. A pickle, mayonnaise, relish, or jelly jar make good choices. The two jars must be identical in size.

Pour ¾ cup of water into one jar. Pour another ¾ cup of water into the second jar. To the second jar add 4 tablespoons of salt. Stir.

Stick a piece of masking tape on each jar and label which one is freshwater and which one is saltwater by writing on the tape. Although it is not actual ocean brine, the saltwater solution will approximate the saltwater found in the sea.

Pour ¼ cup of vegetable oil into each jar. Screw the lids on the jars. Shake each jar lightly several times (be sure to shake each jar the same number of times). This shaking is to simulate the action of the waves in the ocean. The oil in this project is a *constant*. The water is *variable*, comparing both fresh and saltwater.

Make a note of the time. Set the jars on a table and don't disturb them. Observe the jars, waiting for the oil and water to settle out.

Does the oil in one jar settle out more quickly than in the other? The quicker an oil spill can be cleaned up, the less chance it has to have a hazardous effect on the environment.

RESULTS & CONCLUSION Write down the results of your experiment. Come to a conclusion as to whether or not your hypothesis was correct.

SOMETHING MORE Do you live near an ocean or a lake whose water is salty? Repeat the above experiment, but instead of using homemade saltwater, use actual saltwater from the saltwater body near you. Is there any difference between the results of your homemade saltwater and actual brine? If not, then the homemade saltwater was a good representation of actual sea water.

Is there anything that can be added to water—fresh or sea water—to aid in the picking up of oil?

BUILDING BLOCKS

GROWING NATURAL CRYSTAL STRUCTURES

PURPOSE Certain substances just naturally take flat-sided crystalline shapes. Here's how to watch, as you "grow" your own crystals.

OVERVIEW Everything is made up of small particles called atoms and molecules. In some solid substances, these atoms and molecules are arranged together to make three-dimensional patterns which are repeated over and over until they are big enough for us to see with a microscope or a magnifying glass. These substances are called "crystals." Crystals have shapes that are characterized by their smooth, flat surfaces with sharp edges. Crystal-shaped substances include sugar, table salt, gold, silver, topaz, quartz, and copper sulfate.

YOU NEED
- an adult
- salt
- sugar
- 2 short drinking glasses
- thin string or thread
- spoon
- hot water from the tap
- 2 pencils
- magnifying glass (microscope preferable)

Although non-living things do not grow, the molecules of crystals can pile together to "grow" bigger in size. When enough sugar is dissolved into water, sugar crystals will build up or "grow" on a piece of thread or string that is left in the solution until a clump big enough to see with the unaided eye appears.

Examine a few grains of sugar under a microscope. If you do not have a microscope, you can use a magnifying glass that has a high magnification. Observe that the tiny grains of sugar have a cube or block-like shape. This is one kind of crystal shape.

Examine a few grains of table salt under a microscope or a magnifying glass of high magnification. Observe that salt, too, has a cube-like shape and, therefore, it is also called a crystal.

HYPOTHESIS Hypothesize that, since you have observed salt to be a crystal, it, too, can be made to accumulate (build up) and "grow" a large crystal object.

PROCEDURE Fill a short drinking glass with hot water from the tap. Be careful not to burn yourself! Add a spoonful of sugar to the water and stir. Continue to add one spoonful at a time and stir until no more sugar can be dissolved in the water. You can tell when this happens, as sugar will begin to build up at the bottom of the glass and will not dissolve, no matter how long you stir. When a solution is holding as much of a substance as it can, it is called a "saturated solution." A "solution" is a solvent (the material that you use to dissolve) that contains a solute (the material that gets dissolved).

Tie a piece of thread or thin string onto a pencil at its center. Lay the pencil on top of the glass of sugar water and let the string hang down into the water. Set the glass in an out-of-the-way place, where it will not be bumped or moved. Wait two to three days. Then observe the buildup of sugar crystals on the string. We are "growing" a big crystal from many small crystals.

Fill another short drinking glass with hot water from the tap. Use caution handling hot water so as not to burn yourself. Stir in a spoonful of table salt. Continue to add salt and stir until the solution has become saturated (no more salt can be dissolved and excess salt can be seen at the bottom of the glass). Tie a piece of thread or thin string onto the center of a pencil. Lay the pencil on top of the glass and let the string hang down into the solution.

The water and string are *constant*. The solute (the material being dissolved) is the *variable* (sugar and salt). After two or three days, examine the string. Have crystals of salt begun to build up on the string? Was your hypothesis correct?

RESULTS & CONCLUSION Write down the results of your experiments and come to a conclusion as to whether or not your hypothesis was correct.

SOMETHING MORE
1. Can you build your crystal objects even bigger by adding more sugar and salt to the solutions and waiting a few more days? Do not heat the water again, because you don't want to dissolve the crystals that have already formed on the string. You want to add to them.
2. Ice can form crystal structures, too. On a morning when frost makes designs on your house windows or car windshield, use a magnifying glass of high magnification to examine the frost for evidence of crystal shapes.
3. Honey can crystallize and turn into a solid; but can it be restored to a liquid form by warming it?

COOL CLOTHES

TESTING FOR FABRICS THAT "BREATHE"

PURPOSE Sometimes you need to dress to keep warm, other times you want to wear clothing that "breathes" to help you stay cooler. How can we test fabrics for their ability to allow the body to cool itself in summer through evaporation?

OVERVIEW Clothes . . . everybody wears them. Different types of clothing are worn for different seasons, weather, and climates. Years ago, people made clothes from whatever they found in nature. From animals, they got fur, leather, and wool. From plants, they used grasses, wove straw, and grew cotton to make fabric.

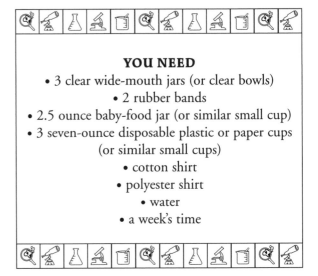

YOU NEED
- 3 clear wide-mouth jars (or clear bowls)
- 2 rubber bands
- 2.5 ounce baby-food jar (or similar small cup)
- 3 seven-ounce disposable plastic or paper cups (or similar small cups)
- cotton shirt
- polyester shirt
- water
- a week's time

Now chemists have developed new materials for clothing. Some of these "synthetics" have greater benefits than clothing made from plants and animals. Rayon, for example, is a synthetic fabric that is strong, yet soft. It is easy to dye and the colors don't fade. In 1939, the DuPont Company began marketing a synthetic fiber called nylon, which quickly became the standard for women's stockings. Nylon was originally developed for its strength and its light weight, perfect for making parachutes. Surprisingly, many of the new synthetic materials are made from *petro*chemicals; in order words, they are are *oil-based* products.

Which types of clothing material are best for keeping warm in winter? Which are best for keeping you cool in summer? Articles of clothing made from polyester fibers are said to allow the vapor of perspiration to pass through easily, keeping the person who wears a polyester shirt cooler than with some other types of material. Perspiration causes evaporation, which is a cooling process.

HYPOTHESIS A piece of polyester shirt fabric covering a bowl of water will allow more of that water to evaporate than will other popular shirt materials.

PROCEDURE Fill three clear wide-mouth jars with an equal amount of water. In order to accurately measure an amount of water for each, fill a tiny jar (for example, a 2.5 ounce baby-food jar) with water until it overflows. Then carefully, without spilling any water, pour the complete contents into one of the jars. Repeat this for the other two jars.

Look at the labels on the shirts in your closet or in the closet of others in your home.

Collect a shirt that is made of polyester and one made of cotton.

Lay a single layer of the polyester clothing over one of the water-filled jars. Stretch a rubber band around the jar to secure it. Lay a single layer of the cotton clothing over one of the water-filled jars. Stretch a rubber band around the jar to secure it.

Leave one jar uncovered. Set the jars in an out-of-the-way place where they will not be disturbed. Let them sit for a week.

The *constant* is the amount of water, the size of the jars (the opening at the top where evaporation takes place), and the period of time. The *variable* is the type of material covering the jars, affecting evaporation of the water in the jar.

After one week, remove the shirts from the jars. Measure the amount of water left in each of the three jars and compare. Did the uncovered jar have the most evaporation? Did the cotton-covered jar have the least? If you have trouble comparing the amounts of water left, pour the contents of each into three smaller or narrower containers (such as disposable plastic or paper cups). Then the water will rise higher in the smaller space and be easier to compare visually. You could also weigh the water if you have a small kitchen gram weight scale.

RESULTS & CONCLUSION Write down the results of your experiment. Come to a conclusion as to whether or not your hypothesis was correct.

SOMETHING MORE Try this experiment using a variety of different clothing materials: rayon, dacron, wool, fur, nylon, and combinations of cotton and polyester.

OUT OF THE MIDDLE

SEPARATING LIQUIDS BY DENSITY

PURPOSE Experimenting with liquids that have different densities.

OVERVIEW Liquids may have different "densities." The "density" of a liquid is a measure of how closely packed together its molecules are, which determines its weight and mass. A liquid that is less dense than another liquid will float on top of that liquid.

Have you ever seen chicken cooking in a pot of water to make chicken soup and noticed a layer of fat floating on the top of the water? Some of the chicken fat is separating from it and the fat floats. Since chicken fat is not easy to digest, some cooks pour some or all of this excess fat off before making the rest of the soup.

In whole unhomogenized milk, fat can also be separated by density. This "cream" is less dense than the rest of the milk. Today, machines separate milk and cream, but farmers used to let whole milk stand for several hours so the cream would separate and rise to the top where it could easily be skimmed off with a spoon.

> **YOU NEED**
> - blue food coloring
> - vegetable oil
> - water
> - food coloring
> - honey
> - 2 clear jars
> - 2 pieces of plastic aquarium tubing, (1ft/30 cm) each
> - plastic food wrap
> - glue
> - drinking glass
> - spoon
> - rubber band
> - pencil

HYPOTHESIS A liquid can be extracted (removed) from a container that holds one or more other liquids, as long as that liquid has a different density than the other(s).

PROCEDURE Honey is denser than water. Water is denser than vegetable oil. We can use honey, water, and vegetable oil to make three separate layers of liquids, all contained in the same jar. The extraction device is *constant*. The density of the different liquids is *variable*.

In a clear jar (a pickle, relish, or jelly jar will work well), pour in enough honey to make a layer about an inch (2.5 cm) high in the jar.

Fill a drinking glass with water. Add a few drops of food coloring (choose blue, or a color that is different from the honey you are using). Stir with a spoon. This will make the water more visible.

Gently and slowly pour the water into the jar of honey until there is enough water to form a second layer about 1 inch (2.5 cm) thick. Next, slowly pour another inch-thick layer, this time of vegetable oil, into the jar. Let the jar sit until the three different layers of liquids are clearly defined.

Let's extract the layer of water, which is in the middle of the liquid layers. To do this, we must construct a device for extracting the liquid.

Seal the top of another clear jar by wrapping several layers of plastic food wrap over it, making a tight seal on the top. Stretch a rubber band around the top of the jar to hold the plastic wrap tightly in place. Poke two small holes in the plastic wrap with a pencil point, at opposite sides. Insert a foot-long (30 cm) piece of flexible plastic aquarium tubing into each hole. Push one tube into the jar until its end is positioned near the bottom of the jar. Position the end of the other tube near the top of the jar. To make a seal, add a bead of glue around the two holes where the tubing goes through, and set aside to dry. The jar must be airtight.

Take the tube whose end extends near the bottom of the jar and stick it into the other jar containing the three liquids. Position the end of the tube to be toward the bottom of the layer of colored water. Place the end of the other tube in your mouth and suck in on it as you would a straw in a soda to drink it. As you pull the air in the jar out through the tube, the liquid will be pulled out of its jar through the other open tube by the vacuum.

You have successfully extracted the middle layer using the concept of differing densities and vacuum suction—an example of chemistry and physics working together!

RESULTS & CONCLUSION Write down the results of your experiment. Come to a conclusion as to whether or not your hypothesis was correct.

SOMETHING MORE
1. Attempt to extract the honey on the bottom of the jar through the vegetable oil.
2. Visit a farm and collect some whole milk in a clear container. Observe the separation of cream over time.

NOT JUST DESSERTS

TESTING TASTE WITH COMBINED FLAVORS

PURPOSE Would combining two different flavors of gelatin dessert create a new flavor, or will the two individual flavors be discernible?

OVERVIEW Food companies are constantly trying to improve the taste of their products and also to come up with new products to sell. Recently, a number of these food products have been made up of combinations of flavored ingredients; cranberry-apple or kiwi-strawberry drink, for example.

Gelatin desserts, available in stores as packaged powders to which you add hot water and then place in the refrigerator to gel, are available in many flavors: lemon, lime, strawberry, cherry, raspberry, peach, and watermelon, to name a few. If we mix two flavors together in equal portions and make a gelatin dessert, do you think your taste buds will interpret the taste as being a brand-new flavor, or do you think you will be able to detect the two separate flavors?

YOU NEED
- an adult
- a box of lemon gelatin dessert powder
- a box of lime gelatin dessert powder
- kitchen measuring cup
- spoon
- bowl
- water
- a cooking pot
- use of stove-top burner
- use of refrigerator

HYPOTHESIS Hypothesize that when two different flavors of gelatin dessert are combined, a person's taste buds will not be able to identify the two individual flavors. Or, hypothesize that a person's taste buds can identify two separate flavors of gel in a combination. What do you think?

PROCEDURE Read the instructions on the box of gelatin dessert. It will probably say, "Bring one cup of water to a boil. Add the powdered gelatin. Stir until the powder is dissolved. Add one cup of cold water. Stir. Pour into a bowl and let cool in a refrigerator."

Since we are going to use the contents of two gelatin desserts, the quantity of water must be doubled. Therefore, the instructions for making our combination dessert would be: Have an adult help you bring two cups of water to a boil on a stove. Add one package of lemon gelatin dessert and one package of lime gelatin dessert. Stir until the powder is dissolved. Add two cups of cold water. Stir. Pour into a bowl and let cool in a refrigerator.

When the gelatin hardens after several hours, scoop some into a bowl and taste. Does the dessert taste like a new flavor? Can you taste both the lemon and lime? Or does it taste like just one flavor (if so, which flavor dominates)?

RESULTS & CONCLUSION Write down the results of your experiment. Come to a conclusion as to whether or not your hypothesis was correct.

SOMETHING MORE
1. Repeat the experiment using different combinations of flavors: Combine lemon and cherry, cherry and raspberry, lime and raspberry, and so on. Which combinations of flavor do you like best? Does one flavor usually dominate, or can you tell what two flavors make up the dessert?
2. Compare sugar-free gelatin desserts to sugar gelatin desserts. Hold a box of sugar-free gelatin in one hand and a box of sugar gelatin in the other. Be sure they each will make the same quantity of dessert (that is your *constant*; the *variable* is the type of gelatin, sugar or sugar-free). Is one lighter than the other? From the nutrition information printed on the boxes, compare the calories of one to the other.

TRICKING THE BRAIN

WHEN A FOOD'S COLOR IS CHANGED

PURPOSE To determine how important color is in our expectations of the taste of a food.

OVERVIEW From our life experiences, we learn to expect something that tastes like lemon to be yellow in appearance. We expect something that tastes like cherry to be red in color. Does color really play a big part in how we expect a food to taste?

In this project, a batch of lemon gelatin will be made, with a spoonful given to each of 10 people. Each person will be asked to take a spoonful and try to identify the flavor. The lemon dessert, however, will not be yellow!

HYPOTHESIS Most people will not be able to recognize the true flavor of a gelatin dessert if the natural color of it has been changed.

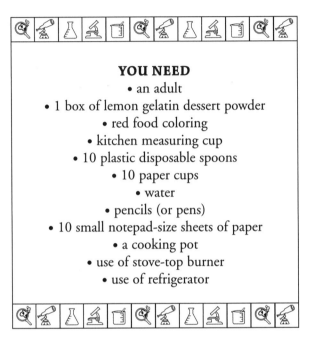

YOU NEED
- an adult
- 1 box of lemon gelatin dessert powder
- red food coloring
- kitchen measuring cup
- 10 plastic disposable spoons
- 10 paper cups
- water
- pencils (or pens)
- 10 small notepad-size sheets of paper
- a cooking pot
- use of stove-top burner
- use of refrigerator

PROCEDURE Following the instructions on a package of lemon-flavored gelatin, ask an adult to help you make a bowl of the dessert. (For safety, it's important that an adult stand by whenever you work around or use a stove.)

Before you place the lemon gelatin liquid in the refrigerator (be careful of splashes), add several drops of red food coloring and stir. Add the food coloring until the lemony-yellow liquid has turned a deep red.

When the disguised lemon gelatin has cooled and hardened, place a spoonful into each of 10 small paper cups. Give 10 people (friends or family members) a cup with a gelatin portion and a spoon. Ask them to each taste the dessert and, without speaking about their choice, to write on a piece of paper the flavor of the gelatin. (Be sure your test subjects aren't being influenced by seeing others' answers.)

Ten people are being asked to give us an idea of how most people will probably answer. Ten is our "sample size." We are using a few people to estimate how a large group of people may respond to the test. A sample size is a smaller group that is tested which, if large enough, will hopefully give us a true picture of a larger group.

$$8/10 = .8$$
$$.8 \times 100 = 80\%$$

When you have tested 10 people and collected your data, determine the percentage of people who were fooled by the unexpected color. To find percentage, simply divide the number of wrong guesses by 10 and multiply the answer by 100. If, for example, eight people guessed wrong, that would mean 80% of those tested were unable to correctly identify the flavor. See the sample math on page 176.

RESULTS & CONCLUSION   Write down the results of your experiment. Come to a conclusion as to whether or not your hypothesis was correct.

SOMETHING MORE

1. Test the concept of "sample size" by testing 20 people (you only need to ask 10 more people and add those results to the first 10). Compare the percentage of wrong guesses to 20. Is the percentage about the same as it was with only 10 people? Do you think that a sample size of 10 people used in the original experiment was enough to get an accurate result?

2. Are some flavors easier for people to identify, even if the color is different? Try a common flavor, for example, orange, and add red food coloring until it is red. Then ask people to identify the flavor. Are more people able to correctly identify orange than lemon, even though both are disguised by a strange coloring?

PHYSICS

INTRODUCTION TO
PHYSICS

Welcome to the fascinating world of physics! This section explores projects in the field of physics. Physics is the science of investigation that tells us the "how" and "why" about nonliving objects. It explains how a refrigerator keeps things cold, why letting the air out of a balloon causes it to fly wildly around the room, and what makes a walkie-talkie work. It tells us why we see a bolt of lightning before we hear its rumbling thunder. Physics helps us unlock the secrets of the physical world around us.

Subjects in physics are numerous, and they include: light, sound, heat, simple machines, forces, magnetism, gravity, friction, acceleration, momentum, time, space, fluidics, pendular motion, wave motion, kinetic and potential energy, work, friction, pressure, weight, conduction, the state of matter (solid, liquid, gas, plasma), electricity, radiation, and many more. Physics is one of the most interesting and motivating science topics.

It is important to understand the laws of physics because so many of its principles are found in other science disciplines, such as astronomy, geology, mathematics, health, engineering, electronics, chemistry, aviation, optics, and even the arts. For instance, meteorology, the study of weather, involves many principles that are explained by physics: convection, evaporation, condensation, temperature, precipitation, tidal action by the forces of gravity, temperature, and erosion. Many of these fields (electronics and structural engineering, for example) are really specialized branches of physics.

Physics affects our daily lives. Its principles are at work when we ride a bicycle, wear a pair of glasses, play a computer game, operate a vacuum cleaner, turn on a bedside light, play a music CD, or call a friend on the telephone. Physics is at work all around us all of the time.

MAGNETIC WATER

THE EFFECT OF WATER ON MAGNETISM

PURPOSE Does water affect a magnetic field?

OVERVIEW Sound waves go through both water and air. In fact, they travel farther and faster in water than they do in air. How about magnetism? Does it go through water, too?

HYPOTHESIS Water has no effect on magnetism.

YOU NEED
- magnet
- 2-liter plastic soda bottle
- masking tape
- metal paper clip
- 2 pencils
- string
- water
- scissors
- an adult

PROCEDURE Ask an adult with a scissors to cut off the rounded top part of a 2-liter bottle. Place a metal paper clip in the bottom of the bottle.

Wrap a strip of masking tape around one end of a six-sided, not round, pencil and then number the sides. Write "1" on the tape on one side, then turn the pencil and write "2," and so on. Tie a piece of string to the middle of the pencil and secure it with a piece of masking tape. Tie the other end of the string to a magnet. Turn the pencil, wrapping the string around it, and set it over the top of the plastic bottle. Slowly, lower the magnet into the bottle. When the magnet is close enough and captures the paper clip, stop! Notice the number on the side of the pencil.

Carefully, lift the magnet straight up without turning the pencil. Remove the paper clip, and lay it back in the bottle in the exact same spot. Fill the bottle half full with water, then slowly lower the magnet into the bottle. Be sure not to turn the pencil, so that the string length is not changed. The string length, the position of the paper clip, and the distance from the magnet to the paper clip are *constants*. The *variable* is the substance between the magnet and the paper clip: air and water.

Does the magnet still attract the paper clip? If so, does it do so from about the same distance above it as it did when the bottle was filled with air instead of water?

RESULTS & CONCLUSION Write down the result of your experiment. Come to a conclusion as to whether or not your hypothesis was correct.

SOMETHING MORE Now test magnetism using saltwater, sugar water, or ice water.

A SWINGING GOOD TIME

PENDULUM MOTION

PURPOSE The properties of pendulums will be investigated.

OVERVIEW When a weight is hung by a wire or a string that is tied to a fixed point (a point that doesn't move), it is called a pendulum. If the weight is pulled to one side and then released to fall freely, it will swing back and forth. Gravity pulls it down, then momentum keeps it moving past the "at rest" hanging point. Eventually, the weight will stop swinging back and forth because friction with the air will slow it down. (Pendulums have been used since 1657 in clocks, because of the regularity of the swinging motion.)

> **YOU NEED**
> - 2 chairs
> - string or strong thread
> - 5 identical large metal washers (for weights)
> - hardbound book
> - long stick or pole
> - scissors

HYPOTHESIS Hypothesize that when the weight (mass) tied to a string is greater than one tied to another string of the same length, the heavier weight will swing longer.

PROCEDURE The *constant* in this project is the length of the string. The *variable* is the mass (or weight) at the end of the pendulum string.

Place two chairs back to back and a short distance apart. Lay a long measuring stick or pole across the tops of both chairs. Tie two pieces of string onto the stick some distance apart so the hanging strings almost touch the floor. Cut the strings to an equal length an inch or two (2–4 cm) from the floor. At the end of one string, tie four large metal washers. At the end of the other string, tie one large metal washer, making sure that the bottom of the washer is at an equal height from the ground as the group of four washers. In starting the pendulums swinging, you must make sure they are both released at *exactly* the same time. To do this, let the washers rest on a hardbound

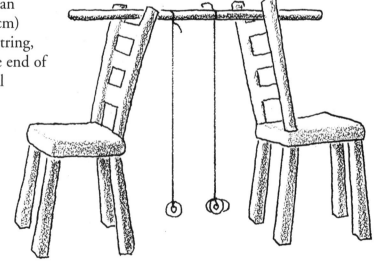

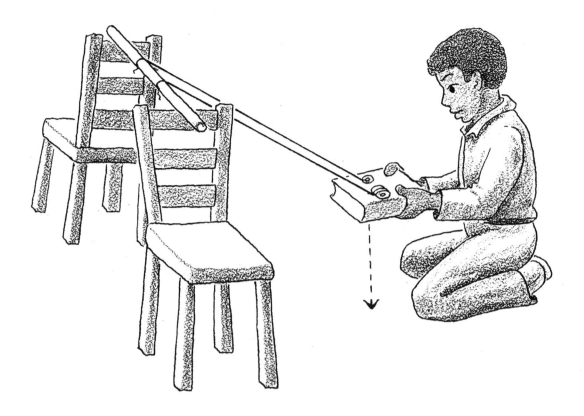

book and lift and pull them both, on the book, to one side of the chairs, perhaps to seat level height. Keep the two hanging strings taut. *Drop* the book down and both pendulums will begin swinging at exactly the same time. What happens then? Do they both swing at the same rate? Does the pendulum that has four washers swing four times longer than the pendulum that has only one?

RESULTS & CONCLUSION Write down the results of your experiment. Come to a conclusion as to whether or not your hypothesis was correct.

SOMETHING MORE
1. How does the length of the string affect the pendulum's swing? If the weights are the same but one pendulum's string is twice the length of the other, will it swing twice as long? Use the same chair setup as above, but take the string that had four washers on it, cut it in half, and tie just one washer to it. Start them swinging at the same time. (You will have to hold one in each hand and let go at the same time as best you can, since you can't get them started together by letting them slide off a book as we did before.)
2. Think of other questions about pendulums that you can investigate and use your chair setup to find the answers. For example, if both strings are the same length and both weights are the same, but one pendulum is pulled back farther/higher when they are set swinging, will the one pulled back farther swing longer?

MAN ON A TIGHT ROPE

WAVE MOTION

PURPOSE Show that energy can travel along a string and do work at the other end.

OVERVIEW Energy can travel in the form of a wave. An uncrested wave in the ocean is energy in motion. The water molecules do not travel along with the wave. That is why a boat will bob up and down when a wave goes by but does not move sideways. Surfers ride the energy of a wave, but not the actual moving water. The water

YOU NEED
- length of string
- 2 chairs
- scissors
- small piece of paper
- pencil

only moves in a circle, but the wave energy travels forward.

If you tie one end of a rope to a fixed object, such as a fence post, pull the rope tight, and then give your end a quick snap up and down, with a fast wrist movement, you will see a wave-like motion travel along the rope to the fixed end. That is wave energy moving along the rope, but any spot on the rope only moves up and down. You can see this easily by making colored markings along the rope and watching them bob up and down. Now, let's track the energy.

PROCEDURE Set two chairs about 4 feet (122 cm) apart. Tie a string tightly from the back of one to the other. Cut a small square piece of paper and fold over one-quarter of it to act as a hook. Hang the piece of paper onto the string near one end by the fold in the paper. Near the other end, hit the string hard with a pencil. You have put energy into the string by making it move up and down. Does that energy travel along the string and flip the piece of paper off the string at the other end?

RESULTS & CONCLUSION Write down the results of your experiment. Come to a conclusion as to whether or not your hypothesis was correct.

SOMETHING MORE Make a colored mark in the middle of a long piece of rope, such as a jump rope or clothesline. Hold one end of the rope and have a friend hold the other. Wave your arm with the rope up and then down, and have your friend do the same but in the opposite direction: when you go up, he goes down. Is it possible to synchronize, or time, both your movements so that the mark in the middle of the rope will not move up or down?

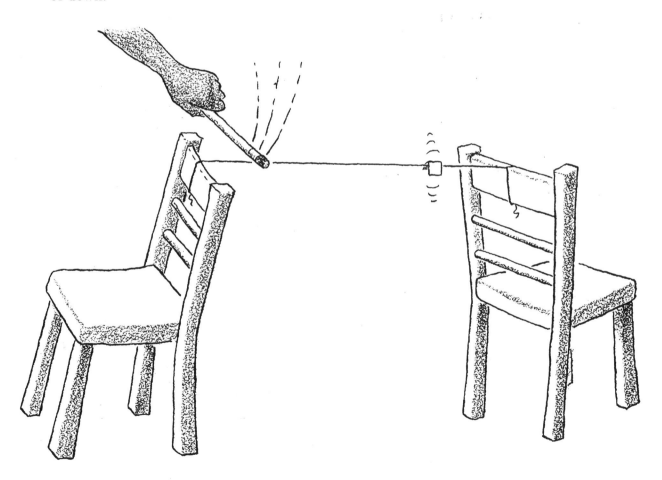

RUB THE RIGHT WAY

FRICTION AND SURFACES

PURPOSE Compare the friction on a dry surface to one coated with oil.

OVERVIEW Friction is the resistance to motion when two things rub together. Friction is often undesirable. It makes machines less efficient where moving parts come in contact with each other. But there are times when friction is helpful. On the road, it's the friction between a car's tires and the road's surface that allows a driver to keep control of the car. If a road becomes covered with water, snow, ice, or spilled oil, the car becomes harder to steer and to stop. This is especially true on a hill.

YOU NEED
- 2 pieces of wood, about 2 feet long (60 cm)
- 2 small plastic butter tubs with lids
- sand
- vegetable oil
- an old rag
- several books
- ruler
- protractor

HYPOTHESIS Hypothesize that if friction becomes less, an object on a slope will need less of an angle for gravity to overcome friction.

PROCEDURE Make a ramp (the slope) using a piece of wood about 2 feet (61 cm) long and 3 to 4 inches (7–10 cm) wide (a 2-by-4 board works well). To raise one end of the ramp, place several books under one end.

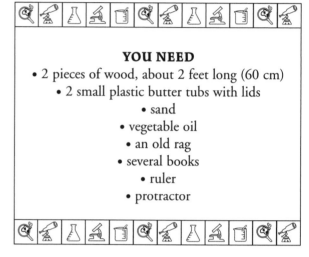

Using an old rag, wipe some vegetable oil onto the board, coating and completely covering the surface. This represents spilled oil on a roadway.

Fill two empty plastic butter tubs with an equal amount of sand, and close the lids.

Place one of the filled tubs in the center of the board. By adding more books or pushing them a little farther under the ramp, slowly make the ramp steeper until gravity overcomes the friction between the surfaces and the tub moves. When this happens, stand a ruler alongside the highest point of the ramp. Measure and write down the height of the ramp at that point. Then, using a protractor at the low end, measure the angle, or slope, of the ramp from the table or floor.

Using books and another board, make a ramp with the same slope as the first ramp. Place the tub in the middle of the board. This time, the tub does not move. Slowly raise the slope of the ramp by adding books until the tub finally moves. Measure the angle of the ramp, using the protractor, and see how much steeper it is compared to the first ramp.

The weight here is now the *constant*, and the surface friction is the *variable*.

What other places can you think of where friction is desirable? Think about walking on patches of ice outside, a newly waxed kitchen floor, or the tile floor in the bathroom when you step out of the shower.

RESULTS & CONCLUSION Write down the results of your experiment. Come to a conclusion about your hypothesis.

SOMETHING MORE Instead of comparing an oil-covered surface to a dry surface, compare a dry surface to one that is covered with ice. Place a piece of wood under the faucet in a sink and run water on it. Then put the wet piece of wood in the freezer and leave it there until the water has turned to ice. Again, find the angle where gravity overcomes resistance and the sand-filled tub moves. Do you think driving a car on an ice-covered road is more dangerous than when the road is dry? Besides driving more slowly, what do people do to help make driving on snow and ice safer?

THE MIGHTY MO

MOMENTUM: A PRODUCT OF FORCE TIMES MASS

PURPOSE Can momentum be increased by increasing the mass of the moving object or by increasing its speed?

YOU NEED
- flour
- salt
- piece of cardboard, 1 foot (30 cm) square
- Ping-Pong ball
- golf ball
- water
- eyedropper

OVERVIEW Momentum is the force with which an object is moving. Objects in motion tend to stay in motion. When you start a ball rolling, it keeps rolling until friction with the surface on which it is rolling and air resistance slow it down. Momentum is a factor of mass and velocity. Mass is a measure of how much "stuff" an object is made of and velocity is how fast an object is moving and in what direction. If either the mass or the velocity is increased, the momentum will be increased, and the moving object will have more force.

HYPOTHESIS Two hypotheses can be stated for this experiment. As the speed of an object increases (speed is affected by the drop point being raised), the momentum increases (as measured by the depth of the hole in soft material). As the mass (weight) of an object increases, the momentum increases.

PROCEDURE We can measure the momentum of a falling ball by dropping it into soft dough. Make a batch of dough by mixing water, salt, and flour. The dough must be thick enough to keep a golf ball from going through a 2-inch-thick (5 cm) batch of it when dropped from a height of about 4 feet (122 cm), but soft enough so that a Ping-Pong ball dropped from the same height will make a small impression.

Cut a piece of cardboard about a foot (30 cm) square. Cover the cardboard with the layer of dough.

Drop a golf ball into the dough from a height of 12 inches (30 cm). The impact will make a depression in the dough. Now hold the golf ball in your hand and raise your arm as high as you can. Drop the ball into another spot in the dough.

Compare the two depressions. Did the ball have more momentum and more force when it was moving faster? Measure the volume of each depression by using an eyedropper to fill each depression with water. Count the number of drops each depression takes to fill it.

In the above experiment, the mass was kept *constant*, but the velocity was increased (the *variable*). Now let's keep the velocity *constant* and increase the mass (the *variable*).

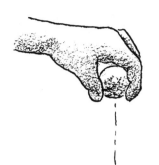

Hold a Ping-Pong ball in your hand and raise your arm as high as you can. Drop the ball into a clear spot in the dough. A Ping-Pong ball and a golf ball are about the same size, but the golf ball has more mass. They were both dropped from the same height, so they traveled at the same distance when they hit the dough. Did the ball with more mass have greater momentum and hit the dough with greater force?

RESULTS & CONCLUSION Write down the results of your experiment. Come to a conclusion about the two hypotheses.

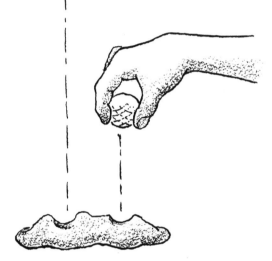

SOMETHING MORE If you have two different velocities (by dropping two balls, each from a different height), can you adjust the mass of one of the balls to make the momentum equal? A small hole can be cut in a Ping-Pong ball to allow different quantities of water added to it, making it heavier (increasing its mass).

HOT ROCKS

HEAT TRANSFER FROM ONE MEDIUM TO ANOTHER

PURPOSE Is there a good way to store solar heat, and release it slowly over time?

OVERVIEW Did you ever touch a rock that had been baking in the sun on a warm summer day? Did it feel hot? Rocks can collect and store heat.

Scientists have been working for many years to harness energy from the sun. Solar energy is being used to heat houses. One design uses hollow roof panels so that the sun warms the air inside. A fan blows the warmed air through a pipe to the basement, which is filled with rocks. As the heated air flows over the rocks, heat is transferred from the air to the rocks, warming them. Then at night, when the collectors no longer gather solar heat, a fan blows air over the rocks, transferring their warmth back to the air. The air is sent to ducts throughout the house to warm each room.

In designing a solar-heated house like this, would it make any difference if huge rocks were used or very small ones? A big rock might have more ability to store heat, but many smaller rocks would have more surface area (they have more sides that would be exposed to the warm air). Find out if a big rock or many smaller rocks would be better at collecting heat, or if rock size doesn't seem to make much of a difference.

YOU NEED

- a scale
- two 2-liter plastic soda bottles
- small rocks (about the size of small coins)
- large rock, about 3 inches (8 centimeters) in diameter
- 2 thermometers
- hot water from a faucet
- pencil
- paper
- clock or watch
- masking tape
- scissors
- an adult

HYPOTHESIS Hypothesize that an equal mass of smaller rocks will absorb heat more quickly than one large rock.

PROCEDURE Have an adult help you by cutting the tops off two 2-liter plastic soda bottles, using a pair of scissors. They should be cut near the top, just at the point where the bottles start to become rounded.

Gather some rocks. One of the rocks should be just large enough to fit inside a 2-liter soda bottle, about 3 inches (8 centimeters) in diameter (across). The other rocks should be small, pebbles about the size of small coins.

Using a scale, find out how much the large rock weighs. Remove it from the scale.

Then pile up smaller rocks on the scale until the same weight is reached. The rock mass will then be held *constant*, and the size of the rocks will be the *variable*.

Set all the rocks on a table for an hour or two until you can be sure they are all at room temperature. Do not put them in direct sunlight.

Gather two thermometers. Before we can use them, we must be sure they are calibrated, so that we can use their readings for comparison. (We might have to adjust the reading of one thermometer to correct it so both thermometers read the same temperature.) Leave the two thermometers at room temperature for several minutes, then read the temperature on each one. If one reads higher than the other, put a small piece of masking tape on it and make a note of the difference in temperature. If it is ½ or 1 degree higher than the other, then subtract this much from its reading when comparing the temperature on it to the temperature on the other thermometer.

Have an adult fill each bottle half full of hot water from a sink. Using a thermometer, be sure the water in each bottle is the same temperature. Be careful working around the bottles of very hot water.

Place the large rock in one 2-liter plastic bottle and the smaller rocks into the other bottle. Be careful not to spash the hot water out and on you.

Put a thermometer in each bottle. After a few minutes, record the temperature on each thermometer. Every three minutes, read and record the temperature on the two thermometers. Make up a table, such as shown in the illustration, to record your data. Continue to record temperatures until they reach room temperature (about 70° Fahrenheit). Remember to make an adjustment of your readings to calibrate the two thermometers.

Did the water in one bottle cool off faster than the other? If so, then the rock (or rocks) in that bottle collected heat faster.

RESULTS & CONCLUSION Write down the results of your experiment. Come to a conclusion about your hypothesis.

SOMETHING MORE Which releases heat more quickly, one large rock or an equal-mass grouping of smaller rocks? In solar heating for a home, it would be preferable to have heat released slowly over a long period of time to keep a house warm all through the night until the sun came up again to add heat back into the system.

SMALLER IS STRONGER

TESTING TENSILE STRENGTH

PURPOSE To discover if an object's strength has any relation to its length.

OVERVIEW The term tensile strength means how strong something is when it is

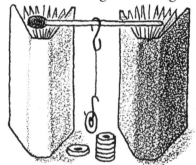

unsupported; how much tension or pressure it can take before it breaks. Steel has great tensile strength. Is tensile strength affected by length?

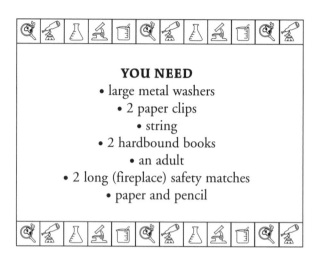

YOU NEED
- large metal washers
- 2 paper clips
- string
- 2 hardbound books
- an adult
- 2 long (fireplace) safety matches
- paper and pencil

HYPOTHESIS As an unsupported span decreases in length, it can support more weight.

PROCEDURE Stand two hardback books upright, opening them slightly. Place them about 10 inches (25 cm) apart. *Have an adult* light and blow out long matches, made specially for fireplaces, so they are safe to use. Lay one match across the books. Bend open two metal paper clips so they form an "S," with a hook at the top and bottom of each clip.

   Tie a paper clip onto each end of a short piece of string. Hang one paper clip from the middle of the match. Push the hook of the other paper clip through the hole of a large metal washer. This makes it easy to add more washers.

   Add washers until the match breaks. Write down how many the match could hold.

   Now repeat the experiment, but this time move the books closer together, about half the distance they were. The *variable* is the length of the span being stressed. Will the shorter unsupported span of the match be able to hold more weight without breaking?

RESULTS & CONCLUSION Write down the results of your experiment. Come to a conclusion as to whether or not your hypothesis was correct.

SOMETHING MORE Can you work out (quantify) the relationship between the length of unsupported match in inches and the number of washers needed to break it?

Up to Speed

ACCELERATION IN A BOTTLE

PURPOSE To show changes in rate of speed.

OVERVIEW Acceleration is an increase in speed. Physicists define it as a measure of the rate of change of velocity over time. To accelerate means to go faster; to decelerate is to slow down.

HYPOTHESIS It's possible to prove that speed and acceleration are different and measurable by constructing an "accelerometer."

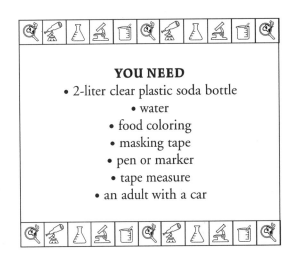

YOU NEED
- 2-liter clear plastic soda bottle
- water
- food coloring
- masking tape
- pen or marker
- tape measure
- an adult with a car

PROCEDURE Partially fill a 2-liter clear plastic soda bottle with water. Add some food coloring so that you will be able to see the water's movement better. Screw the cap on tightly. Place masking tape along one side of the bottle's circumference. Draw a scale on it in millimeters or ¼-inch increments.

Ask an adult with an automatic-shift car to take you for a short drive. (Manual-shift cars could be jerky and uneven during acceleration.) Open the car's glove compartment and use the door as a shelf. Lay your "accelerometer" on it. Fix it there with masking tape or rubber bands. On the tape, mark the water level when the car is not in motion.

When you are ready (remember to fasten your seat belt), have the driver accelerate. Observe how far up the scale the water moves. The faster the car accelerates, the steeper the slope of the water up the side of the bottle. The amount of water in the bottle has remained *constant*, but the acceleration of the car has *varied*.

Next, have the driver hold a steady speed, like 40 miles (63 kilometers) per hour, on a highway. Is the water level at the same mark as it was when the car was at rest? Even though the car is traveling at quite a good speed, the acceleration is zero.

RESULTS & CONCLUSION Write down the results of your experiment. Come to a conclusion as to whether or not your hypothesis was correct.

SOMETHING MORE What about deceleration, when the car is slowing down and coming to a stop. Can your accelerometer also be used to compare rates of deceleration?

BAD MANNERS

HEAT CONDUCTION AND HEAT SINKING

PURPOSE Is there a way to make something cool more quickly, like a drink that is too hot?

OVERVIEW Metal is a good "conductor" of heat. That means it makes an easy path that heat can travel along. When a metal frying pan is placed on a stove burner, the heat from the burner is conducted (carried) through the bottom of the pan and heats the food inside it.

Metal is sometimes used to cool things by conducting heat away from an object. In electronics, transistors and integrated circuits ("chips"), which are found in televisions, stereos, and computers, get hot, but heat can damage them. Often metal is made in the shape of fins and attached to transistors and integrated circuits in order to carry the heat away from them. These cooling fins, called heat sinks, help transfer the heat to the surrounding air and keep the transistors and integrated circuits cool. Sometimes a small fan is used to get rid of the heated air. Does your computer have a fan in it?

YOU NEED

- 2 identical containers (coffee mugs or tea cups)
- hot tap water
- 2 thermometers
- masking tape
- spoon
- clock or watch
- paper and pencil

Have you ever been served a hot cup of tea or hot chocolate that was too hot to drink and someone told you, "Leave the spoon in. It might be bad manners but it will help cool the drink faster." They are thinking that, since metal conducts heat, the spoon will carry some of the heat away from the drink. The spoon is indeed hot to the touch, so it does conduct heat away from the drink.

However, since the handle of the spoon is not designed like a heat sink, the heat in the spoon doesn't efficiently transfer to the surrounding air, so you may want to hypothesize that leaving the spoon in the hot liquid won't make a significant difference.

HYPOTHESIS Hypothesize that leaving a spoon in a hot drink will not make any noticeable difference in its rate of cooling, reducing the temperature faster.

PROCEDURE Gather two thermometers. Before we can use them, we must be sure they are calibrated, that is, we may need to adjust the temperature readings of one thermometer so both thermometers correctly read the same. Leave the two thermometers at room temperature for several minutes, then read the temperature on each one. If one reads higher than the other, put a small piece of masking tape on it and make a note of the difference in temperature. If it is ½ degree or 1 degree higher, then subtract this much from its readings when comparing the temperature on it to the temperature on the other thermometer.

Fill two coffee cups of equal size with equally hot tap water. (Be careful working with and around very hot water.) Place a thermometer in each cup. Put a metal spoon in one of the cups. After one minute, read the temperatures on the two thermometers and write them down. Every minute, write down the temperatures you read. Be sure to make any adjustment of your numbers to calibrate the two thermometers. Continue to make readings until the water in the two cups reaches room temperature.

Did the water in the cup with the spoon in it cool down faster, or wasn't there any noticeable difference?

RESULTS & CONCLUSION Write down the results of your experiment. Come to a conclusion as to whether or not your hypothesis was correct.

SOMETHING MORE Can you find a way that will measurably cool the cup of hot water? Purchase some transistor heat sinks at your local electronics shop and affix them to the cup with rubber bands. Try using larger spoons, such as a ladle.

WATT?

COMPARING LIGHT OUTPUT AND POWER
CONSUMPTION

PURPOSE Determine if a 100-watt light bulb gives off as much light as two 50-watt bulbs.

OVERVIEW Incandescent light bulbs, the kind used in most household lamps, are rated by the amount of power they use, but the amount of light they give off is really the most important thing to know. Light bulbs are rated by the number of "watts" they use. A watt is a unit of measure of electric power, that is, how much electrical energy is used. It would take the same amount of electrical energy to light one 100-watt bulb as it does to light two 50-watt bulbs, so the cost would also be the same. But, does a 100-watt light bulb give off as much light as two 50-watt bulbs?

> **YOU NEED**
> • an adult (for safety when working with electricity or hot light bulbs)
> • camera
> • 2 lamps
> • 1 hundred-watt light bulb
> • 2 fifty-watt light bulbs
> • a room that can be made completely dark
> • an index card or stiff piece of paper
> • dark marker

HYPOTHESIS Hypothesize that a 100-watt light bulb will give off about the same amount of light as two 50-watt light bulbs.

PROCEDURE Place two lamps side by side on a small table, dresser, or any object that will hold them in a room that can be made dark. Before plugging the lamps into an electric outlet, screw a 50-watt bulb in each lamp. Be very careful plugging the lamps into the outlet. You can leave the lamp shades on or take them off, but whichever you do, you must do the same when you use the single 100-watt bulb later. If the lamps have different shades, then you must remove both shades.

Fold an index card or small piece of paper in half, making a "V" shape. Turn it upside down so it will stand up. On one side, write "1" with a dark marker. On the other side, write "2." Place it on a table, nightstand, or dresser on the side of the room opposite the lamps. Stand the card so that the 1 is visible.

Turn the lamps on. Stand with your back to the lamps, but be sure that your body is not blocking the light from shining directly on the card on a table or dresser. Face the card and the rest of the room to take a picture. Be sure the camera does not have a flash, or that the flash is turned off. The camera must also be one that does not have an automatic sensor for lighting. Take a picture, focusing on the index card. You may want to set the camera on a table or something to keep it still, and to ensure that the camera will still be in the same position for the next picture. The camera position and everything in the room will remain *constant*. The only *variable* will be the light bulb(s).

Turn the lamps off. Unplug one of them from the electric outlet, unscrew the 50-watt bulb, and replace it with a 100-watt bulb. Plug the lamp back in and turn it on. Turn the index card around, so the side with "2" on it is showing. Again, stand with your back to the lamp and take a picture, with the index card as the focal point.

If you have to send the film away to be developed, write down on a piece of paper that the photo with the #1 on the index card was taken with two 50-watt bulbs, and the one with #2 was taken with one 100-watt bulb. That way you won't have to remember which photo matched which lighting experiment.

Compare the two pictures. Do objects in the pictures have about the same brightness, or are there differences?

If you can borrow a light meter from a photographer or your school's science teacher, try to measure the amount of light given off by two 50-watt bulbs and compare it to the light given off from one 100-watt bulb.

RESULTS & CONCLUSION Write down the results of your experiment. Come to a conclusion about your hypothesis.

SOMETHING MORE

1. Even if two 50-watt bulbs give off about the same amount of light as one 100-watt bulb, do you think two 50-watt bulbs are better for lighting a room? By "better" we mean that the light is more evenly distributed and less harsh, making it easier to read, work, or play in a room when there are two lights on opposite sides of the room rather than just one real bright one.
2. Audio power (volume) is also measured in watts. Does a stereo sound louder when its two speakers are placed next to each other, or spread far apart?

ROOM FOR BRIGHTNESS

REFLECTED LIGHT

PURPOSE Show that a room is better lit when the room's walls are painted in bright colors compared to a room where the walls are dark. (Bright colors make a room safer, reduce eye fatigue when reading or working, and make the room a more cheerful, pleasant place to be.)

OVERVIEW In a house, some rooms are brighter than others, not just because they have more indoor lighting or windows to let sunlight in, but because the walls, ceilings, and floors are more brightly colored. In a kitchen, people need lots of light to work with food. A bright bathroom makes it a safer place. A living room, bedroom, or den, however, may have darker, more deeply colored carpeting and dark walls or paneling for a quiet feeling of richness and luxury.

YOU NEED
- a room with light, brightly colored walls and that can be made completely dark
- a room with dark-colored walls and that can be made completely dark
- camera (an instant camera is preferred, but not required)
- lamp
- tape measure
- an index card or stiff piece of paper
- dark marker
- a friend

Bright colors, such as white and yellow, reflect much of the light that hits them. When walls, ceilings, and floors are bright in color, more light is reflected (bounced) off those surfaces, and the light spreads around the room.

HYPOTHESIS Photographs can be used to show how a room that has bright colored walls is brighter than a similar room that is darkly colored.

PROCEDURE Find two rooms about the same size in a house; one room that has light colored walls and another room that has dark walls. The rooms must be able to block any light coming in from outside the room, such as car lights or street lights through a window, even the glare of a television set from another room. Do this experiment at night to reduce outside light from leaking in behind curtains or blinds.

Take an index card or stiff piece of white paper On one side, write "#1" with a dark marker. On the other side, write "#2."

In a room with light walls, place a lamp on a table, dresser, or any object that will raise it up to the height of a normal table. Place the table and lamp against a wall. Turn the lamp on. Using a tape measure, stand 4 feet (1.2 m) in front of the lamp, with your back to it. Have a friend stand 10 feet (3.5 m) from the lamp, 6 feet (1.8 m) in front of you, facing you and holding the index card with the #1 side facing the camera. You are standing *between* your friend and the lighted lamp. Take a picture of your friend. (Do not

use a camera that has an automatic flash or an automatic lens adjustment for light levels.)

Next, in a room with dark walls, place the same lamp on a table, dresser, or any object that will raise it to the same height as it was in the lighter colored room. Place the table and lamp against a wall. Turn the lamp on. Again, using a tape measure, stand 4 feet (1.2 m) in front of the lamp, facing away from it. Have your friend stand 10 feet (3.5 m) from the lamp, face you, and hold the index card with the number #2 side facing the camera. Take a picture of your friend.

If you take or send the film for developing, tell them not to "adjust" prints. Also, write yourself a reminder that the #1 card photo was taken in a light-colored room and the #2 one was taken in a dark-colored room. The light source and distance of your friend from the camera remain *constant*. The *variable* is the color of the walls.

Compare the two pictures. Even though the same amount of light was used in both pictures, did the picture of your friend come out darker in the room that had the darker walls?

RESULTS & CONCLUSION Write down the results of your experiment. Come to a conclusion as to whether or not your hypothesis was correct.

SOMETHING MORE Do you think the color of the ceiling and carpet on the floor also affects how light is reflected in a room?

Down-Range Shooter

TRAJECTORY: CURVED PATH THROUGH THE AIR

PURPOSE The purpose of this experiment is to determine the angle of trajectory that will give the greatest distance.

OVERVIEW When you throw a stone a little upward and away from you, you know that it will not keep going in that direction, but will slowly curve and begin to fall to the ground. The path of an object hurled through the air is called its trajectory. This path is caused by the motions of the stone, moving forward and moving upward at first, then downward. The stone moves upward and forward because of the force of your throw. But, because the stone has weight, the earth's gravity eventually causes it to curve and fall down.

What determines where an object will land when it is thrown or launched? The force at which it is thrown and its upward angle are both factors.

The trajectory of an object is very important to the military when they use artillery. If a cannon is to hit its target, the operator has to know the right angle to tilt the gun upward.

HYPOTHESIS Hypothesize that the launch angle of an object will affect the distance it will travel away from the launching device.

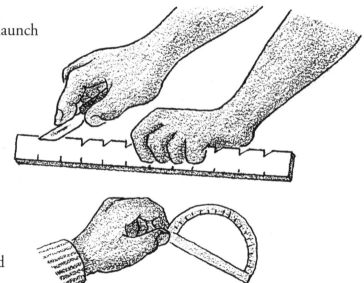

PROCEDURE Because of the hazard of using a sharp tool, have an adult cut a small notch at each inch or centimeter mark on a wooden ruler with a utility knife or razor.

Stretch a rubber band from one end of the ruler to one of the notches at a marking, giving it a good stretch, but not to its maximum stretch potential. Hold the ruler lengthwise with one hand near the edge of a table. With the other hand, push the rubber band out of the notch until it launches. Place a domino on the floor to mark the spot where it landed. Always keep safety in mind; do not launch the rubber band while anyone is standing in front of the ruler.

Then raise the end of the ruler by placing dominos under it. Experiment with different heights (elevation). By launching the rubber band from the same marking, the launch force is kept *constant*, and only the angle is *variable*.

Set a protractor on the table and measure the angle the ruler is elevated upward before each launch. What is the angle that shoots the rubber band the farthest distance from the ruler? What is the angle that, if the angle is further increased, the rubber band will not travel any farther (this is the optimum angle for distance)?

Note: If the rubber band gets caught on some of the other notches in the ruler as it launches, you can put tape over them, or make a horizontal cut in a straw and cover the notches.

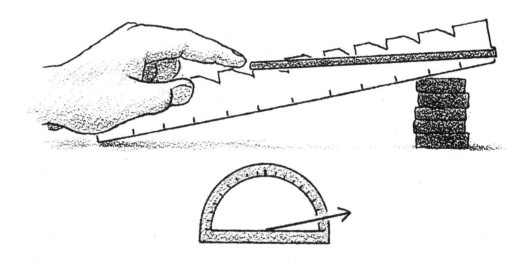

RESULTS & CONCLUSION Write down the results of your experiment. Come to a conclusion as to whether or not your hypothesis was correct.

SOMETHING MORE
1. The distance the rubber band will travel depends on both the launch angle and the launch force. Try launching the rubber band from different notches, which changes the force. The more the rubber band is stretched, the more force it will have when it is launched. What combination of tilt angle and launch force (marked notch) makes the rubber band travel the farthest? The highest?
2. Make a game by having a friend place a domino on the floor while you try different combinations of force and tilt to land the rubber band as close as you can to the target. Then reverse places with your friend, and see who can come closest with the least number of tries.

GET A HANDLE

WHEEL AND AXLE, A SIMPLE MACHINE

PURPOSE Understanding the wheel and axle concept and what a great advantage a screwdriver handle gives you because it is a "simple machine."

YOU NEED
- screwdriver with a large handle
- pair of pliers
- a friend

OVERVIEW Simple machines is the term used in physics to refer to a group of tools that make it easier to do work. Levers, inclined planes, pulleys, wedges, screws, and wheel-and-axles are examples of simple machines. With the simple machine called a wheel and axle, movement over a bigger distance gives a stronger force over a smaller distance.

Imagine trying to open a door if the door knob is missing and only the small shaft is there! The door knob is like a big wheel; the knob covers a bigger distance when it is turned but makes it easy to turn the tiny shaft. Think about steering a car without the steering wheel or closing a submarine's watertight hatch without the wheel on the door.

A wheel and axle tool may not actually have a wheel but simply a "spoke" that is rotated in a circular direction, like a wheel. An example of this type of wheel and axle is a pencil sharpener. When you turn the handle, you are covering a larger distance than the turning sharpening blades inside, but a greater force is gained at the blades. Using a socket wrench is another example, where you turn the handle over a larger distance in order to turn a nut a smaller distance, but with greater force.

Sometimes the opposite is needed—a little distance and a lot of force yields a smaller force but a greater distance. An example of this is swinging a baseball bat. At the handle, you put a lot of force into the bat and turn over a small distance, and the other end of the bat moves over a greater distance, giving it more speed.

Show the concept of wheel and axle using a screwdriver and a few friends. A screwdriver is a simple machine—a wheel and axle. Turning the bigger handle gives a bigger force at the smaller blade end.

HYPOTHESIS No matter how much I try, I will not be able to turn a screwdriver by the blade using only my hand while a friend holds the handle.

PROCEDURE Have a friend hold the handle of a fairly large screwdriver. Tell your friend to try to keep it from turning. Grab the blade with one hand and try to turn the screwdriver while your friend holds the handle. Even if your friend is weaker than you, you will not be able to turn the screwdriver. Try to grasp and turn the shaft using two hands instead of one. Are you able to turn it at all?

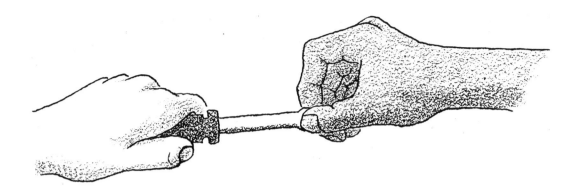

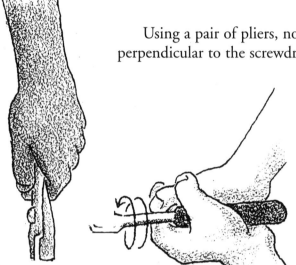

Using a pair of pliers, now try to turn the blade (hold the pliers perpendicular to the screwdriver shaft). Is your friend still able to hold the handle and keep it from turning? What if your friend uses two hands?

The pliers are a wheel and axle, too, and the pliers form a much bigger spoke of the wheel than the screwdriver handle. The longer the length of the turning spoke, the more force you get from it, but the more distance must be traveled.

RESULTS & ONCLUSION Write down the results of your experiment. Come to a conclusion as to whether or not your hypothesis was correct.

SOMETHING MORE Try to turn a long thin screw into a piece of wood with your bare hands by turning the shaft. Is it impossible? Then try using a screwdriver. Is it easy to do, or easier? If the wood is very hard, try using the pliers to help turn the shaft while you press down on the screwdriver. What happens now?

BALANCE THE BOOKS

FIRST-CLASS LEVER, A SIMPLE MACHINE

PURPOSE How can you manage to raise something that is to heavy for you to lift, or that you want to lift using less force?

OVERVIEW Simple machines is a term used in physics to refer to a group of tools that make it easier to do work. Levers, inclined planes, pulleys, wedges, screws, and wheel-and-axles are examples of simple machines.

    With the simple machine called a lever, movement over a bigger distance provides a stronger force at the other end, but moving over a smaller distance. This is done by placing a support called a fulcrum under a long shaft or board. When the fulcrum is placed closer to the load (the object to be moved), it is called a first-class lever (there are three classes of levers—see the following project). A pry bar is an example of a first-class lever tool.

    See the first-class lever drawing below. A push down on the end of the lever that extends farther out from the fulcrum will yield a gain in force at the other end. However, a much greater distance is covered in order to raise the object only a small distance.

> **YOU NEED**
> • 7 heavy books (encyclopedia volumes, for example)
> • piece of lumber, 1 foot (30 cm) wide by 4 feet (120 cm) long
> • rope
> • bathroom scale

HYPOTHESIS It takes less effort to lift a group of heavy books with a first-class lever than to lift them by hand.

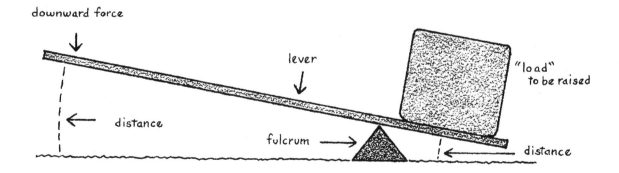

PROCEDURE To get an idea how hard it is to lift a heavy book against gravity, pick up a heavy book while keeping your arm straight, then hold it at arm's length for one minute.

Gather seven heavy books (encyclopedia volumes, for example). Tie six of the seven books together with a piece of rope. Place them on a bathroom scale to see how much the group of books weighs.

Place the one loose book underneath the board, about one foot (30 cm) from an end. This book will be the fulcrum. Place the tied books on the board at the end nearest the fulcrum. Press down on the other end of the board.

Were you able to raise the pile of books with little effort? Even though they were only raised a short distance, it would have been much harder to lift the books the same distance straight up off the ground yourself. Remember putting them on the scale?

RESULTS & CONCLUSION Write down the results of your experiment. Come to a conclusion as to whether or not your hypothesis was correct.

SOMETHING MORE

1. If you have a small brother or sister, remove the pile of books and have him or her sit on the board, and use the lever to raise this load.
2. Is it harder to lift an object as you move the fulcrum farther away from the load and closer to the end where the effort (the force) is being applied?

WE ARE #2

SECOND- AND THIRD-CLASS LEVERS

PURPOSE Learn to use a second-class lever (a simple machine) to reduce the force required to lift a heavy object.

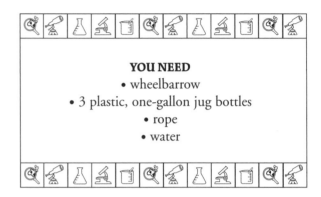

YOU NEED
- wheelbarrow
- 3 plastic, one-gallon jug bottles
- rope
- water

OVERVIEW A lever is made up of a long shaft or board that rests on a support called a fulcrum. The object you are trying to move is called the load. With a lever, either force is gained and distance is lost or distance is gained and force is lost.

A seesaw is a lever. Some seesaws allow the fulcrum to be moved from the middle balancing point. If you sit on a seesaw and the fulcrum is closer to the other end of the board, a person sitting on that end will be easier for you to lift than if the seesaw had the fulcrum in the middle. This is an example of a first-class lever (see the previous project). A first-class lever is useful for lifting heavy objects a short distance.

There are three classes of levers, first class, second class, and third class. A third-class lever is the opposite of a first-class lever. In a third-class lever, the fulcrum is close to where the force is applied. Sweeping with a broom is an example of a third-class lever. Your one arm applies a force, moving a small distance. Your other arm is the fulcrum, the point that the lever swings around. The other end of the lever has less force, but makes a big gain in the distance it moves. When you cast a fishing line into the water, you are using the concept of a third-class lever. Your one arm is the fulcrum and the other arm applies a lot of force over a short distance. The end of the pole has less force but moves quickly over a longer distance to throw the line out into the water.

First-Class Lever

Second-Class Lever

In a second-class lever, the fulcrum is actually the point on which the lever rests, and instead of pushing down with force, you lift up (applying an upward force). Like a first-class lever, this, too, is useful for lifting heavy objects to a short height.

HYPOTHESIS It is easier to lift a heavy object by using a second-class lever, and the closer the load is to the fulcrum, the easier lifting becomes.

PROCEDURE First, fill three plastic one-gallon jugs with water. Water weighs a little more than 8 pounds per gallon. Try gently lifting all three jugs. Careful! They're heavy!

Now, place the three jugs (one at a time) in a wheelbarrow at the end near the wheelbarrow's handles. Lay them in a row and use a piece of rope to tie them together and to the handles of the wheelbarrow. This will keep them from sliding when you lift the wheelbarrow up.

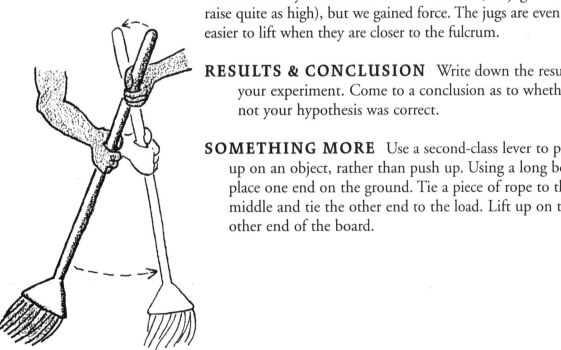

Lift the wheelbarrow by its handles. You will find that the jugs of water (including some of the weight of the wheelbarrow) is easier to lift then just trying to lift the jugs by themselves.

To make them even easier to lift, untie the jugs and move them to the front of the wheelbarrow. Now they are almost over the wheel, which is the fulcrum. Again, lift the wheelbarrow by its handles. We lost distance (the jugs didn't raise quite as high), but we gained force. The jugs are even easier to lift when they are closer to the fulcrum.

RESULTS & CONCLUSION Write down the results of your experiment. Come to a conclusion as to whether or not your hypothesis was correct.

SOMETHING MORE Use a second-class lever to pull up on an object, rather than push up. Using a long board, place one end on the ground. Tie a piece of rope to the middle and tie the other end to the load. Lift up on the other end of the board.

Third-Class Lever

BOTTLED FORCE

KINETIC AND POTENTIAL ENERGY

PURPOSE Let's see if we can find a way to store "work" energy.

YOU NEED
- children's wooden building blocks
- 2-liter plastic soda bottle
- piece of wood 1 foot (30 cm) wide by 4 feet (120 cm) long
- thick book
- water

OVERVIEW Energy can be placed in one of two groups, kinetic energy and potential energy. Kinetic energy is the energy of work being done. It is the energy of movement. When a bowling ball is rolling down an alley, the energy of its motion is kinetic energy. Potential energy is "stored-up" energy. It means something has the ability to do work, but the energy is not being used at the moment. If a rock is sitting high on a hilltop, it has potential energy. Because of gravity, the resting rock has the potential, or ability, to release energy. If the rock is given a push, its potential energy is easily turned into kinetic energy . . . as it rolls down the hillside.

We use the word mass to describe how much "stuff" an object has in it. The more mass an object has, the heavier it will be. A Ping-Pong ball and a golf ball are both about the same size and shape, but the golf ball has more mass. Think about how much more mass a bowling ball has compared to a same size ball of cotton candy!

HYPOTHESIS The more mass an object has, the more potential energy it will have when it is raised up, and the more kinetic energy it will have when gravity causes it to move down. This can be proven by comparing the work done by objects that are the same size and shape, but have different masses.

PROCEDURE Lay a book about an inch (2–3 cm) thick face down on the floor. Place one end of a board about 1 foot wide by 4 feet long (30 × 122 cm) on the book, making a ramp with a gentle slope.

On the floor, about 1 foot (30 cm) from the end of the ramp, stack three or four children's wooden building blocks on top of each other.

Hold an empty 2-liter soda bottle at the top of the ramp. The bottle has potential energy (stored energy), because gravity can pull it down. Let go of the bottle, but be careful not to give it a push. Just let gravity start it rolling. Does it push over the wooden blocks? If it doesn't, remake the stack but this time use one less block. If it does, add another block to the stack. Repeat rolling the bottle and adding or taking away blocks until you find out exactly how many blocks the empty bottle will push. Do not stack the blocks more than six high. If more blocks are needed, start another pile of blocks behind the first, building a thicker wall.

Now, fill the plastic bottle with water. Be sure the cap is on tight. We are keeping the slope of the ramp *constant*, and the *variable* will be the mass of the bottle. As before, place the bottle at the top of the ramp and find out the maximum number of blocks it can knock down. Remember not to stack the blocks more than six high. Make more stacks of blocks behind the others, making the wall thicker.

When the bottle is filled with water, it has more mass. Did the filled bottle have more potential and kinetic energy than when it was empty and had less mass?

RESULTS & CONCLUSION Write down the results of your experiment. Come to a conclusion as to whether or not your hypothesis was correct.

SOMETHING MORE
1. What can you fill the bottle with to give it more mass than water, giving it the ability to do even more work (pushing even more blocks)?
2. Change the slope (the incline) of the ramp. How does the angle of the ramp affect the bottle's kinetic and potential energy?
3. At what angle does the force into the blocks remain unchanged? At some point, the bottle will begin putting energy into the floor and no more into the blocks.

WATER MAKER

SOLAR RADIATION

PURPOSE How could we change snow to water if the temperature was below freezing?

OVERVIEW If you were stranded in the woods or in a place where there was lots of snow and ice and you needed water to drink, how could you get it to melt?

On a sunny day when there is snow on the ground, you may notice the snow in places starting to melt, even though the air temperature is below freezing—32° Fahrenheit or 0° Centigrade. Where do you see this happening? Is the ice melting because the sun is hitting it? Would the melting stop if a black plastic bag was placed over it to block the sunlight getting to it, or do you think the black color would collect even more sunlight and turn it into heat that would melt the ice faster?

YOU NEED
- 3 clear cereal bowls
- 12 ice cubes
- clear plastic food wrap
- black plastic trash bag
- sunny day when the outdoor temperature is cold
- clock or watch
- paper and pencil

HYPOTHESIS Hypothesize that a black covering will absorb sunlight and the heat will make the ice melt even faster.

PROCEDURE Place three cereal bowls outside on a sunny, but cold, day. Put four ice cubes in each bowl. Cover one bowl with clear plastic food wrap. Cover another bowl with a black plastic trash bag. Leave the third bowl uncovered. Our *variable* is the color of the plastic covering. Temperature, location, amount of sunlight, and the ice are held *constant*. We are *assuming* that either the thickness of the food wrap and the plastic bag is the same or, if not the same, that the thickness will not affect the results. What do you think will happen to each bowl of ice?

After setting the bowls outside in a sunny place, check them every fifteen minutes. Write down the time and your observations (recording what you see happening) in each bowl. If you don't see any change, write down that that there is no change.

After a time, water may appear in some of the bowls. If ice appears in more than one bowl, you can find out in which bowl the ice melted faster by "quantifying" (measuring) the amount of water in each bowl or by comparing the water in each bowl after you remove the ice cubes.

RESULTS & CONCLUSION Write down the results of your experiment. Come to a conclusion as to whether or not your hypothesis was correct.

SOMETHING MORE

1. You may wish to continue your experiment by making covers of different colors, red, green, yellow, and others. Is there a difference in the amount of ice melted between a bowl of ice that is air tight (covered by plastic wrap) and a bowl that is not air tight (covered by a piece of colored construction paper), even if both colors are the same?
2. Does the thickness of the cover act as an insulator? Try comparing various cover thicknesses.

AN UPHILL BATTLE

KINETIC ENERGY AND THE TRANSFER OF ENERGY

PURPOSE Demonstrate that energy can be transferred from object to object, and defy gravity.

OVERVIEW An energy force can travel like a wave, which means that it can be passed from one object to another. The force of the energy transferred can even be stronger than the force of gravity, so that the energy can be made to travel uphill, where it is possible for it to do more work.

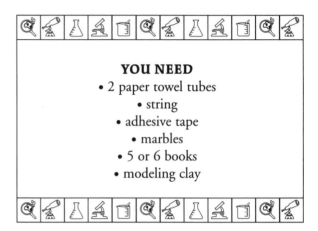

YOU NEED
- 2 paper towel tubes
- string
- adhesive tape
- marbles
- 5 or 6 books
- modeling clay

HYPOTHESIS Hypothesize that energy does pass through objects and this force can be transferred with enough strength to travel uphill.

PROCEDURE By using adhesive tape at the sides, position a piece of string over the opening of one end of an empty paper towel tube. Fill the tube with marbles. Lay a thick book (such as a dictionary or encyclopedia volume) down. Tilt the open end of the paper towel tube filled with marbles up on the book. The other end of the tube, with the piece of string, should be at the bottom to keep the marbles from rolling out. Placing modeling clay on top of the book will hold the paper towel tube in place.

Stack four or more books face down on the table. Using modeling clay, tilt the other empty paper towel tube up onto the books, making a ramp. The bottom ends of both paper towel rolls must face each other, as shown in the drawings on the next page.

Roll a large marble (or two smaller ones together) down the steep paper towel tube. This rolling force is called kinetic energy, the energy of work being done. When the

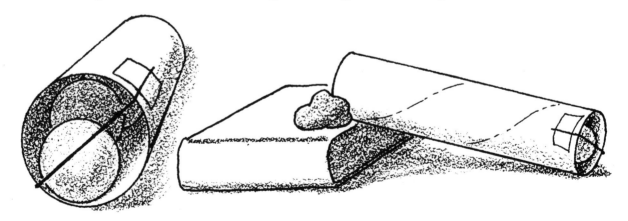

marble comes out of the bottom of the roll, it will hit the first marble in the next tube filled with marbles. The energy will pass from the rolling marble to the first marble, and then up through all the marbles. All the marbles in the filled tube are touching each other, and while these marbles do not move, the energy passes through them. When that energy gets to the last marble at the top, the force will move the marble. Can you see it move?

Now, repeat the experiment, this time changing the slope (the angle) of the empty striking tube. Remove two of the books to lower the slope of the tube. Keep everything else *constant*. The only *variable* is the change in the slope of the striking tube. Roll the large striking marble down the tube again. Is the weaker force of the striking marble still able to move the marble at the end of the filled tube?

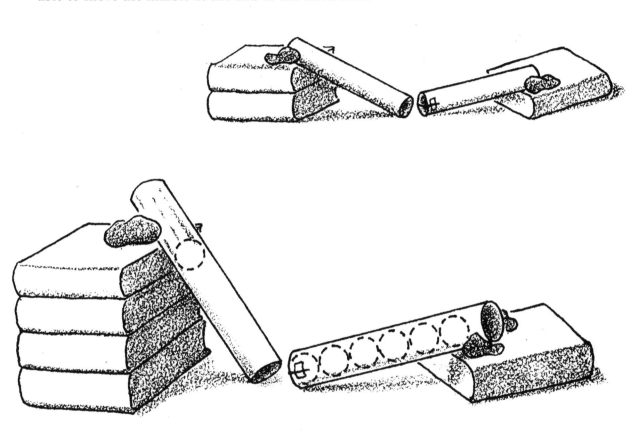

RESULTS & CONCLUSION Write down the results of your experiment. Come to a conclusion as to whether or not your hypothesis was correct.

SOMETHING MORE Can you make the force so strong that it will knock the marble off the end? You can increase the force by using a larger striking marble (increases mass and momentum), and you can make the angle steeper for the striking marble. If you can get the last marble to roll out of the tube, how far can you get it to travel?

CELLULAR CAN

TRANSMITTING SOUND BY VIBRATING MATERIALS

PURPOSE To improve the sound of the traditional homemade "tin-can" toy phone.

OVERVIEW Sound is formed by an object moving back and forth, or vibrating. These vibrations move molecules in the air by first compressing them and then causing them to spread apart. In order for us to hear something vibrating, the object must be quivering with enough force for our ears to detect it (loudness). It must also be vibrating between about 16 and 20 thousand times per second, which is the frequency response of the human ear.

YOU NEED
- an adult
- 2 small metal (soup) cans
- 2 large metal (juice) cans
- string
- hammer
- nail
- a friend

You can often feel the vibrations that are making a sound. Lightly touch a string on a guitar or a harp after it has been plucked. Lay a piece of paper on top of the speaker in a car and turn up the volume on the car radio.

A popular toy children often make is a "telephone," put together using two metal cans and a string pulled tight between them. A small hole is punched in the bottom of each empty can through which a piece of string is tied and knotted. When the string is pulled tight, speaking into one can causes the can bottom to vibrate. These vibrations then travel along the taut string and vibrate the bottom of the other can, converting the vibrations back into sound. The vibrations of your voice are therefore "transmitted" to the person on the other end of the toy-telephone system, and he or she can hear you.

Can you improve on this toy, making the sound either clearer or louder?

HYPOTHESIS Using larger cans instead of the usual smaller "soup" cans will improve the sound transmission of a homemade tin-can telephone system. (We are defining "improve" to mean either louder or clearer sound.)

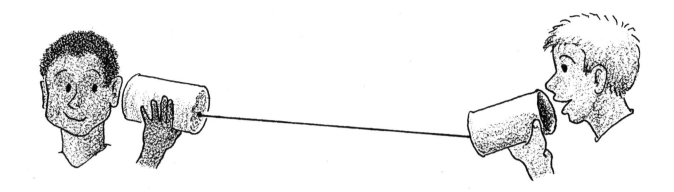

PROCEDURE Make a set of toy "can telephones" using a piece of string and two small, empty cans with one lid removed; use cans that are the size soup usually comes in. Have an adult check the can rims to be sure there are no sharp edges that might hurt you. Also, ask the adult to punch a small hole in the middle of the bottom of each can, using a hammer and nail. Push one end of the string into the can through each hole far enough to be able to tie a knot in the string inside the can. Knot it several times, making a knot big enough so it won't pull out through the hole. Pull the string tight and hold a "secret" conversation with your friend on the other end.

   Now make a set of can telephones using two larger size cans, the kind that fruit juice might come in. Is there any difference in sound quality or volume between the telephones using the larger cans?

RESULTS & CONCLUSION Write down the results of your experiment. Come to a conclusion as to whether or not your hypothesis was correct.

SOMETHING MORE
1. Can you think of any other kinds of material to use instead of string that might work better? Replace the string with monofilament line (fishing line). How about thick monofilament line compared to thin line (different "pound test" strengths).
2. Try using cans that have short sides, such as those that pineapple or tuna fish come packed in, to improve sound.

SINGIN' IN THE SHOWER

ACOUSTICS: THE BEHAVIOR OF CONFINED SOUND

PURPOSE To find out whether different rooms in your house have different acoustics (sound qualities).

OVERVIEW A branch of physics that studies the behavior of sound is called "acoustics." You often hear the word acoustics when someone is talking about the characteristics of sound in a particular place. Smooth, hard surfaces reflect sound waves, bouncing the waves off the object. Hardwood floors, walls, and glass are examples of things that reflect sound. Other materials absorb (soak up) sound waves rather than reflecting them or do not reflect all the sound that strikes them. These include carpeting, curtains, and couches.

When sound is reflected off objects, it can create either an echo or a reverberation. An echo is a distinct repeat of a sound. When sound bounces off an object far away, an echo is often heard, such as shouting into a high cliff. The farther away the reflecting object is, the longer will be the delay between a shout and the echo. A short echo may be heard if you stand far back from the side of a brick building, such as your school might have, face the large brick or concrete wall, and give a sharp yell.

The term reverberation, or simply reverb, is used to describe the sound of thousands of echoes mixed together, each with a different delay. Reverb is a wash of sounds rather than separate distinguishable sounds. It is caused by sound bouncing many times off of many different objects. You will hear a reverb effect if you talk in an empty room that has bare walls and floor. Some sound will bounce only once before reaching your ear, while other sound waves may bounce from wall to wall two, three, or several times before they reach your ear.

Reverberation and echoes can make listening difficult when a person is speaking, as a lecturer in a large hall or a pastor in a church would do; but a little reverb can make some kinds of music sound more interesting, giving them a fuller sound.

Rooms in libraries and hospitals are places where architects and builders try to reduce the reverberation of sound so as to keep the rooms quieter. Theaters are designed to keep sound from bouncing around, so that a person speaking on stage can be more easily heard and understood.

YOU NEED
- portable battery-operated cassette tape or CD player
- portable battery-operated cassette tape recorder with built-in microphone
- blank cassette tape
- tape or CD with your favorite song on it
- bathroom that is not carpeted, or an uncarpeted kitchen or long empty hall
- a room with carpeting, window drapes, and upholstered furniture or cloth material (such as a couch or bed)
- tape measure

Where you live, the room that probably reflects sound the most is the bathroom; and in that room, the shower is the most reverberant. Have you noticed that effect?

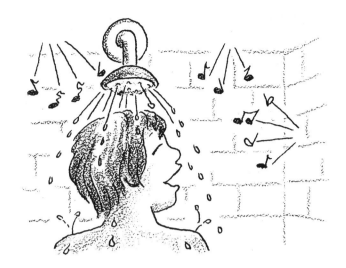

HYPOTHESIS A sound recording made in a bathroom, which has a lot of reflective surfaces, will sound different from a recording made in a room that is heavily furnished and carpeted.

PROCEDURE Place a battery-operated tape recorder on the floor of a bathroom, a kitchen, or any room that does not have carpet and upholstered furniture. Place a battery-operated tape or CD player on the floor of the same room at a distance of six feet or more. Put a blank tape in the recorder. Put a music tape or CD containing your favorite song in the player. Start recording on the tape recorder, and play the song on the other player. Let the recorder and player run for about one minute. Stop them both.

Set up the two machines in another room, one that is carpeted, has drapes on the windows, and has a bed with covers or has upholstered furniture, as you would find in a living room. Place the tape machines at the same distance from each other. The song, the tape machines, and the distance apart are kept *constant*. The *variable* is the environment the recorders are in. Again, start recording on the one machine and play the song on the other. After one minute, stop the tapes and rewind both of them.

Listen to the recording you made. Compare the "acoustics," or sound qualities, of each recording. Write down a description of both rooms and the things that are contained in them.

RESULTS & CONCLUSION Write down the results of your experiment. Come to a conclusion as to whether or not your hypothesis was correct.

SOMETHING MORE
1. Lift the lid of a washing machine and give a yell, then kneel in front of a couch and yell; describe the difference in the two sounds.
2. Compare a recording made inside your house to one made outside.

EAR OF THE BEHOLDER

PLEASANT SOUNDS VERSUS "NOISE"

PURPOSE The purpose is to determine whether there is a difference in the opinions of young people and those of an older age as to what normal-living sounds they consider pleasant and unpleasant.

OVERVIEW Some sounds are thought of as pleasing, while others are "noise." The difference between a pleasant and an unpleasant sound may be in the mind of the listener. Hitting a fence with a stick may be noise, but if you walk along a picket fence and run the stick against it, the regular repetitive sound may be pleasing to you but more than annoying to the home owner who is sitting on his porch listening to you scratching his fence!

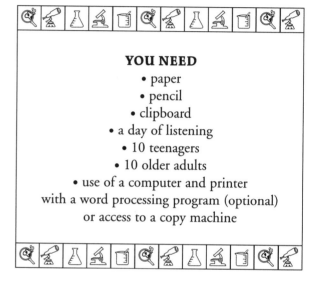

YOU NEED
- paper
- pencil
- clipboard
- a day of listening
- 10 teenagers
- 10 older adults
- use of a computer and printer with a word processing program (optional) or access to a copy machine

Sometimes pleasant sounds can be unpleasant, depending on the circumstances. The sound of a telephone ringing during the day can be pleasant; it could be a friend's expected call. The sound of a telephone ringing at three o'clock in the morning can be annoying and may be alarming. The sound of a doorbell ringing during the day may be pleasant, but in the middle of the night may be a worry or even frightening.

HYPOTHESIS When young people and older people are surveyed regarding a list sounds they think are pleasant or unpleasant, the results will be different between the different age groups.

PROCEDURE For one whole day, pay attention to all the sounds you hear. Carry paper, a pencil, and a clipboard to make a list of all the daily sounds around your home and neighborhood. Some sounds you may not have paid much attention to before, for example: toast popping up in a toaster, a door chime, a church bell, popcorn popping, a car horn, the crackling of a fire in a fireplace, the telephone ringing, birds chirping, the next door neighbor's dog barking, an umpire or referee blowing a whistle during a sporting event, insects buzzing in your ear, the screech of car brakes, and a friend blowing air across the top of a soda bottle.

After you have made up your list, think about other sounds you sometimes hear; a babbling brook, rap music playing loudly on a boom box, someone sitting at a table "drumming" a pencil in beat with a song in his head.

Take your notes and make a list of fifty sounds. Alongside the items, make three columns and head them pleasant, unpleasant, and no response. Make twenty copies of your list (or use a computer to make up and run off copies).

Give your survey to ten adults and ten teenagers, and write their names at the top. Ask each one to mark one column for each item on the list. Tally their marked answers, totalling the pleasant, unpleasant, and no response items for all the adults, then do the same for the teens. Which age group found which sounds to be pleasant or unpleasant? Are there sounds that they agreed on?

Mr. Brown

	Pleasant	Unpleasant	No Response
Robins	✔		
Crows			✔
Garbage truck		✔	
Neighbor's radio		✔	
Neighbor's dog		✔✔	
Microwave beep	✔		
Fridge hum			✔
Rap music		✔	
Jazz music	✔		

RESULTS & CONCLUSION Write down the results of your experiment. Come to a conclusion as to whether or not your hypothesis was correct.

SOMETHING MORE Rearrange the results of your survey based on male and female, rather than on age group.

THE SOUND OF TIME

AMPLIFYING SOUND

PURPOSE Sound is sometimes faint and hard to hear; how can it be amplified to improve hearing?

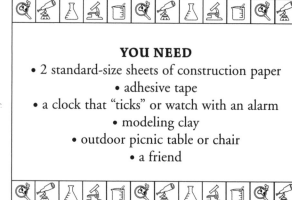

OVERVIEW Sound waves traveling through the air can be gathered to make them louder. They can also be directed (focused) in one direction to make them louder. Have you ever seen a band shell behind a large orchestra playing outside?

One way that sound is directed is by using a megaphone. A megaphone is a horn-shaped device used to increase the sound of a person's voice. Cheerleaders at a football game or the lifeguard at a beach often use megaphones. Early record players, made before the invention of electronic amplifiers, used such horns to make the music louder for listeners.

A megaphone works in reverse, too. It can gather sound and allow a person to hear weaker sounds better. Think about the shape of your outer ear, which is responsible for gathering sound. At a football game on television, you might notice a technician standing on the sidelines holding a large curved dish? This parabolic dish has a microphone attached to pick up what the players are saying.

HYPOTHESIS Hypothesize that by using a paper megaphone at the source and one at your ear, you will be able to hear a sound louder than one that, without these devices, you are able to hear not at all or just barely.

PROCEDURE Roll a piece of paper into the shape of a horn and use adhesive tape to keep it in place. Make another horn so you have two of them.

On a quiet, calm day, go outside and find a place (table, bench, stoop) to mount your sound source. You will need a clock that has an audible "tick" or a watch with an alarm, and some modeling clay in order to stand the watch on its side.

Make sure the clock is ticking or turn the watch alarm on so that it produces its beeping sound. Move away as far as you can from the clock or watch until you can just barely hear the sound. Then stop and hold one of the horns to your ear. Can you hear the sound any better?

Now have a friend hold the other horn in front of the clock or the watch with the large end toward you. Does the beeping get even louder? The source of the sound is *constant*; our *variables* are two megaphone devices.

Note: If you do this experiment on a windy day, it could affect your results. When doing science projects, it's important to control *all* the variables, which means keeping all things constant (the same) except for those that are changed on purpose. If the wind is constant, that is, if the wind speed and direction are the same when you listen with and without the horn, maybe the results of the experiment can be trusted. But if the wind is gusting or swirling, it will very likely change the results.

RESULTS & CONCLUSION Write down the results of your experiment. Come to a conclusion as to whether or not your hypothesis was correct.

SOMETHING MORE Does frequency (cycles per second) have an effect on the ability of the megaphones to amplify a sound? Use a music-instrument keyboard and compare a low note to a high note, both with and without the aid of the megaphones.

BLOWN AWAY

FLUIDICS: AIR FLOW AROUND SHAPES

PURPOSE Determining how air flows around objects could sometimes be very helpful to know.

OVERVIEW It is important to understand how moving air behaves. Airplanes lift off the ground because of the way air travels past the wings, which have a special shape. When two tall buildings are close together, wind can speed up as it travels between them, causing a windy condition that may be undesirable.

HYPOTHESIS The shape of an object affects how moving air flows around it.

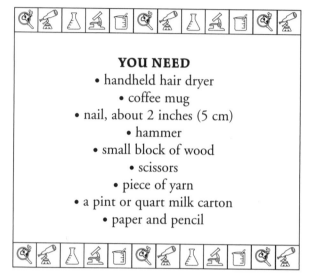

YOU NEED
- handheld hair dryer
- coffee mug
- nail, about 2 inches (5 cm)
- hammer
- small block of wood
- scissors
- piece of yarn
- a pint or quart milk carton
- paper and pencil

PROCEDURE Prove that the shape of the object affects how moving air flows around it.

Using a hammer, drive a 2-inch-long (5 cm) nail partially into a small piece of wood as shown. Near the head of the nail, tie a piece of yarn tightly onto the nail. Cut the yarn so it is about 3 inches (8 cm) long. This will be our "air-flow indicator."

Place a round coffee mug on a table. Place the air-flow indicator that you made about 2 inches behind it.

Hold a handheld hair dryer in front of the mug and turn it on at the highest speed. Use a cool setting if it has one. The fast moving air splits, hugs the mug as it travels around it, and comes together behind the mug. The yarn will stand out straight like a flag or a windsock in a strong breeze, showing that air is moving quickly.

Move the air-flow indicator to various spots along the side of and behind the mug to find places where the air is moving. On a piece of paper, draw a diagram of the mug and hair dryer. Make it a view looking down from the top of the mug. Mark spots on the paper to show where there is moving air, as detected by your air-flow indicator.

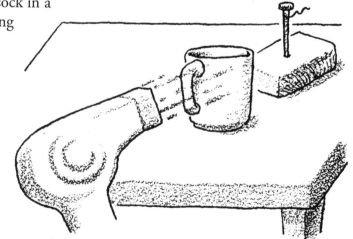

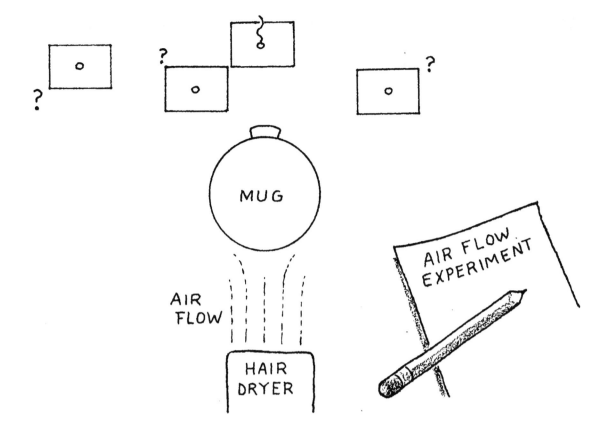

Use arrows to show the direction of its flow. Do you see a pattern of the air flowing around the mug?

The velocity of the moving air will be held *constant*. Changing the shape of the object in the stream of air flow will be the *variable*. What if you turn the handle of the mug to one side or the other?

Note: Since fast moving air flows around a rounded object and meets behind it, maybe hiding behind a tree or telephone pole to block wind is not as effective as you might think!

Now, replace the mug with a rectangular-shaped object, such as a pint or quart carton of milk. Again, move the yarn air-flow indicator around the carton and draw a diagram showing the air flow around it.

RESULTS & CONCLUSION Write down the results of your experiment. Come to a conclusion as to whether or not your hypothesis was correct.

SOMETHING MORE Making the piece of yarn longer will allow it to become an indictor of air speed. The farther out the yarn is blown, the stronger the air flow. Now you can use the device to compare the strength of air flow in addition to direction.

BALANCING ACT

OBJECTS AT REST TEND TO STAY AT REST

PURPOSE We want to find out whether objects at rest will remain at rest if balanced forces are applied.

OVERVIEW One of Sir Isaac Newton's laws of nature is that "objects at rest tend to stay at rest," which means that things that are not moving will stay that way unless an "unbalanced force" pushes (or pulls) on them. An unbalanced force is a push on an object that is stronger in one direction than a push from the opposite direction.

Balanced forces occur when equal forces coming from opposite directions are applied to an object. A book lying on a table has balanced forces acting upon it; the table is pushing up and gravity is pulling down. If the forces are equal, but they are not at exactly opposite angles, the resulting force will be unbalanced. In other words, the book may slide down the slanted table.

YOU NEED
- an adult
- a 9-inch (21 cm) wooden dowel, an inch or more (3 cm) in diameter
- hand wood saw
- 3 small nails
- hammer
- thin string
- scissors
- broom handle or yardstick
- 2 chairs of equal height

HYPOTHESIS Objects at rest tend to stay at rest when balanced forces are applied to them.

PROCEDURE To put together a device to prove, or disprove, the above hypothesis, ask an adult to help by cutting a wooden dowel into three 3-inch-long (7 cm) cylinders. The dowel should be at least 1 to 1½ inches (3–4 cm) in diameter. If the dowel is purchased at a hardware store or hobby shop, the sales clerk may offer to cut the dowel to size for you.

With a hammer, tap a small nail into the top of each dowel at exactly the middle. To find the middle accurately, you can use two pieces of string or thread. Lay one piece across the end of the dowel and another straight across it, at a 90-degree angle. The point where the two pieces cross each other is the middle.

Tie one end of a 3-foot-long (91 cm) piece of string onto the nail of one of the dowels. Do the same for the other two dowels.

Place two chairs equal in height back to back (such as matching kitchen or dining room table chairs), but separate them by about 3 feet (91 cm). Lay a broom handle across the top of the chair backs (a yardstick or any long, stiff pole will also work).

Tie the loose end of the string of one of the dowels to the center of the broom handle, so that the dowel hangs down, but does not touch the floor.

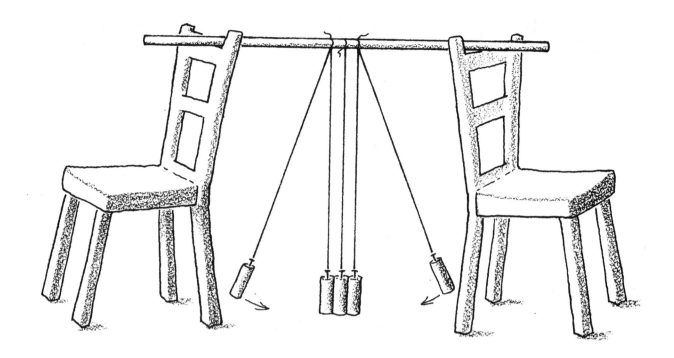

Hang another dowel on the right and another one on the left of the first dowel, so they are side by side. Tie the ends to the broom handle so that all three dowels are hanging straight and just touching alongside each other when they are not moving.

Take the left dowel in your left hand and the right dowel in your right hand. Pull them both away from the center hanging dowel until they are each about a foot (30 cm) away from the center dowel. Let the dowels in each hand go at exactly the same moment (this may take some practice), so they will both hit the center dowel together.

If only one dowel should swing into the center dowel (which is at rest), the "unbalanced force" will push the center dowel and make it swing, too. But, if both swinging dowels apply equal force in opposite directions, the experiment should result in a balanced force on the center dowel so that it remains at rest.

RESULTS & CONCLUSION Write down the results of your experiment. Come to a conclusion as to whether or not your hypothesis was correct.

SOMETHING MORE Show balanced and unbalanced forces in the game of "tug of war." Tie a ribbon onto the center of a long rope. Place a brick or some object on the ground to mark a spot, and lay the rope over it, with the ribbon on top of the brick. Have several friends grab one end of the rope and several grab the other for a game of tug of war. When equal pulling force is on both sides, the ribbon will stay hovered over the brick. When the pulling force becomes unbalanced, the ribbon will move toward the friends who are exerting the stronger total force.

FLOATING ALONG

BUOYANCY: THE ABILITY TO STAY UP

PURPOSE Let's figure out why things that are heavier than water can float.

OVERVIEW Why do things float? An object may float in water if it is light and weighs less than water. A Ping-Pong ball will float because it weighs less than water.

But why does a heavy boat float? Big ships are made from steel, and steel is much heavier than water.

The "buoyancy" of an object is its ability to float on the surface of water (or any fluid). Water gives an upward push on any object in it. The amount of force pushing upward is equal to the weight of the water that the object "displaces" (takes the place of). So, if a boat or ship is designed to displace an amount of water that weighs more than the boat, it will be able to float. For something to be buoyant, its shape is very important.

YOU NEED
- modeling clay
- large bowl
- water
- small kitchen food scale (gram weight scale)
- small bowl or cup
- kitchen measuring cup that has a pour spout
- thin piece of thread

HYPOTHESIS An object that is heavier than water can be made to float.

PROCEDURE Fill a large bowl with water, but don't fill it all the way to the top. Take a small amount of modeling clay and use your hands to roll it into a ball that is about 2 inches (5 cm) in diameter. Place the ball on the surface of the water and let go. The clay ball is heavier than water. Does it float or sink?

Take the ball out of the water. Use your hands to mold the same clay into the shape of a small boat. It should have a flat bottom and sides.

Now, place the boat on the surface of the water. It floats, even though it is the same amount of clay. While holding the weight (mass) of the clay *constant*, the *variable* has been its change in shape.

You can take this project further by capturing and weighing the water that is displaced by the ball of clay. To do this you will need a kitchen measuring cup that has a pour spout. Set a small bowl or cup under the spout to catch the water that spills out.

Fill the measuring cup with water until water begins to spill out of the spout. When the water stops overflowing, empty the small bowl that caught the water. Dry it out.

Shape the clay into a ball. Tie a piece of thin thread onto the ball and slowly lower it into the water. The water it displaces will spill out into the bowl.

When the water stops overflowing, remove the bowl and weigh it on a small kitchen food scale. Write down the weight.

Dry the bowl and weigh it. This is to get the "tare weight," the weight of the container that had been holding the water. Subtract this tare weight from the weight of the bowl with the water in it. The difference is the weight of the displaced water.

Also weigh the clay ball. Compare the weight of the clay ball to the weight of the water that it displaced.

RESULTS & CONCLUSION Write down the results of your experiment. Come to a conclusion as to whether or not your hypothesis was correct.

SOMETHING MORE Weigh the amount of water the clay boat displaces. Compare it to the amount of water the same clay in the shape of a ball displaces. Do you think the weight of the water displaced by the boat will be less than the weight of the water displaced by the ball?

FLYING IN CIRCLES

AIR FRICTION: SOMETIMES GOOD, SOMETIMES NOT

PURPOSE Set up some demonstrations showing how air friction (resistance) affects falling objects.

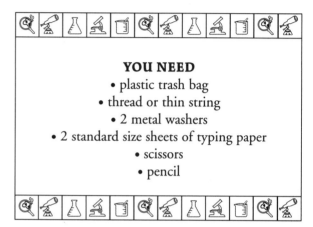

YOU NEED
- plastic trash bag
- thread or thin string
- 2 metal washers
- 2 standard size sheets of typing paper
- scissors
- pencil

OVERVIEW When we see or hear the word "friction" we usually think about it taking place between two surfaces. As the project on page 186 explained, friction is the resistance to motion when two things rub together. Friction can also occur, however, between air and any object that moves through it. Air friction causes resistance, which pushes against the object.

Car manufacturers try to design cars that are "streamlined," which means the cars are shaped to let air flow smoothly around them without offering much resistance. This reduction in air friction is desirable because it then takes less energy to move the car. This saves fuel. The car will get more "miles (or kilometers) per gallon"—go farther on less gasoline. Streamlined cars save gasoline (an important resource), the cost of gasoline at the fuel pump, and the car will also put less pollution into the air.

Designers of aircraft, just like the designers of cars, try to make their crafts have as little resistance to the air as possible, but sometimes, air friction is desirable. When sky divers jump out of an airplane, their parachutes need to have a lot of air resistance to slow their descent and land them safely on the ground.

HYPOTHESIS Air friction can be increased and decreased simply by changing an object's shape.

PROCEDURE First, we'll compare how air friction affects two sheets of typing paper, keeping the material and height *constant* and shape the only *variable*. Fold one of them into a paper airplane shape and crumple the other into a ball. Stand in a clear area in a room. Stretch your arms out to your sides, holding the airplane nose down in one hand and the paper ball at the height of the airplane nose in the other. At exactly the same time, drop them.

Next, with a scissors, cut a section of plastic the size of the sheet of paper out of a plastic bag. Take a pencil or nail and carefully poke a small hole near the edge at each corner. Cut four pieces of thread or thin string, each 2 feet (61 cm) in length. Tie one end of each piece to each hole in the plastic. Tie the loose ends of the four threads to a metal washer. The washer is our sky diver, and the plastic bag is his parachute.

Now, cut another piece of plastic the same size, put a washer inside, and wrap and tie it into a bundle using 8 feet of the same thread or string. Holding the parachute and wrapped plastic out so they are the same height from the floor, let them go. Here again, shape is the only *variable*.

In order to further demonstrate the difference streamlining makes, do one more drop. In one hand, hold your sky diver. In the other hand, hold the paper airplane, with its nose facing the ground. Outstretch and raise your arms so the bottom of the sky diver is at the same distance from the ground as the nose of the airplane. Let go of both objects at the same time. Does the sky diver's parachute encounter much more resistence, from friction with the air, than the streamlined paper airplane?

RESULTS & CONCLUSION Write down the results of your experiments. Come to a conclusion as to whether or not your hypothesis was correct.

SOMETHING MORE Would it make a difference if the shape of the parachute was square or round instead of rectangular? Would another shape have even more air resistence?

POP A TREAT

THE PHYSICS OF POPCORN

PURPOSE If it's moisture that causes popcorn to pop, is it measurable?

OVERVIEW Smelling the distinct aroma of freshly popped popcorn probably brings to mind a trip to a movie theater to see a great movie. Popcorn is a healthy and tasty food. The kernels of corn used to make popcorn have a strong airtight outer covering that seals moisture inside. When heat is applied, the moisture turns into superheated steam. This pressure buildup eventually bursts through the outer coat, expanding the contents to about thirty times its original size. Of course, the moisture escapes, but how much? Is it possible to quantify the amount lost during the popping process?

YOU NEED
- an adult
- kernels of unpopped popcorn
- 2 brown-paper lunch bags
- ruler
- pencil
- a microwave oven
- 2 paper plates
- adhesive tape
- oven mitts

HYPOTHESIS Hypothesize that the moisture in a serving size of popcorn kernels, which causes the kernels to pop when heated and escapes as steam, is not measurable—even though we are able to see it as steam.

PROCEDURE Tape a small paper plate onto each end of a ruler, to keep them from moving, and make a balance scale by placing a pencil at the middle of the ruler with the paper plates.

Put fifty kernels of unpopped popcorn in a small brown paper lunch bag. Put fifty kernels in another lunch bag. Place one bag at the center of each paper plate.

Try to balance the two bags by adding kernels to the lighter of the bags. When you have the two bags balanced, remove one of the bags, being careful not to bump the ruler, pencil, or the other bag.

Fold the very top of the bag closed, to keep the popping kernels inside the bag. Place the bag in a microwave oven and have an adult help you set the controls and pop the kernels in the bag.

When the popping is done, take the bag out (use oven mitts to prevent being burned) and open the bag. Do you see steam coming out? This is visual proof that there was water

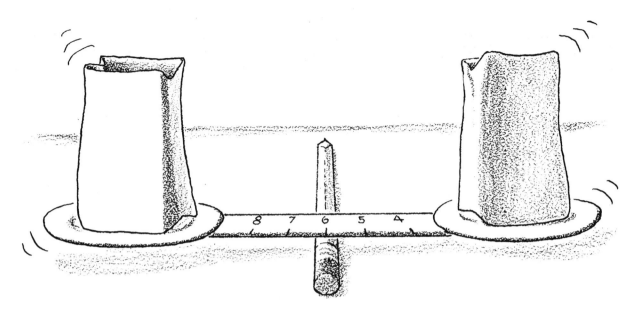

in the popcorn kernels, which was heated to steam and has now just been released. The question is whether or not the lost moisture is measurable.

Place the bag back onto the balance scale, positioning the bag in the center of the plate as before. The number of kernels in the microwaved bag has remained *constant*, and the moisture content is the *variable*.

It's okay if there are a few kernels that remain unpopped. Can you detect any noticeable difference in weight? If so, was the bag of popcorn lighter than the bag of unpopped kernels? Eat the popcorn. Enjoy!

RESULTS & CONCLUSION Write down the results of your experiment. Come to a conclusion as to whether or not your hypothesis was correct.

SOMETHING MORE The reason some kernels of corn don't pop can be because there is a scratch or break in their airtight coating, which lets steam escape slowly and prevents sufficient pressure buildup. You may want to try an experiment and see if you can prevent kernels from popping by first scratching their surface or carefully poking them with the sharp point of a drawing compass (use caution when handling sharp tools).

UNWELCOME GUSTS

COMPARING AND MEASURING WIND STRENGTHS

PURPOSE Over a week's time, we want to determine which day had the strongest gust of wind.

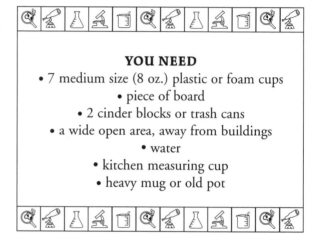

YOU NEED
- 7 medium size (8 oz.) plastic or foam cups
- piece of board
- 2 cinder blocks or trash cans
- a wide open area, away from buildings
- water
- kitchen measuring cup
- heavy mug or old pot

OVERVIEW People have harnessed the powerful force of wind to help them do many useful things. Windmills have been used to pump water and make electricity. Boats can sail around the world by using sails whose large surface area captures the wind's power.

But, sometimes this wind force works against us. On extremely windy and gusty days, huge bridges are sometimes closed to vehicles with large surface areas, such as tractor trailers and motor homes, because of the danger. Playing beachball or volleyball in a strong wind can either help your team or hinder it, depending on whether or not you are downwind.

On a windy day, have you ever tried to carry a big piece of plywood or poster board, or a small bag holding only something light, like a greeting card? Have you ever helped your parents put garbage cans out at the curb on a windy trash day? If no one is home when the trash is collected, you could come home to find the cans scattered all over. The empty cans, being lighter without trash, are easily blown all over the yard and even into the street, causing a hazard to motorists, by strong gusts of wind. Can you think of other times when the force of the wind is not welcome, or is even harmful?

Wind velocity is important in air travel. In physics, the word "velocity" means both speed and direction. Airports use wind socks to get a relative indication of wind direction and speed.

You can build a simple weather instrument to detect wind gusts and get a comparative indication of their strength by using water-filled paper cups.

HYPOTHESIS Hypothesize that you can put together a simple device that will allow you to determine the force of the strongest wind gust of the day.

PROCEDURE Find an open area away from buildings or other structures that might block the wind. A spot in your own backyard would be good, if place is available.

Set two cinder blocks upright on the ground several feet apart. If you don't have cinder blocks, you can use same-size milk crates, or buckets, or trash cans turned upside down. Across the top of any such "risers," lay a long piece of wood.

Set seven 8-ounce paper cups (or plastic cups) in a row on the board. Leave one empty and, using a measuring cup, pour 1 ounce of water in the second cup, 2 ounces in the next, 3 in the next, continuing up to 7 ounces. If your measuring cup is marked in milliliters, use increments of 50 (that is, 50 ml, 100 ml, 150 ml, 200 ml, and so on).

On the board or in an open place nearby, place a heavy mug or old pot. This will be used to capture any rainfall for the day. If you find rain in it, don't record that day's results because they won't be valid.

At the end of each day, observe which cups have blown off the board. Write down how many cups blew off. The lighter cups are more sensitive to the force of the wind.

The next day, set them up again, and refill the cups with water (some water will probably have evaporated). The contents and positions of all of the cups must be kept *constant*. The wind gusts should be the only *variable* in the project. At the end of the day, record which cups have blown off the board.

Do this every day for a week or two, or as long as you wish. Look at your recorded observations for each day. Did your paper-cup system work as a weather instrument to allow comparisons of the strongest gusts of wind that occurred each day?

RESULTS & CONCLUSION Write down the results of your experiment. Come to a conclusion as to whether or not your hypothesis was correct.

SOMETHING MORE What if you found a heavy and a light cup knocked over, but one in the middle still standing? Do you think the results of that day should not be used, as there may have been interference from squirrels, birds, or other animals seeking water?

A LOPSIDED PINWHEEL

BALANCING POINTS OF ODDLY SHAPED OBJECTS

PURPOSE How to discover the balancing point of irregularly shaped objects.

YOU NEED
- a pushpin
- piece of thin cardboard, oak tag, or standard size construction paper
- cardboard box, standing at least a foot (30 cm) high
- scissors
- thread
- metal washer
- pencil

OVERVIEW The balancing point of a square or circle is easy to find. You just need to measure. It's right at the center of it, as long as the object is basically two-dimensional or flat; that is, doesn't have a significant amount of depth (a rock or glob of clay is definitely three-dimensional).

The balancing point, however, is not always in the center. It's the point at which, if an axle is placed through it, an object can be spun like a wheel and it will stop at a different spot every time. Is it possible to find the balancing point of something flat, but that has an odd unsymmetrical shape?

HYPOTHESIS Hypothesize that you can find the balancing point of an irregularly shaped piece of stiff paper or cardboard.

PROCEDURE Draw an irregular shape on a piece of thin cardboard, oak tag, or construction paper and cut it out with scissors. You may draw something like the six-sided shape shown here. Although the cutout shape will be really three-dimensional (it has some depth, or thickness, as well as length and width), for the purposes of our project, this third dimension is so small we can assume it will not affect the results.

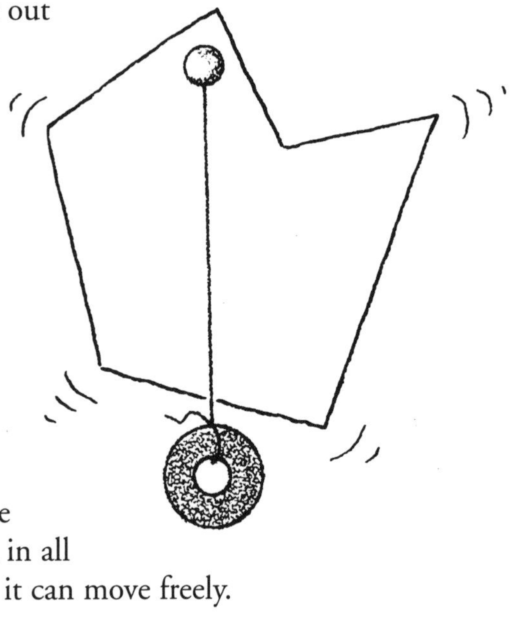

Set a cardboard box on a table. Near one edge at the top of your shape, place a pushpin through your object and into the side of the cardboard box. If you don't have a cardboard box, you can use a cork bulletin board or a piece of plywood, as long as it is kept perpendicular to the ground (standing up straight). Do not push the pin in all the way. Swing the object back and forth to be sure it can move freely.

Tie one end of a piece of thread onto the pushpin, and tie a metal washer to the other end. If you don't have a washer, use any object as a weight to cause the string to hang straight down (a large paper clip, for example). We are going to use gravity to make sure the line we draw will be perpendicular (at a 90-degree angle) to the ground. The thread must also hang straight down and be hanging freely, not hung up on anything. With a pencil, draw a line tracing the path of the string across the object.

Next, take out the pushpin, turn the object about 90 degrees (it does not have to be turned an exact amount), and push the pushpin into a point near the top edge and through to the cardboard box. Again, hang a thread from the pushpin and draw a line tracing the path of the string as it falls across the surface of the object. The shape of the object is our *variable*; gravity and the line with the washer hanging down are *constant*.

Where the two lines intersect (where they cross) is the balancing point of the shape. How do you know this?

First, you can verify it by turning the object once again and repeating the hanging of the thread from the pushpin, drawing a third line. That line, too, should cross at the same spot where the other two meet. Other similar lines will also cross there.

Second, prove that this is the balancing point by pushing a pushpin through that intersecting point and into a stick, making a pinwheel-like toy. Give the object a spin a number of times. Each time it should stop at a different point.

RESULTS & CONCLUSION Write down the results of your experiment. Come to a conclusion as to whether or not your hypothesis was correct.

SOMETHING MORE
1. Place numbers all around the edges of your shape to make a spinning "fortune wheel" game (in this case, "Hexagon of Fortune"). You and your friends can guess what number it will stop on when given a good spin. Try turning your object into a pinwheel by bending up some of the edges to catch the wind.
2. Draw and cut out more objects, each with a different numbers of sides or some irregular shapes. Find the balancing point of each object and prove it. Or you and your friends can guess where the balancing points will be and find out, using the methods above, who comes closest.

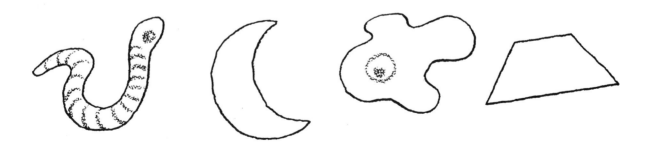

GET THE POINT

CHANGES AFFECTING SURFACE AREAS

PURPOSE To study surface area differences.

OVERVIEW A famous trick from long ago in India was for a person to lay down on a bed of nails. Ouch! How could they do that without the nails sticking right into them? Physics, that's how!

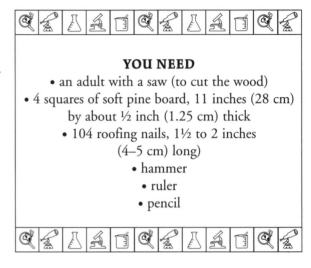

YOU NEED
- an adult with a saw (to cut the wood)
- 4 squares of soft pine board, 11 inches (28 cm) by about ½ inch (1.25 cm) thick
- 104 roofing nails, 1½ to 2 inches (4–5 cm) long)
- hammer
- ruler
- pencil

The term "surface area" refers to the total area of an object exposed to the space surrounding it. Imagine a sailboat trying to get anywhere with a sail only 2 feet (61 cm) by 2 feet. Its surface area would be only 4 square feet (360 cm square), certainly not enough to catch any meaningful wind. The large surface area of a big sail is needed to really capture and harness wind power.

Let's get back to the man on the bed of nails. The surface area of the pointed end of a large nail is certainly not very big. But, what if there were a thousand nails all fairly close together? If a person lies gently on the bed, the weight of the person could be distributed over the total surface area of all the nail points. Lying on a bed of nails doesn't sound like something you would want to do, but with the help of physics and "surface area," it seems not as painful as you might think.

Women wearing very tiny high (spike) heels, perhaps only ¼ inch or 1 centimeter square, have been known to break the toes of a dance partner. Imagine even an average-size grown woman concentrating almost all her weight on two such little square heels! Each of those little heels would have a very powerful downward pressure!

We can expose the "bed of nails" trick as a fraud by proving that when weight is distributed over a lot of nails compared to just a few, there is less force per nail tip because of the total increase in surface area of the combined tips.

HYPOTHESIS When a weight is divided over a greater surface area (many nails), each nail will make a smaller impression in a piece of wood under it.

PROCEDURE Have an adult cut some soft pine board into 11-inch (28 cm) squares. The boards should be thin, no bigger than about ½-inch (1.25 cm) thick.

With a ruler, make marks all the way around the edge of one of the pieces of wood at 1-inch (2.5 cm) increments. Then draw lines from the points on one side to the other

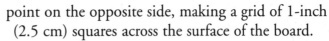

point on the opposite side, making a grid of 1-inch (2.5 cm) squares across the surface of the board.

Lay the board outside on the ground. Using a hammer, pound a flat head roofing nail at each spot where lines intersect. There will be 100 intersecting points. The nails must be long enough to go through the board and stick out the other side, extending through at least ½ inch (about 1.25 cm). When pounding the nails in, they will stick harmlessly into the ground.

Lay another piece of pine wood on a hard surface, such as a sidewalk or paved driveway. On top of it, lay the board with nails, with the nails facing down. Next, place another pine board on top. This board will help ensure that none of the nails will back out when weight is put on them. Now stand on the boards. Jump up and down once. Remove the top two boards and observe the nail depressions made in the bottom board.

Now we want to keep the weight *constant*, but use fewer nails, making the surface area the *variable*. So, lay the fourth board on the ground and pound four nails into it, one near each corner, perhaps 1 inch (2.5 cm) in from the sides.

Turn the board with the nail depressions in it over so its smooth side is facing up. Lay the board with only four nails on top of it, with the nails facing down. As before, lay the other piece of pine on top to keep the nails from backing out. Then stand on the boards and jump up and down once.

Remove the boards. Examine the board with the nail depressions in it. Are the nail depression marks deeper when all your weight was distributed by only four nails compared to when the surface area of 100 nails distributed your weight?

RESULTS & CONCLUSION Write down the results of your experiment. Come to a conclusion as to whether or not your hypothesis was correct.

SOMETHING MORE Try measuring the depth of the impressions. Use a toothpick.

BREAK THE BEAM

EXPLORING SOME CHARACTERISTICS OF LIGHT

PURPOSE The purpose is to understand how a light security system works.

OVERVIEW Can you see a beam of light? You can certainly see a lit light bulb, the sun, a candle's flame, or any source of light. You can also see objects because light is shining on them. But, you are normally not able to see the light beam itself. The path of the beam through the air can, however, be seen by filling the air with tiny particles so the light will reflect off them.

> **YOU NEED**
> • lamp
> • handheld mirror
> • modeling clay
> • small piece of cardboard
> • flashlight
> • several facial tissues
> • dark room
> • a friend
> • table

In a dark room, lay a flashlight on a table and shake several facial tissues in the air. The light will reflect (bounce) off of the tiny particles of tissue, allowing you to see the path of the light beam. Similarly, have you ever seen the rays of sunlight shine from behind breaks in clouds? Have you ever seen the light beams coming from the headlights of the car you were riding in on a dark, foggy evening?

Because we can't actually see a beam of light, some home security systems use light to detect someone walking through a room. A light source shines into an electronic

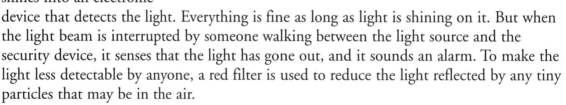

device that detects the light. Everything is fine as long as light is shining on it. But when the light beam is interrupted by someone walking between the light source and the security device, it senses that the light has gone out, and it sounds an alarm. To make the light less detectable by anyone, a red filter is used to reduce the light reflected by any tiny particles that may be in the air.

HYPOTHESIS We can detect a person walking in another room using a light source and a mirror.

PROCEDURE   Set up a demonstration of how a home security system might work. Lay a hand mirror on its side on a piece of cardboard. With modeling clay, build a base around it so the mirror will stand up by itself, as shown.

Set the mirror on a table or bookshelf, and adjust it so that the light from a lamp is reflected into another room. It should be a room that you can make fairly dark. Stand against the wall and look out the door at the mirror. Have a friend adjust the mirror until you can see the lamp in it. Then you know the mirror is lined up. This demonstrates another characteristic about light; light travels in a straight line unless something interferes.

Go into the dark room and close the door until it is only open enough to let a slit of light in to shine against the wall opposite the door.

Watch the light on the wall as you have your friend walk around the room. Can you detect when your friend steps in the path of the light?

RESULTS & CONCLUSION   Write down the results of your experiment. Come to a conclusion as to whether or not your hypothesis was correct.

SOMETHING MORE   You can tell the direction of a person walking through the room by adding a second mirror a few feet to either side of the first mirror, so that a second light spot shines on the wall. Then, when a person walks by, he will break one beam before the other. The beam that is broken first tells you in which direction the person is walking.

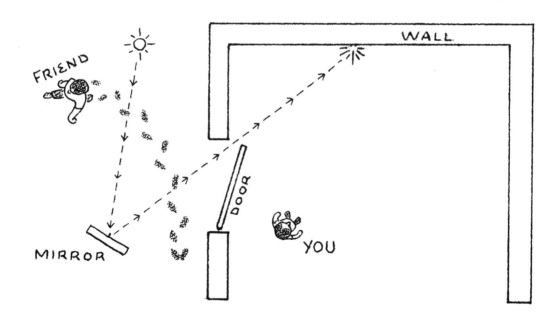

Now Soft / Now Loud

AMPLIFYING SOUND THROUGH REFLECTION

PURPOSE To understand and demonstrate how sound vibrations can be amplified through the use of a "sounding board."

OVERVIEW A sound something makes can often be made louder by focusing it, reflecting it, or making a second object vibrate or resonate.

Did you ever see a cheerleader using a megaphone? A megaphone is a large horn with a small opening at one end and a large opening at the other. Sound is focused by a megaphone. Speaking into the end with the small opening makes the user's voice louder. It can also be used in reverse, holding the small opening end up to your ear to collect distant or faint sounds and make them louder (see the project on page 220).

Another way to amplify sound (make it louder) is to cause the vibrations to be expanded to another object. The hollow wooden body of an acoustic guitar gives the vibrating strings of the instrument more volume and better tone quality.

A third way is to use something called a "sounding board." The sounding board in a piano reflects the sounds of the vibrating piano strings, making the sound louder.

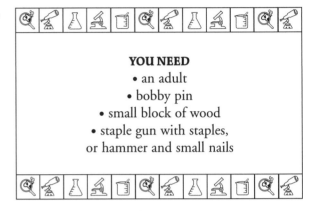

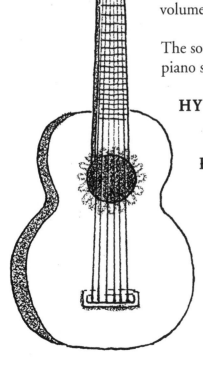

YOU NEED
- an adult
- bobby pin
- small block of wood
- staple gun with staples, or hammer and small nails

HYPOTHESIS Hypothesize that sounds from a vibrating body can be amplified by adding a sounding board.

PROCEDURE Take a bobby pin, the flat metal hairpin used to hold one's hair in place, and bend one of the prongs out until it makes a 90-degree angle (so that the bobby pin forms an "L" shape). Normally, one prong of a bobby pin is straight and the other contains zigzag curves. With your thumb and index finger, tightly hold the bobby pin near the bottom of the straight prong, holding only about ½ inch (1.25 cm) of the prong. Use the thumb of your other hand to sharply flick the end of the curved prong, making a downward stroke. Listen closely to hear the faint sound.

We are going to keep the vibrating bobby pin *constant*; the *variable* will be the addition of a block of wood to act as the sounding board.

Now, ask an adult to help you mount the bobby pin on a small block of wood. The wood should be about 1 inch (2.5 cm) thick by 5 or 6 inches (13–15 cm) square or rectangular. (The exact length and width are not important.) Mount the bobby pin by placing two staples from a staple gun or two small nails (brads) to attach the bobby pin to the wood block. The nails can be tapped partway into the wood then bent over the pin, using a hammer. About ½ inch (1.25 cm) of the straight prong should be mounted flush against the wood block, and the rest of the bobby pin should rise above the block. If staples are used, give them a tap with the hammer to ensure that the bobby pin is firmly touching the wood. Sharply flick the end of the curved prong with your thumb, with a downward stroke. Is the tone you heard before louder now?

RESULTS & CONCLUSION Write down the results of your experiment. Come to a conclusion as to whether or not your hypothesis was correct.

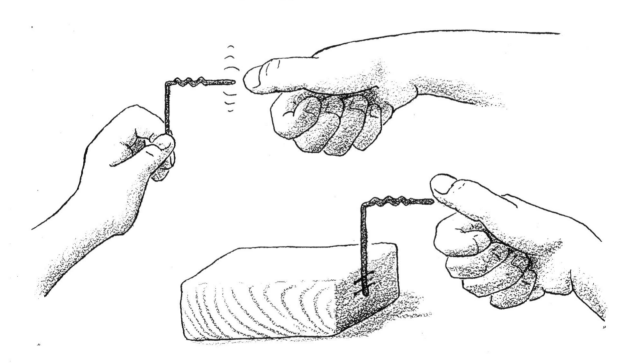

SOMETHING MORE
1. Will increasing the size of the wood block amplify the sound even more? At what size does further increase make no difference in the sound?
2. Can you make the sound even louder by resting the board on a large wooden table, holding it tightly against a wall, or against a large metal pan?

PLANT FIRST AID

COLLECTING LIGHT TO BENEFIT PLANTS

PURPOSE To increase the amount of light available to a houseplant not getting direct sunlight.

OVERVIEW We have a houseplant that sits on a table where it does not get much light. The table is not near any windows in the room, and the room is sometimes a little dark because of an overhang on the porch outside the only window in the room.

Plants need light. To help the plant out, we constructed a simple device to capture light and bathe the plant in more light than it would normally receive. Since light travels in straight lines but can be reflected, we constructed a three-sided cardboard reflector to collect the light that missed the plant and bounce it back toward the plant.

YOU NEED
- 2 large pieces of cardboard
- 2 similar house plants, or batches of growing seedlings
- aluminum foil
- adhesive tape
- black paint or construction paper
- art supplies (optional)
- scissors
- 2 months' time

HYPOTHESIS A plant exposed to more light, by having a reflector surrounding it, will grow better than one that does not have the reflector. (We consider "growing better" to mean the plant will have either bigger or more leaves, or will be healthier and grow taller.)

PROCEDURE Obtain two houseplants of the same type that are similar in appearance: about the same height and number and size of leaves. (You could also grow your own.)

Find a location in your home that gets good light but not direct sunlight.

Take a large piece of cardboard, big enough to go around three sides of one houseplant and as tall as the plant—or cut one from a larger piece of cardboard. Bend the cardboard in two places to make "wings" that can be angled so the cardboard can stand up by itself, as shown. In the same way, construct a second three-sided cardboard stand.

To make the stands more attractive, since the project will take some time, use your art supplies to draw, paint, or otherwise decorate the backs of the shields, the convex side that will be facing away from the plants.

Line the inside (the concave side) of one of the cardboard stands with aluminum foil (shiny side out); use pieces of adhesive tape or glue to keep it in place. Paint the inside of the other cardboard stand black, or cover it with black construction paper.

Set up the plants and shields in the location you've found for the project. Position the wings of the cardboard stands mostly open, but closed enough so the cardboard will stand on its own. Place one plant on the concave inside of each cardboard stand so that the two plants will receive the same amount of normal room lighting and not be shaded.

The plants must also be cared for equally. Be sure to water the plants regularly. When you water them, each plant must receive the identical amount of water.

The *constants* in this project are the room temperature and the amount of water they receive. The *variable* is the amount of reflected light each plant receives.

RESULTS & CONCLUSION Write down the results of your experiment. Come to a conclusion as to whether or not your hypothesis was correct.

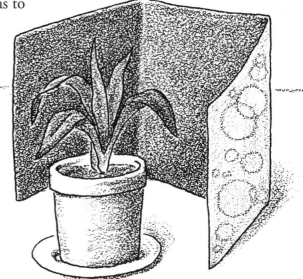

SOMETHING MORE If your reflector worked, can it be made smaller so that it is more attractive in a room, yet still gives the same results? Try cutting the size of the reflector in half.

HOT LIGHT

COMPARING WASTE HEAT FROM BULBS

PURPOSE Let's see if using a higher wattage incandescent light bulb to increase brightness also produces more waste heat energy.

OVERVIEW If we want more light in a room, we could change the wattage of the light bulbs used in lamps in the room. Although brightness is really measured in units called "lumens," light bulbs are often sold by wattage; the rating is listed on the package. A "watt" is a unit of electrical energy. Bulbs that are brighter require more electrical energy to use them, so they have a higher wattage rating, based on consumption. Consumers have a good idea of the brightness of a bulb by comparing its wattage rating. A 15-watt bulb is commonly used in refrigerators. A 25-watt bulb might be found in a small bedside lamp. A 75- or 100-watt bulb is used in overhead fixtures in a kitchen or workroom or in large living room lamps where strong light for reading is needed. Other wattage bulbs available are 40 and 60 watts.

> **YOU NEED**
> - an adult
> - lamp
> - thermometer
> - wooden stick
> - clear adhesive tape
> - 25-watt incandescent light bulb
> - 100-watt incandescent light bulb
> - ruler
> - clock or watch
> - pencil and paper

While we get more light from higher wattage light bulbs, we may also be getting more of something else that is unwanted—heat. Some energy is given off from light bulbs in the form of heat, which is wasted. Does a 100-watt incandescent light bulb give off more waste heat than a 25-watt light bulb?

HYPOTHESIS An incandescent bulb that produces more brightness (has a higher wattage rating) also produces more heat.

PROCEDURE Safety is always the first concern when doing any science project. Because light bulbs can get very hot, and it is important to be very careful working with electricity, have an adult unplug and plug in the lamp and remove the light bulbs as needed.

Using clear adhesive tape, attach a thermometer to a wooden stick or dowel, and position the sensitive tip of the thermometer 2 inches (5 cm) from the end of the stick. You can use any kind of stick: an ice-pop stick, a tongue depressor (available at your local pharmacy), a wooden dowel (found in a hardware store or hobby shop), or a small twig from a tree. The adhesive tape should be clear or positioned so that it does not interfere with your reading of the numbers on the thermometer.

Find a lamp on which the lampshade can be easily removed. Once an adult unplugs the lamp from the wall outlet, unscrew the light bulb and replace it with a 25-watt bulb. Carefully reinsert the lamp's plug and turn the lamp on.

Hold the wood and thermometer device against the side of the bulb, as shown. Only the wood, which does not conduct heat, should be touching the bulb. Do not touch the thermometer glass itself while you are holding the device, and do not hold the device over the bulb, to avoid excess heat building up in your hand.

Holding the thermometer device parallel to the tabletop, wait for three minutes. Then, read the temperature and write it down.

Turn the lamp off. Wait about 10 minutes for the bulb to cool off and for the thermometer to return to room temperature. Remember, a glass light bulb may be hot, but not look hot.

Our *constant* is the distance the thermometer is from the bulb surface, and the *variable* is the wattage of the bulbs.

Carefully unplug the lamp from the electric receptacle. Unscrew the 25-watt bulb and replace it with a 100-watt bulb. Plug the lamp back in; turn it on and again hold the thermometer by the bulb and wait three minutes. Be very careful around the bulb. It is hot! Write down the temperature.

Compare the temperature readings from the two bulbs. Does the bulb that is brighter also produce more heat?

RESULTS & CONCLUSION Write down the results of your experiment. Come to a conclusion as to whether or not your hypothesis was correct.

SOMETHING MORE

1. Find the temperature of bulbs having 25, 60, 75, and 100 watts and see if there is a mathematical relationship between the wattage and the temperature.

2. Find a lamp that uses a fluorescent bulb, in your home or at a friend's, and use your thermometer device to see if it gives off as much heat as an incandescent bulb of the same wattage rating.

CRASH!

THE RELATIONSHIP BETWEEN MASS AND FORCE

PURPOSE It often happens that objects that are at rest, that is, not moving, are hit by moving objects and forced to move. What happens when the objects struck have different masses?

OVERVIEW Sir Isaac Newton did experiments to find the mathematical relationship between the mass of an object and how fast it moves when a given force strikes it. Mass is how much "stuff" makes up an object. Newton found that the larger the mass of an object, the smaller will be its movement when a given force is applied.

Imagine a soccer ball filled with air and another one that is filled with sand. If you kicked each soccer ball with the same amount of force, the ball with more mass (filled with sand) would not move as far as the one with less mass (filled with air). You might hurt your foot on the ball with more mass, too!

> **YOU NEED**
> - an adult
> - ladder
> - soccer ball
> - bowling ball
> - golf ball
> - several thick hardback books
> - 2 wooden boards, 2-by-4-inch by 8 feet (240 cm) long
> - hammer
> - 6 long nails
> - ruler

HYPOTHESIS A soccer ball will move farther than a bowling ball when the same force is applied to each.

PROCEDURE Let's strike a bowling ball (in place of a sand-filled soccer ball) and a soccer ball with the same force and measure how far they move. If Sir Isaac Newton is right, the soccer ball, which has less mass than the bowling ball, will move farther. (Be very careful handling the bowling ball. It could hurt your foot if it should fall on it. Have an adult help you if the ball is too heavy for you to handle safely.)

We need to have a force that will be exactly the same every time, so we can be sure each ball is struck with an identical force. This is our *constant*. To do this, construct a ramp with the long two 2-by-4 inch wooden boards, making a "V" shape. Rolling a golf ball down the "V" channel will cause it to strike whatever object is at the bottom of the ramp with the same force every time. If we let go of the golf ball at the same place on the ramp each time, the force of gravity will ensure that the ball is rolling at the same speed every time it reaches the bottom of the ramp.

Nail two 8-foot (240 cm) long 2-by-4-inch pieces of lumber together, making a "V" shaped channel. This will be our wooden ramp.

Outside, set up a ladder. Rest one end of the ramp on the third or fourth rung of the ladder. At the ground end of the ramp, place a bowling ball so that it is touching the end of the ramp. The ground must be flat and level.

You'll get the most action if the bowling ball is struck in its middle, some small distance above the ground. Place books underneath the end of the ramp to raise it until it is positioned at the middle of the bowling ball. You may need to place a few books along the sides of the ramp to keep the "V" shape facing up.

Pick a spot along the ramp to let go of a golf ball and start it rolling down the ramp. To get the most speed out of the ball, you can let it go from the high end of the ramp. Be sure, however, that you let the ball go from the same spot every time. Also, don't give the golf ball a "push" start, because you would not give it an even push every time. Just let go of the ball and gravity will start it rolling.

If the bowling ball moves when it is hit, use a ruler to measure how far it moved.

Now we want to see how far a soccer ball, which has much less mass, will roll when the same force is applied to it. The different masses of the two balls is the *variable* in our project.

Release the golf ball. If the soccer ball moves a lot, it may be easier to use a tape measure, yardstick, or meterstick than a ruler to measure the distance it rolled.

If neither ball moved, increase the slope of the ramp by moving up one rung on the ladder, giving more speed, hence force, to the rolling ball.

RESULTS & CONCLUSION Write down the results of your experiment. Come to a conclusion as to whether or not your hypothesis was correct.

SOMETHING MORE Repeat this experiment using different balls at the bottom of the ramp; try a baseball, basketball, and a tennis ball. Can you predict which one will roll farthest?

BIGGER WATER

TEMPERATURE'S EXPANSION/CONTRACTION EFFECTS

PURPOSE What happens when water freezes?

YOU NEED
- empty metal soup can
- water
- use of a freezer
- small bowl

OVERVIEW Many things expand or contract when they change temperature. Have you ever noticed, when standing by a railroad track, why there are gaps in the rails at certain intervals? The spaces in the rails allow them room to "grow," in case they expand; otherwise, the rails would buckle. Track engineers know exactly how big the gaps should be to allow for this rail expansion.

If you have electric baseboard heat in your home, you may have heard the crackling sounds it makes when the metal fins heat up or cool down. That's because the fins are expanding and contracting. Gaps in the roadway of bridges are also there to allow for expansion and contraction from temperature changes.

HYPOTHESIS The same amount of water takes up more space when it is frozen.

PROCEDURE Fill an empty soup can with water. (Be careful of sharp can edges.) Set the can in a small bowl, and place it in the freezer section of a refrigerator. The bowl will catch any water that might spill from the can. Add more water if necessary so the water level in the can is at the very top. Leave the can of water in the freezer overnight.

In this experiment, the quantity of water is being held *constant*, and the temperature is our *variable*.

Take the can of ice out of the freezer in the morning. The volume of water that fit into the can when it was a liquid is now too big for the can. The ice has risen above the top of the can because of the expanding water and its push against the bottom of the can.

RESULTS & CONCLUSION Write down the results of your experiment. Come to a conclusion as to whether or not your hypothesis was correct.

SOMETHING MORE Quantify how much more volume the ice takes up than it did as a liquid by using displacement, which is explained in the project on page 226. Hold the can tightly to melt the ice slightly around the edges of the can so the ice will come out as one block. Dip the block in a container of water and measure the water that it displaces.

LOOK AT THE SOUND

LIGHT SPEED FASTER THAN SOUND SPEED

PURPOSE Prove that sound travels much slower than light through the medium of air.

YOU NEED
- an adult with a car
- a straight, mile-long, open stretch of road

OVERVIEW Lightning streaks across the sky. Wait! It's only then you hear the rumble of thunder. You hear a jet plane flying high overhead. You look up immediately, but it's already way past you. You're at a baseball stadium, far from home plate. The batter's ready. There's the pitch! It's a hit, and the ball starts to soar. Then, you hear the crack of the ball against the bat!

Why do we see things before we hear them? Could it be because the speed of light is faster than speed of sound through the air? (Actually, light travels 186,000 miles per second, so when something happens we see it almost instantly. Sound travels through the air much more slowly, only about 1,100 feet per second—764 miles per hour at 32° Fahrenheit—slightly faster at higher temperatures.)

HYPOTHESIS We can prove that sound travels more slowly than light through air.

PROCEDURE Find an open stretch of road at least a mile long. Some evening, as you stand safely off to the side of the road, have an adult with a car drive one mile away, then turn the car around and turn the headlights on and "beep" the horn at the exact same time. Do you see the flash of the headlights before you hear the sound of the horn?

The *constants* are the distance and the time the headlights are turned on and the horn is sounded. The *variable* is the time it takes for the light and sound to go from car to you.

RESULTS & CONCLUSION Write down the results of your experiment. Come to a conclusion as to whether or not your hypothesis was correct.

SOMETHING MORE
1. Does wind direction have an effect on the travel of sound through the air?
2. Does sound take so long to reach your ears that, in the above experiment, the driver could blink the lights on and off several times before you even hear the horn?
3. What things can transmit sound but not light, or light but not sound? Think about a supernova or a railroad track.

WORK = FORCE × DISTANCE

THE WEDGE, A SIMPLE MACHINE

PURPOSE To show the relationship between the distance a wedge is moved forward and the height of an object sitting on top of the wedge is raised.

OVERVIEW A "wedge" is one of those "simple machines" we talked about. A wedge is an object in the shape of a triangle. A doorstop and the metal head of an axe are examples of wedges.

When an axe or chopping maul is used to split firewood, the worker swings the tool over a large distance to strike the wood with great force. That force is turned into the small distance covered by the wedge, as the axe moves down into the wood to split it. In science, "work" is a measurement equal to "force" times "distance."

When a force is applied to a wedge, the force moves the wedge forward, but it also moves anything resting on top of the wedge into an upward direction (at a 90-degree angle to the forward movement of the wedge).

A wedge can be used to lift very heavy objects a short distance. House movers sometimes use wedges between the sill plate and the foundation to raise a house up so steel girders can be slid under it.

> **YOU NEED**
> - a wide strip of thick cardboard, about 12 inches (30 cm) long
> - two rulers
> - small, light cardboard box (shoebox or a similar size)
> - scissors
> - pencil
> - paper
> - 1 or more heavy books

HYPOTHESIS Using a wedge increases the amount of force in a perpendicular direction, but we pay for it in a decrease in distance.

PROCEDURE Draw a right triangle on a thick piece of cardboard. Make the triangle about 2 inches (5 cm) tall by about 12 inches (30 cm) in length. The hypotenuse of the triangle will form a long, gently sloping ramp. Use scissors to cut the triangle out.

Place a small, light box on a table. A shoebox would be perfect. At one end of the box, stack one or two heavy books. That will keep the box from sliding.

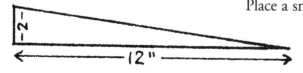

At the other end, place your cutout wedge so that its pointed tip just slips under the box. Lay a ruler alongside the box, with the zero mark on the ruler at the edge of the box where the wedge touches the box. The length of the ruler should face away from the wedge (running parallel to the side of the box).

Push on the wedge so that it slides 2 inches (5 cm) under the box. Use another ruler to measure how high the end of the box is raised above the table.

On a piece of paper, draw two vertical columns. Label the heading on one column "distance wedge moved" and the other column "height raised." Write the measurement under the first heading and the distance the box was raised in the second column.

The *constant* in this project is the incline (the slope) of the wedge, the box it is lifting, and the force applied. The *variables* are the distance the wedge is moved inward and the height it pushes up on the box.

Now push the box forward another inch or centimeter, and record the height raised. Continue to push the wedge under the box at each increment, until the top of the wedge is reached. Write down the distance and the height for each move increment.

RESULTS & CONCLUSION Write down the results of your experiment. Come to a conclusion as to whether or not your hypothesis was correct.

SOMETHING MORE A wedge doorstop is a stationary wedge that is applying a force equal to the force needed to keep the door from closing.

A nail is also a wedge. Can you imagine pushing something into a piece of wood that doesn't come to a point? The smaller the nail, the easier it is to wedge into the wood, because it has less wood material to push out of the way. Try pushing a nail into a piece of wood by hand. Then try pushing a thumbtack with a head on it into the same piece of wood. Is the thumbtack much easier to push in?

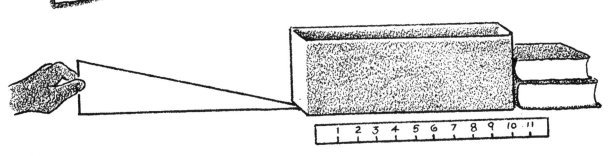

WATER SHOOTER

COMPRESSING A FLUID

PURPOSE Let's learn a little about "hydraulics."

OVERVIEW Hydraulics, from the Greek word meaning "about water," is the study of liquid in motion. A part of hydraulics deals with compressing a liquid, used in machines where great pushing or lifting strength is needed. A force pushing on any part of an enclosed liquid creates an equal pressure per unit of area on everything the liquid touches. By using a system of pistons (cylindrical containers filled with a liquid), great force can be achieved.

YOU NEED
- squeeze bottle with spout top
- a piece of heavy board
- water
- ruler

HYPOTHESIS When water is compressed and forced to flow out of an opening, the velocity of the water will be much greater if the opening is small than if it is large.

PROCEDURE Outside, remove the spout and fill the squeeze bottle with water. Set the board on its side and tilt the container against it. Let water leak out until it stops; the angle will keep most of the water inside. Then with your hand, strike the side of the bottle, forcing water out through the opening. Watch how far the stream of water shoots.

Again, fill the squeeze bottle with water, set it against the board and let the water leak out. This time, screw on the spout. Keeping the volume of water *constant* (by tilting) as well as the striking force used on the bottle, our *variable* will be the diameter of the opening through which the water escapes. The spout makes the opening much smaller. Strike the side of the container again, using the same amount of force as before. Does the stream of water travel farther with the spout on? Does that mean the velocity of the water coming out was greater?

RESULTS & CONCLUSION Write down the results of your experiment. Come to a conclusion as to whether or not your hypothesis was correct.

SOMETHING MORE Compare the amount of water coming out of the bottle with the spout off and with it on. Use a measuring cup to quantify the volume of water in the bottle before and after each strike. Perhaps, with the spout on, less water is coming out? Did you strike the bottle with the same force each time? Can you find a way to be sure?

SIPHON FUN

WATER DRAINS TO OWN LEVEL

PURPOSE Discover how a siphon works.

OVERVIEW A hose or tube can be used to create a "siphon," a device that drains liquids. A siphon will drain liquid from a higher to a lower level, even if it first has to travel uphill! A hose placed with one end underwater in an above-ground swimming pool and the rest draped over the side and down to the ground will drain water out of the pool. To get the flow started, it may be necessary to suck on the low end of the hose. Once the flow begins, gravity pulls the liquid down, creating a vacuum in the tube that draws the liquid up and through the tube.

YOU NEED
- two 2-liter soda bottles
- long piece of aquarium tubing
- several books
- water

HYPOTHESIS Water can be made to rise above its level through the use of a siphon.

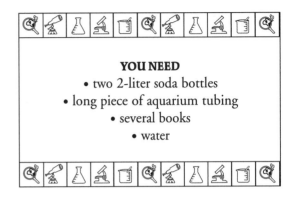

PROCEDURE Stack books on a table. Fill a clear plastic bottle with water and place it on the books. Set an empty bottle near it, but on a lower level—*not* on the books. Insert one end of plastic tubing, available at pet shops, into the bottle of water. Be sure there is space around the tubing in the bottle's neck (if it is air-tight, the siphon will not work). The end of the tubing should touch the bottom of the bottle. Suck on the other end of the tubing, as you would a soda straw, to get the water flowing, then insert the tube into the empty bottle. Push the tubing in so it touches the bottom of the bottle.

Held *constant* is gravity, the volume of water, the lack of air in the tube system, and the bottles. The motion of the water from higher to lower bottle is the *variable*.

RESULTS & CONCLUSION Write down the results of your experiment. Come to a conclusion as to whether or not your hypothesis was correct.

SOMETHING MORE
1. Once the lower bottle is filled, do you think that the siphon would work in reverse? What if the full bottle was now raised higher than the one on the books?
2. Does it take the same amount of time for the bottle to empty each time the experiment is done, so that it could be used as a sort of "water clock"?

WHIRRING BUTTON

TORQUE: CHANGING THE DIRECTION OF FORCE

PURPOSE To learn about torque and changing the direction of a force. A force pulling outward can be changed into a force at a 90-degree angle and made to do work, causing a button on a string to spin.

OVERVIEW A force can push or pull an object along a straight line. When a force is used to rotate, or turn, an object, physicists have a special name for the force. They call it "torque."

Torque has a direction associated with it. Look at these drawings. As your wrist turns a screwdriver clockwise, the force rotates the screw forward into the wood. That torque, or force, is in a different direction from the turning force applied by your wrist. The same is true when a wrench is used to turn a nut on a bolt.

YOU NEED
- ruler
- scissors
- 2 identical, large flat buttons, with two or four holes
- cotton thread
- a friend

HYPOTHESIS A change in the length of string used to cause a button to spin will cause a change in the rate of the rotating button.

PROCEDURE Loop a piece of cotton thread through a hole in a large button, and then back through another hole. Cut the thread to a length of 2 feet (61 cm) and then tie the ends together. In the same way, loop a piece of cotton thread through an identical button, but cut the length

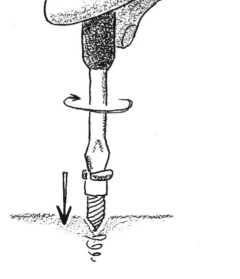

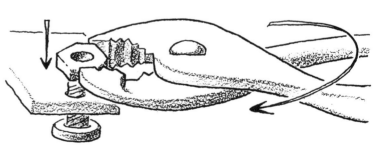

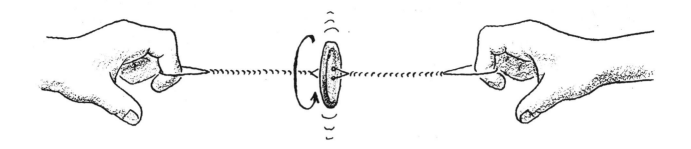

of this piece of thread to 4 feet (122 cm), and then tie the ends together.

Hold the looped thread between two hands, moving the button to the middle of the thread. Move your hands together so that the button hangs down, and use a circular motion with your hands to swing the button around and around, winding up the thread, until it has wrapped many, many times. Have a friend hold the second button and longer string, and wind the thread in a similar way, giving it the same number of turns as you do.

Note: If your flat buttons have four holes instead of two, you can place the thread through two diagonal holes, as shown.

At the same time, both you and your friend pull outward with each hand, and the thread will begin to unwrap, causing the buttons to spin. The outward pulling force of your hands is being changed into the rotating motion of the button.

The mass of the buttons and the number of winding turns was held *constant*, and the length of the string was the *variable*. We are "assuming" that the force pulling outward on both button devices is equal. Repeat the test, exchanging whirring buttons.

Does one device spin faster than the other? Do the spinning buttons set up vibrations in the air causing a tone that is audible—that you can hear? If so, is the pitch higher on one than the other? Is the higher pitch coming from the button that is rotating faster?

RESULTS & CONCLUSION Write down the results of your experiment. Come to a conclusion as to whether or not your hypothesis was correct.

SOMETHING MORE
1. Experiment using different threads: does string or monofilament line (fishing line) work better or worse in rotating a button? What effect does changing the size of the button have on the speed of rotation?
2. Can you think of other places in our daily lives where torque force is used?

TOY STORY

TORQUE-ENERGY STORAGE IN A HOMEMADE TOY

PURPOSE Determine the optimum (best) number of rubber band windings for an ice-pop toy.

YOU NEED
- 3 ice-cream pop sticks
- rubber band
- hardbound book

OVERVIEW This simple, old-time, homemade toy demonstrates three concepts of physics: potential energy, torque, and elasticity. A stick is placed inside the loop of a rubber band and turned, so the band is wound up. The wound band has "potential" energy; that is, stored energy that, when released, becomes "kinetic" energy. As with the whirring button in the previous project, the concept of "torque," a twisting force, is also demonstrated.

The more a rubber band is twisted, the more potential energy it can store. But is there a point where additional winding does no more good, or can even be bad?

HYPOTHESIS A certain number of elastic band turns will consistently give the best results.

PROCEDURE Hold one ice-cream stick in each hand and place a rubber band around them. In the middle of the rubber band, place a third stick.

Turn the center stick, winding the rubber band tighter and tighter. Count the number of turns. After it is wound many times, carefully place the toy under a book on a table. Lift up the book and the toy will dance.

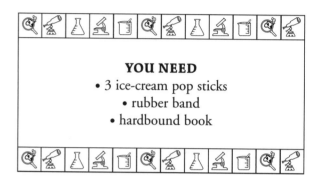

Wind the toy again, this time making five more turns than before. The elastic band and the sticks are *constants*, while the number of turns is the *variable*. Does the toy dance better with the extra twists?

Experiment by adding more and more windings. Is there a limit to the torque energy stored in the elastic band beyond which there is no benefit?

RESULTS & CONCLUSION Write down the results of your experiment. Come to a conclusion about your hypothesis.

SOMETHING MORE At what point does the toy have potential energy? Kinetic energy? What effect does using different rubber bands (longer or thicker) have on the energy stored? (For fun, surprise family and friends with hidden, dancing torque toys of all sizes!)

WALLS DON'T MOVE

NEWTON'S THIRD: ACTION AND REACTION

PURPOSE Understanding the physics concept of work through force and distance.

OVERVIEW Newton's Third Law of Motion explains that if one body exerts a force on a second body (action), the second body exerts an equal force in the opposite direction (reaction),

back to the first body. In other words: For every action there is an equal and opposite reaction. Imagine yourself and a friend floating in a swimming pool, in two inner tubes touching each other. If you push your friend's tube away, the force will push back and yours will move, too. Astronauts in orbiting spacecraft push against walls in order to float backward. Work, in physics, is defined as: work = force × distance. Since anything multiplied by zero is zero, if either force or distance is zero, then work equals zero.

HYPOTHESIS According to the physics definition of work, it is possible that no work is done, no matter how much effort is used.

PROCEDURE Wearing shoes that won't slip, stand facing a wall and push on it as hard as you can. The wall doesn't move, and you don't move. Force × distance = zero. No work was done (no distance, no work). Even if you pushed long enough to work up a sweat and you were out of breath from trying, technically no work was done because nothing moved. Although effort or force was applied, no work was accomplished!

Now, put on roller or in-line skates. Face the wall and push against it. Again, the wall doesn't move, but a force equal and opposite to yours pushes back, causing you to roll away from the wall. The wheels reduced friction, you rolled . . . and work was done!

RESULTS & CONCLUSION Write down the results of your experiment. Come to a conclusion as to whether or not your hypothesis was correct.

SOMETHING MORE Measure the distance you traveled from the wall by pushing on it. If you push harder (apply more force), does the distance increase? Is the distance you travel in relation to the force you apply?

SANDWATER

EROSION CAUSED BY FRICTION OF GLACIAL ICE

PURPOSE Without taking hundreds of years, we can demonstrate the erosive effect of a glacier.

YOU NEED
- sand
- 2 paper cups
- water
- use of a freezer
- an old painted board
- a pair of heavy gloves or mittens

OVERVIEW There are places in the world where the heat of summer is not enough to completely melt the snow that has fallen during the winter. Some of the snow that does melt into water makes its way deep into the snow, where it turns into ice. As each year goes by, more and more layers of ice are built up, and the underlying layers become pressed tighter and tighter. A "glacier" is formed.

Glaciers can be as small as a few acres. Ice-sheet glaciers can spread out like continents. The Antarctic ice sheet is about 5 million square miles in area, about one and a quarter times the area of the United States.

Often, glaciers form on the side of mountains. When they become heavy enough, they begin to slide down the mountain slope. This movement is very slow, perhaps only a few inches or centimeters a day. But as this tremendous mass moves, it picks up stones and other materials that it then rubs against the rocks and ground underneath, causing erosion. The incredible force of glacier movement can change the way the terrain looks; it can even shear off the sides of mountains and change a "V" shaped valley into a "U" shape. The friction and force of glacier ice acts like sandpaper, eroding away even very hard rocks.

HYPOTHESIS Sand embedded in ice will cause abrasions in a surface it rubs against.

PROCEDURE Fill a paper cup with water. Place it in a freezer. Line the bottom of another paper cup with sand. Fill the cup with water, and place it in a freezer.

When the water has completely turned to ice in the two cups, take them out of the freezer. Remove the ice from the cups by turning the cups upside down until they slide out.

Pull on a pair of gloves or mittens to protect your hands. Pick up the blocks and turn them back over (sand side down). Hold a block of ice in each hand. Pushing fairly hard, rub both blocks of ice with equal strokes on an old painted board.

After several minutes, examine the area of the board that the two ice blocks were rubbed against.

Does the area rubbed by the "sand-ice" block look different from the area rubbed with the smooth ice? Are there scratches? Rub your figures gently over the board. Does one feel more abrasive than the other?

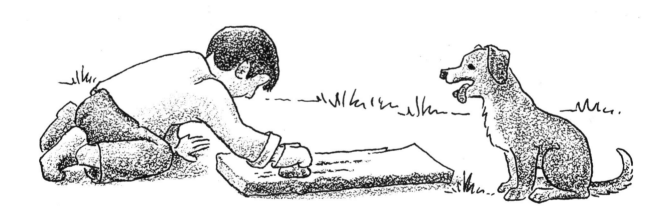

RESULTS & CONCLUSION Write down the results of your experiment. Come to a conclusion as to whether or not your hypothesis was correct.

SOMETHING MORE
1. As you increase the rubbing pressure, do the gouged-out, scratched areas get deeper? Do you think a heavier glacier would cause more erosion than one of less mass?
2. Make a comparison of the abrasion caused by a block of ice with fine sand particles embedded in it to one with coarse sand.

BACK IN SHAPE

THE CHARACTERISTICS OF ELASTICITY

PURPOSE The purpose is to find the effect of weathering and stretching on the elasticity of a rubber band.

OVERVIEW One characteristic of a material is a measure of its "elasticity." Elasticity is the ability of a material to return to its original shape after it has been stretched or pressed together. Balloons and rubber bands are very elastic. Can you think of other examples?

Have you ever seen a rubber band wrapped around a newspaper or something else that has been outside for some time? Have you ever seen an old rubber band that has been wrapped around something in an attic for many years? Can you observe cracks in the bands? Are they able to be stretched? Do they snap back to a smaller shape?

YOU NEED
- 2 identical rubber bands
- 2 paper clips
- large empty milk carton
- water
- clothesline
- nail or awl, to poke a small hole in the milk carton

HYPOTHESIS After a rubber band has been stretched and exposed to outdoor weathering elements for several days, the elasticity of the rubber band will be affected, and it will not return to its original shape.

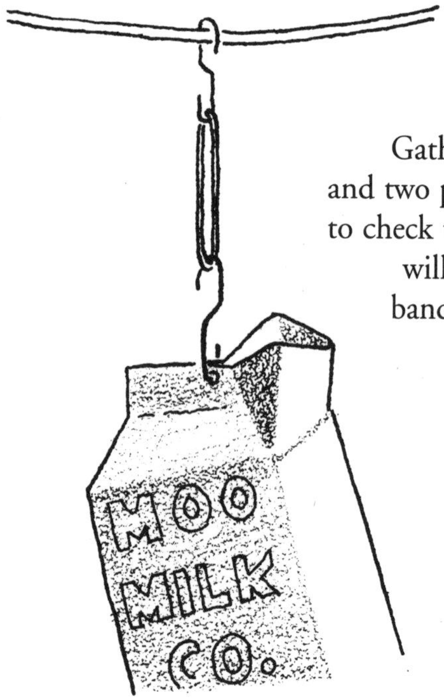

PROCEDURE For this project, we'll need a device to test the elasticity of material.

Gather two identical rubber bands, a large empty milk carton, and two paper clips. Lay the two rubber bands on top of each other to check that they are as equal in shape as possible. The rubber band will be our *constant*. Our *variable* will be to stretch one rubber band and expose it to weather, while the other will remain unstretched and indoors, protected from weathering.

Bend open the paper clips to make "S" shaped hooks. Carefully poke a hole in the top of a large empty milk carton, and insert a paper clip hook through it.

Hang another paper clip hook on an outdoor clothesline and drape a rubber band on the bottom part of the paper clip hook. Hang the milk carton on the rubber band using the paper clip hook in the carton, as shown at left.

Pour some water into the milk carton. This will create a weight to stretch the rubber band. We want to stretch the rubber band a lot, but not to the breaking point. Since rubber bands are not all the same, we can't tell you how much water to add to the carton. (Science is not always like a food recipe!) Slowly add more water to the milk carton until it looks like the rubber band is well stretched, but not in danger of breaking.

Leave the rubber band stretching device hanging on the clothesline for three or four days. Then, carefully, take the device apart and remove the rubber band. Line it up next to the other identical one that you had put aside indoors and compare them. Has the stretched one changed shape? Is it able to completely return to its original shape?

Inspect the stretched rubber band closely. Are you able to see any cracks, discolorations, or other signs of deterioration caused by the experiment?

RESULTS & CONCLUSION Write down the results of your experiment. Come to a conclusion as to whether or not your hypothesis was correct.

SOMETHING MORE Can you use your stretching device to test the elasticity of other materials or objects?

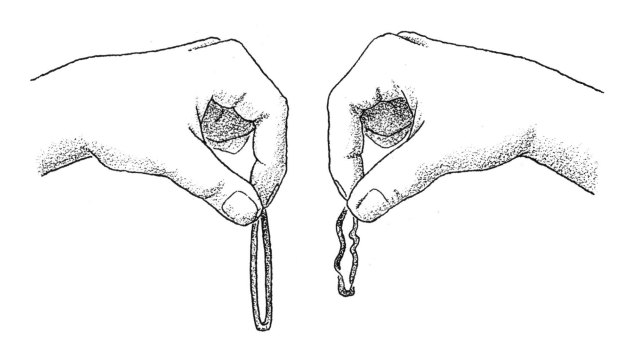

DON'T FRET

CHANGING PITCH BY VARYING STRING TENSION

PURPOSE An understanding of frequency change through an increase in tension on a stretched rubber band.

OVERVIEW Some musical instruments have strings that vibrate in order to make sounds: guitar, banjo, violin, and harp, to name a few. A string is pulled taut and "plucked." The plucking force applied to the string causes it to vibrate. The mechanical vibrations are converted to sound by our ears.

As a string is pulled tighter by tuning pegs on the instrument, the frequency of its vibration increases and the notes sound higher in pitch. On a guitar and bass guitar, strings are kept under tension as they are stretched across a long wooden neck. The instrument has "frets" that the musician places his fingers against to shorten the strings that are played, changing the pitch of the sound.

YOU NEED
- large rubber band
- piece of board about 1 foot (30 cm) long
- nail
- small play bucket
- different size stones
- scissors
- hammer

HYPOTHESIS The more a rubber band is stretched, the higher the pitch it makes when it's made to vibrate.

PROCEDURE Hammer a nail partway into a piece of wood about 1 foot (30 cm) long and several inches or centimeters wide. The wood should be ½-inch (1.25 cm) thick or more. Don't pound the nail all the way in. Set the board near the edge of a table.

With scissors, cut a large rubber band in half. Tie one end to the nail and the other end to the handle of a small toy bucket, the kind a young child might use in a sandbox or to play with on the beach.

Drape the rubber band and bucket over the board lengthwise and off the end of the table, so that the bucket hangs in the air.

Put a few stones in the bucket to put tension on the rubber band. With your finger, pluck the length of rubber band that is stretched across the board. Like the string on a guitar or violin, the band will vibrate, producing a sound that you can hear.

Add a few stones to the bucket to stretch the rubber band even more. Pluck the band again.

Is the note sound higher or lower than before? The rubber band is the *constant* in the experiment, and the amount it is stretched is the *variable*.

RESULTS & CONCLUSION Write down the results of your experiment. Come to a conclusion as to whether or not your hypothesis was correct.

SOMETHING MORE

1. Can you add or take away stones from the bucket to match a note from the rubber band to a piano, organ, or guitar in your home? You must have a "musical ear" to be able to tell when a note on your instrument is in tune with one on the real instrument. If you do not have a good ear for matching notes, have a friend who is taking music lessons help you. Someone who has music training may do best at matching notes.

2. **Challenge Project:** Our musical scale consists of 12 notes in an octave. Take your project further by constructing 13 rubber band systems, each one stretched to be in tune with a different piano note (the 13th note being one octave higher than the beginning one).

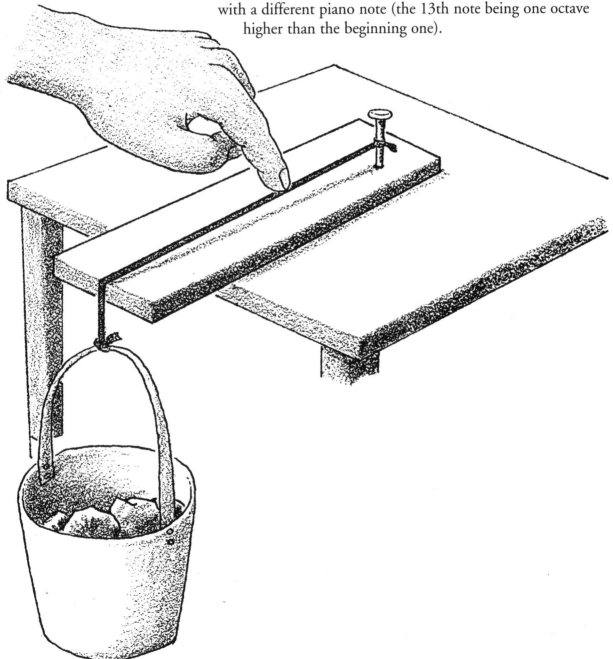

SPACE SAVER

THE CONCEPT OF VOLUME

PURPOSE Learn that an object's weight (mass) can remain the same, regardless of its shape.

OVERVIEW Space in landfills, where towns and cities get rid of their trash and garbage, is limited. When things can be compressed so they take up less room, landfill space is preserved.

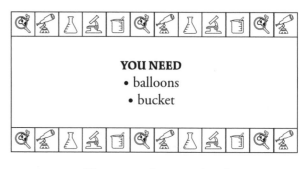

YOU NEED
- balloons
- bucket

The volume of an object is a measure of how much space it takes up. Tin cans and aluminum soda cans, those that are not returned to stores for the deposit, are among the items collected and recycled so the metal can be reused. Cans in a recycling truck can take up a lot of room. If they were crushed, they would have far less volume, so they would take up much less space. But, they would still weigh the same.

HYPOTHESIS Objects can be made to have less volume but still keep the same mass.

PROCEDURE Instead of crushing soda cans to demonstrate volume, we'll use balloons. Inflate some, making each balloon about the size of a soda can. In a bucket, put in as many balloons as you can fit.

Now, take the balloons out of the bucket and lay them on a table. Count them. Lay the same number of uninflated balloons next to them. Compare the difference in the volume of the uninflated balloons to the inflated balloons—much different, right?—yet both weigh about the same. (Since air actually has some weight, the inflated balloons do weigh more, but the amount is negligible—not an important, easily measured, difference.)

RESULTS & CONCLUSION Write down the results of your experiment. Come to a conclusion as to whether or not your hypothesis was correct.

SOMETHING MORE Quantify the volume by how much water can be stored in a balloon. Does each balloon hold one quart? Buckets are usually sold by the number of quarts they can hold. Does a 12-quart bucket hold 12 quart-filled water balloons?

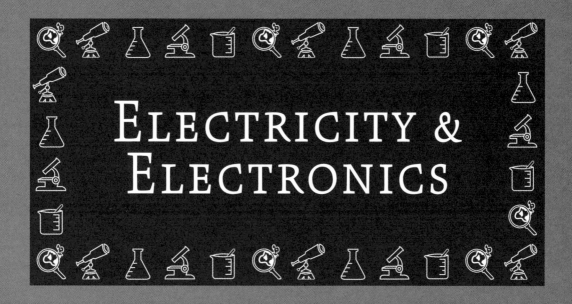

ELECTRICITY & ELECTRONICS

INTRODUCTION TO
ELECTRICITY & ELECTRONICS

This portion of the book deals with a wide variety of topics related to electricity and electronics. Choose from a subject area that you like best. We suggest making a "schematic diagram" of projects that use electrical circuits. This will enhance your display visually, and increase understanding. A schematic diagram is a pictorial layout of an electrical circuit, showing the arrangement of components and how they are connected. Symbols are used to represent the various components. Some standard symbols are shown in the back of the book.

No one knows what electricity is. We have learned how to generate it and how to make it do work. We understand its properties, how it behaves, and what takes place at the atomic level. But we really don't know what it is.

Electricity refers to the movement of electrons through a conducting medium (a pathway) such as copper and silver. Electron movement is energy that we can put to work to improve our daily lives.

The difference between what we call electricity and electronics is small. Generally, electronics is considered to be a branch within the science of electricity. Electronics deals with electricity as it moves through and is affected by certain devices. These devices include resistors, capacitors, coils, transistors, and integrated circuits.

The human race has harnessed electric power to perform tasks from illuminating a simple light bulb to making a calculating machine called a computer which can do math operations at tremendous speeds.

Electronics is among the most rapidly changing sciences. Technological advancements are made every year. Consider how far computer technology has come in the relatively short time since the first commercially available home computers were introduced around 1977.

In most homes today you will find a wealth of electronic marvels: computers, stereos, televisions, radios, telephones, laser music discs, copy machines. Electrical appliances have enhanced our standard of living: washing machines, hair dryers, vacuum cleaners, toasters, microwave ovens, electric can openers, and refrigerators.

Many specific topics fall under the blanket category, "electricity and electronics." Topics in this book include electromagnetic forces, static electricity, current flow, motors and generators, resistance and capacitance, generating electricity, solid state electronics, and radio frequency energy. You have only to make your selection, and begin your project.

SECTION 1
ELECTROMAGNETIC FORCES

Magnetism is an electromagnetic force that occurs between certain materials in nature. Magnetism can be found in rocks called "lodestones" (sometimes referred to as "magnetite"). Lodestones exert an attractive force on materials containing iron. Iron can be turned into a magnet by stroking it with a lodestone. It can be said that we inhabit a magnet. Early experimenters, around (1200 AD), determined that the planet we live on is a huge magnet.

Electricity and magnetism are related. It was discovered that, when an electric current flows in a wire, the needle of a compass placed next to the wire will be deflected. The same holds true in reverse; when a magnetic field is moved past an electrical conductor, current is generated. This concept is the basis for electric motors and generators.

ATTRACTIVE FORCE

RELATIONSHIP OF WIRE TURNS TO ATTRACTION IN ELECTROMAGNET

PURPOSE Does the voltage strength passing through a wire affect the strength of the magnetic field?

OVERVIEW When current passes through a wire, a magnetic field is built up around the outside of the wire. You can make a simple electromagnet (a magnet that attracts only when it is connected to a power source) by wrapping wire around a nail and connecting one end of the wire to the positive side of a battery terminal and the other to the negative.

HYPOTHESIS Hypothesize that the magnetic field will be stronger if the voltage is higher.

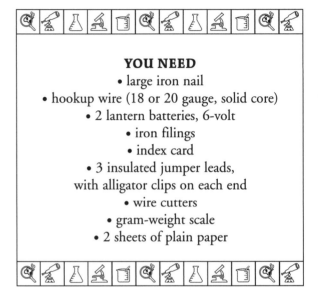

YOU NEED
- large iron nail
- hookup wire (18 or 20 gauge, solid core)
- 2 lantern batteries, 6-volt
- iron filings
- index card
- 3 insulated jumper leads, with alligator clips on each end
- wire cutters
- gram-weight scale
- 2 sheets of plain paper

PROCEDURE Cut a length of hookup wire, about 18 or 20 gauge, to a length of about 3 to 4 feet (90–120 cm). Wrap the wire in a spiral motion around a large iron nail. Strip 1 inch (2.5 cm) of insulation off each end of the wire to expose the bare wire inside. Using an insulated jumper lead with alligator clips on each end, attach an alligator clip to one of the ends of the wire. Connect the other alligator clip to the positive terminal of a 6-volt lantern battery. Using another insulated jumper lead with alligator clips, attach an alligator clip to the other end of the wire that is wrapped around the nail. Connect the other alligator clip to the negative terminal on the battery.

Note: Since the wire that is wrapped around the nail is almost a dead short, having very little resistance to current flow, the battery will not last very long before it begins to lose its power. For that reason, only connect the alligator clips to the battery while the experiment is actually being done. One alligator clip can be connected at all times, since no current will flow unless both are connected.

To prove that the hypothesis is correct, the strength of the electromagnet must be measured. This can be done by seeing how many iron filings the electromagnet can collect. The iron filings that are collected can be weighed.

Pour some iron filings onto a sheet of typing paper. To keep the electromagnet from getting dirty, rest an index card on top of the iron filing pile. Hold the point of the nail on top of the index card and connect the battery. Slowly pull the card and nail up away from the iron filing pile. Be sure the nail point touches the index card. Some filings will be hanging underneath the index card, attracted by the magnetic field. Hold the card and nail over a second clean sheet of typing paper to catch the iron filings. Turn the electromagnet off by disconnecting one of the alligator clips on the battery. The iron filings will fall onto the paper. Lightly shake loose any filings that stick to the index card. Weigh the filings by placing the paper onto a gram weight scale. Write down the weight registering.

Repeat the experiment, but this time use 12 volts instead of 6 volts. Two 6-volt batteries can be connected together to give a total of 12 volts. Connect a jumper lead with alligator clips on each end to the positive terminal (+) of one battery and the negative terminal (–) of the second battery. Connect the two clips attached to the electromagnet to the two empty terminals on the batteries. Use fresh iron filings for the second test to avoid possible magnetized filings. Use the index card again to gather iron filings. Weigh the filings gathered. Compare the weights of the iron filings collected the first and second times.

RESULTS & CONCLUSION Write down the results of your experiment. Come to a conclusion as to whether or not your hypothesis was correct.

SOMETHING MORE Is there a direct relationship between the number of turns of wire on the nail and the amount of filings it collects? For example, will twice as many turns collect twice as many iron filings?

FILED UNDER CURRENT

MAGNETIC LINES OF FLUX AND MAGNET'S DC POLARITY

PURPOSE Does the direction (polarity) the current is flowing in the wire make a difference in the shape of the magnetic field?

OVERVIEW When electric current flows through a wire, a magnetic field is established surrounding the wire. This field has a pattern of lines called "flux lines," or "lines of force," by early experimenters. The pattern can be seen by sprinkling iron filings onto an index card and placing the magnetic source underneath. When the index card is tapped, the iron filings shift and align themselves with the magnetic field, and the pattern made by the lines of force becomes visible.

YOU NEED
- spool of solid conductor hookup wire
- 1.5-volt "D" cell alkaline battery
- "D" cell battery holder
- index card
- 3-inch iron nail
- powdered iron filings
- wire cutters

HYPOTHESIS Hypothesize that the direction of current flow through a wire does not affect the pattern shape of the magnetic lines of force, that the pattern will be the same regardless of the polarity of the source voltage supplying power to the wire.

PROCEDURE Cut a 2-foot (6 cm) length of solid conductor hookup wire and strip about ¼ inch (.6 cm) of insulation off both ends. Wrap 25 turns of wire around an iron nail about 3 inches (7.6 cm) long. Twist the positive wire coming from the battery holder to one end of the wire coiled around the nail. Connect the negative wire to the other end of the coiled wire. The reason for coiling the wire around a nail is to strengthen the magnetic field. The strengthened field makes the iron particles line up more distinctly. An "electromagnet" has just been constructed.

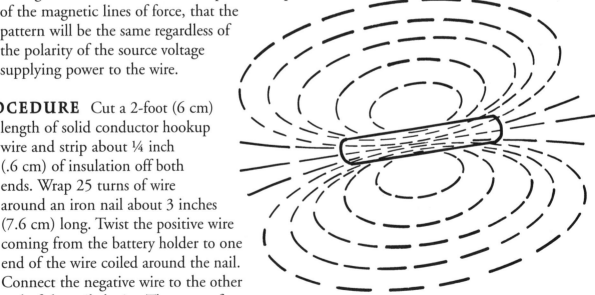

Magnetic lines of flux surrounding magnet

Lay the coiled wire-nail assembly flat on a table. Sprinkle powdered iron filings on an index card. Place the index card on top of the nail. Put a battery in the battery holder. Tap the index card several times until the iron filings form an observable pattern.

Next, without disturbing the iron filings and the coil underneath, reverse the positive and negative battery leads. You may want to use a double pole switch to reverse these leads. Observe whether or not the pattern changes and reach a conclusion about your hypothesis.

Note: Once the electric current is removed, some iron filings that were piled on top of each other may fall. When power is reapplied, they may align themselves identically again due to gravity.

RESULTS & CONCLUSION Write down the results of your experiment. Come to a conclusion as to whether or not your hypothesis was correct.

SOMETHING MORE

1. Why doesn't AC (alternating current) work with this experiment?
2. Does the magnetic field produce more lines of flux at the ends of the nail when the voltage to the coil of wire is increased? What about the lines along the sides of the nail?
3. Does the shape of the pattern change as the number of windings are increased, or if the nature of the wire (gauge, composition) is changed?
4. Can you diagram an "end on" field? In other words, place the magnet in a vertical position?
5. Is there a way to focus the lines of flux?
6. Put a paper clip next to a magnet. How does it affect the pattern of the lines of force?

SHORT STOP IN A MAGNETIC FIELD

ELECTRICAL INSULATORS NOT NECESSARILY MAGNETIC INSULATORS

PURPOSE Are materials that are insulators to electrical flow also insulators, or shields, for magnetic flow?

OVERVIEW All materials conduct electricity to some degree. Insulators are materials that do not conduct electricity well. They have a resistance so high that they block current flow. Magnetic insulators are materials which do not allow magnetic fields to pass. They shield magnetic fields and do not let magnetism affect objects on the other side.

HYPOTHESIS Hypothesize that electrical insulators are not necessarily magnetic insulators.

YOU NEED
- powdered iron filings
- wax candle
- an adult with matches
- plastic sandwich bag
- magnet
- ohmmeter
- old ashtray
- small brown-paper lunch bag
- 12-inch square of aluminum foil
- glass test tube
- iron frying pan
- water
- graphic art materials (to make display chart)

PROCEDURE Sprinkle some powdered iron filings into an old metal ashtray or metal lid of any wide-mouth jar. Have an adult assist in lighting a candle and dripping a few drops of the hot wax into the iron filings. The filings will stick to the wax, making several tiny balls. We will use these iron balls and a magnet to test the magnetic insulating ability of several materials.

Using graphic art supplies, make a display chart listing materials to be tested for electrical and magnetic insulation properties: aluminum, glass, iron, and water, for example.

Use an ohmmeter to check the resistance of each material and record your results on the chart. Fill in the chart with either "YES" if it is an insulator, or "NO" if it is not an insulator. If the ohmmeter needle does not move, then it is an electrical insulator. If the meter indicates the resistance is only a few ohms, then it is an excellent electrical conductor.

Next, test each material for its magnetic insulating ability. To test the plastic bag, place one of the iron-wax balls inside the bag. Place a magnet on the outside of the bag and try to move the ball inside. If the ball is able to be moved, then the bag is not a magnetic insulator. Use the same procedure to test a brown-paper bag and a glass test tube. Then fill the glass test tube with water and attempt to move the ball. To test a sheet of aluminum and an iron frying pan, hold it flat (horizontally), place an iron-wax ball on top, and try to move the ball by moving a magnet around underneath.

RESULTS & CONCLUSION Study the charted results of the data. Come to a conclusion as to whether or not your hypothesis was correct.

SOMETHING MORE

1. Test other materials such as tin, zinc, copper, rubber (use a balloon).
2. Test combinations of materials, a layer of rubber on top of a layer of aluminum, for example.
3. What affect does distance have on magnetism?
4. Test some materials that fall somewhere between being an electrical insulator and an excellent conductor.

RUST IN PIECES

COMPARING MAGNETIC PROPERTIES OF
IRON AND RUST

PURPOSE Does iron rust have different magnetic properties than iron?

OVERVIEW When iron is exposed to damp air, a chemical process takes place, changing the iron to "iron rust" (hydrated iron oxide). The process of oxygen in the air combining with iron is called oxidation. During our procedure, we will collect a magnetic load of rusted filings and compare it with a magnetic load of regular filings.

YOU NEED
- iron filings
- water
- magnet
- gram-weight scale
- index card
- 2 paper cups
- ice-cream stick

HYPOTHESIS Hypothesize that one group will weigh more than the other or that they will be equal.

PROCEDURE Cut two small paper cups in half sideways and throw away the top parts. Put several teaspoons of iron filings in one shortened paper cup, and several more in the second paper cup. Add water to the iron filings in one cup and let the filings soak for about an hour. Drain off the water and let it dry overnight.

In the morning, the rusty iron filings will be stuck together. Use a popsicle stick to thoroughly loosen the different particles.

Place an index card over the top of the paper cup containing the iron filings that were not exposed to water. Lay a magnet on top of the index card. Slowly lift the card and magnet. Iron particles will be clinging to the bottom of the card. Drop the iron particles onto a gram-weight scale. Measure the weight of the particles collected.

Repeat the procedure with the rusty iron filings. Is there a significant difference between the amount of unrusted iron filings and rusty iron filings collected?

RESULTS & CONCLUSION Write down the results of your experiment. Come to a conclusion as to whether or not your hypothesis was correct.

SOMETHING MORE
1. Measure the collected filings by volume.
2. Is iron rust a better or worse conductor of electricity? What effect does this have on outdoor metals that should remain good conductors of electricity (such as a lightning rod and its grounding system)?

DIRECTIONAL FLUX

INDUCING CURRENT USING SOUTH OR NORTH MAGNETIC POLES

PURPOSE How do magnetic poles effect current flow?

OVERVIEW Electricity and magnetism have similar characteristics. Each, for example, has a polarity. Magnets have a north and south pole. Electricity has positive and a negative polarity. In magnetism, *like* poles repel each other and *unlike* poles attract. This is true of electricity, too. Current flows when there is a difference in electrical potential, but not when both are exactly alike.

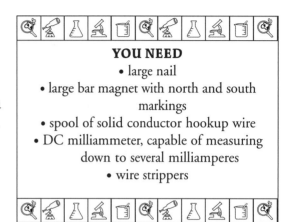

YOU NEED
- large nail
- large bar magnet with north and south markings
- spool of solid conductor hookup wire
- DC milliammeter, capable of measuring down to several milliamperes
- wire strippers

HYPOTHESIS Hypothesize that there is a polarity in the current flow induced in a wire which is cutting the lines of force in a moving magnetic field.

PROCEDURE Cut a 3-foot (91 cm) length of solid conductor hookup wire. Strip ½ inch (1.3 cm) of the insulation off each end. Wrap the wire in a spiral coil around a large nail, keeping the wire turns tight against each other and against the nail. Connect the two bare ends to the terminals of a DC milliammeter.

Using the north pole of the magnet, quickly stroke the magnet along the coil of wire in one direction only. Observe which direction the needle jumps on the meter (toward the positive or toward the negative). Using the south pole of the magnet, quickly stroke the magnet along the coil of wire in the same direction as you did with the north pole. Observe which direction the needle jumps on the meter. Was this direction opposite to when the north pole end of the magnet was used?

RESULTS & CONCLUSION Write down the results of your experiment. Come to a conclusion as to whether or not your hypothesis was correct.

SOMETHING MORE Does it matter whether you stroke the magnet over the coils from left to right or from right to left?

STROKE OF GOOD LUCK

INDUCING MAGNETISM IN IRON BY STROKING WITH PERMANENT MAGNET

PURPOSE What affects the strength of induced magnetism in iron?

OVERVIEW Any metal object attracted by a magnet becomes magnetic itself, as long as it is in contact with a real magnet. If a strong magnet comes in contact with one end of an iron nail, the other end displays magnetic characteristics and becomes capable of attracting yet another nail, forming a chain. This effect is only temporary. When the strong magnet is removed from the first nail, the second nail falls away from the first.

YOU NEED
- iron nail
- strong permanent magnet
- iron filings
- plastic sandwich bag
- typing paper
- gram-weight scale
- paper and pencil

An iron nail or piece of steel can be turned into a permanent magnet by stroking it with a strong magnet. The more the metal is stroked by the magnet, the stronger it becomes, but it can never become stronger than the original stroking magnet. How many strokes does it take for a soft-iron nail to show signs of becoming a magnet? Does a nail stroked 100 times have twice as much magnetic strength as one stroked only 50 times? What is the relationship between the number of times stroked and the strength of the magnetic field?

HYPOTHESIS Hypothesize that the strength of the induced magnet increases the more it is stroked.

PROCEDURE Pour a pile of iron filings onto some paper. Place an iron nail in a small plastic bag. Avoiding the seam, hold the side of the bag tightly against the nail. Dip the nail, head first, into the filings, then lift it out. No iron particles should adhere to the bag, indicating that the nail has no magnetism. Remove the nail from the bag.

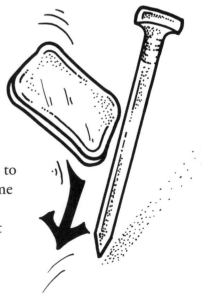

Using a strong magnet, stroke the nail 25 times. Be sure to use the same pole on the magnet and always stroke in the same direction. Start at the head end of the nail and stroke down. At the bottom, move the magnet away from the nail. Bring it back to the nail's top, touch the nail, and again stroke in a downward motion.

After 25 strokings, place the nail back into the bag and lower it into the iron filings. Slowly lift the bag straight up. Hold the bag low over a sheet of paper and remove the nail. Collect the iron particles that fall from the bag, weigh them on a gram-weight scale and record the results on a chart.

Remove the filings from the scale and hold them aside. Do not put them back into the pile because they may be magnetized and interfere with the accuracy of the project.

Stroke the nail 25 more times. Again, lower the nail in the bag into the iron filings and weigh the amount collected. Record it on the chart.

Repeat the stroking and weighing procedure for 100, 500, and 1,000 strokes. Examine the data recorded on the chart. Is there a relationship between the number of strokes and the amount of iron filings attracted?

RESULTS & CONCLUSION   Write down the results of your experiment. Come to a conclusion as to whether or not your hypothesis was correct.

SOMETHING MORE
1. Is the relationship between the number of strokes and the amount of iron filings attracted by the nail linear or exponential?
2. How many strokes does it take before a soft-iron nail becomes observably magnetic?
3. Is there an easier way to induce magnetism? Can we simply place it in the presence of an electromagnet?

DON'T LOSE YOUR COOL

MAGNETISM LOSS DUE TO HEAT

PURPOSE What effects does temperature have on induced magnetism?

OVERVIEW Heat removes magnetism. In this project, we will create three magnets from soft-iron nails, then attempt to note any observable changes in magnetism after being subjected to hot and cold temperatures.

HYPOTHESIS Hypothesize that the magnetic abilities of iron decrease with exposure to extreme temperatures.

YOU NEED
- 3 soft-iron magnets
- strong permanent magnet
- iron filings
- typing paper
- 2 bowls
- plastic sandwich bag
- gram-weight scale
- cold water
- ice cubes
- boiling water

PROCEDURE Stroke a soft-iron nail 300 times with a strong permanent magnet. Always stroke it in the same direction: from the top down, moving the magnet away from the nail once at the bottom. Touch the top again and stroke down. Be sure to use the same pole of the magnet when stroking. Repeat this procedure for each of three soft-iron nails.

Place one nail into a plastic sandwich bag. Lower it into a pile of iron filings. Slowly lift the bag straight up. Hold the bag close over a sheet of typing paper. Slowly pull the nail away and collect the iron particles that fall. Weigh the iron filings on a gram weight scale. Repeat this procedure for all three nails.

The amount of filings collected by each nail must be as equal as possible. If a nail is magnetically weaker than the others, stroke it a few more times and compare the amount of filings it attracts.

Place one nail in a bowl of cold water. Add ice cubes. Have an adult boil water and pour it into another bowl. Place a nail in the boiling water. Leave the third nail at room temperature as "the control nail." Let the nails remain in the water for about one hour, until the hot water has become cooler and the cold water less cold. Repeat the procedure of using iron filing attraction to measure the strength of the nails' magnetism. Is there any observable difference in the nails' magnetic abilities?

RESULTS & CONCLUSION Write down the results of your experiment. Come to a conclusion as to whether or not your hypothesis was correct.

SOMETHING MORE

1. Have an adult place a magnetized nail in an oven and heat it to 300° or 400° Fahrenheit. When removed from the oven and cool, check the nail's magnetic ability.
2. Is there a relationship between the length of time the magnet is exposed to high heat and its magnetic ability? Vary time and temperature and compare magnetic attraction. Graph it on a chart.

SECTION 2
STATIC ELECTRICITY

Sliding across a fabric car seat and touching the metal door handle on a cold, dry day in winter may give you a shock. Clothes stick together when they are taken out of the dryer. These phenomena are caused by "static electricity," stationary electrical charges on objects.

Static charges can be caused by friction between two materials, such as glass and silk. Static caused by electrical disturbances in the atmosphere can be heard in an AM radio. A hissing sound in a radio, similar to escaping steam, is caused by small atmospheric charges. Strong electrical noises in a radio, sounding like loud sharp cracks, can be caused by a discharge, or arcing, of electricity in the atmosphere. Such sounds are likely to be caused by nearby electric motors and from lightning.

Static buildup occurs in materials where electrical charges do not move freely, as is true of metal conductors. The charges are called "static" because they have accumulated but are not moving. Electrons flow quickly, however, when a material with a static charge discharges, thus removing the electrical potential. Electrical potential is the difference in the charge between two materials.

TOO CLOSE FOR COMFORT

STATIC ELECTRICITY ON TV SCREENS

PURPOSE To find out if TV sets emit static electricity.

OVERVIEW There has long been a debate about whether sitting too close to a TV set (or computer screen) is a health hazard. Besides light, there may be other electromagnetic fields present which may or may not be a problem for humans. This project will detect the presence of one unseen energy field that emanates from a TV set's picture tube, namely static electricity.

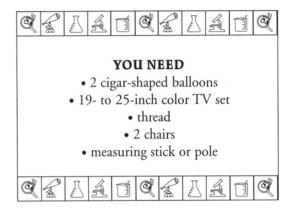

YOU NEED
- 2 cigar-shaped balloons
- 19- to 25-inch color TV set
- thread
- 2 chairs
- measuring stick or pole

HYPOTHESIS Hypothesize that TV sets will give off static electricity which can be detected with a balloon.

PROCEDURE Blow air into a cigar-shaped balloon. Tie a thin piece of thread around its center so that it balances on the thread. Tie the other end to the center of a yardstick. Place two chairs in front of a TV set. For best results, a larger size color TV set should be used, as larger size sets require higher picture tube voltages (typically 25,000 to 30,000 volts). Suspend the balloon so that it hovers directly in front of the TV screen. Do this by placing a rod or measuring stick across the backs of the two chairs.

First, position the chairs so that the balloon is 12 inches (31 cm) away from the front of the TV screen. Turn the TV on. Note any effect on the balloon, such as a movement away from or towards the TV set. Touch the balloon to a metal grounding point, such as a refrigerator or metal plumbing fixture to remove any static charge on the balloon. Repeat the procedure, positioning the balloon 2 feet (61 cm) from the screen, and then repeat it at a distance of 3 feet (91 cm).

Turn the TV set off. Bring another balloon near the balloon suspended on a thread. Is there an attraction or repulsion? Does the TV set have a static electric field around it that you were able to detect by charging a balloon?

RESULTS & CONCLUSION Write down the results of your experiment. Come to a conclusion as to whether or not your hypothesis was correct.

SOMETHING MORE Measure the ability of a TV screen to charge a balloon at different distances by first exposing a balloon to a TV screen, then measuring the distance the balloon must be from a piece of thread before the thread is moved by the static field of the balloon. Start several feet away from the set, moving 1 foot closer each time. End by finally touching the balloon to the screen and then testing its ability to attract or repel a suspended piece of thread.

SNAP, CRACKLE, POP

DETECTING APPROACHING THUNDERSTORMS

PURPOSE To find out ways of predicting a thunderstorm from your home.

OVERVIEW Lightning is a very dangerous natural phenomenon, taking the lives of many people each year. One popular scientific company even markets a device designed to detect approaching lightning strikes.

Lightning can strike as much as 20 miles in front of a thunderstorm and has been known to move through an area at speeds of 75 miles per hour. Obviously, advance warning could save lives. People working outdoors in the open, or on the beach or playing golf, may be caught off guard by dangerous storms and not have sufficient time to seek shelter.

Water droplets in clouds each carry a small electrical charge. As these droplets combine and grow larger, the electrical charges also add together. If the voltage becomes high enough, sparks discharge through the air. Sparks may arc from one cloud to another or from a cloud to the ground. These lightning arcs cause static-electric disturbances in the atmosphere. On an AM radio, these disturbances are heard as a sharp cracking sound.

One of the drawbacks of radio waves that use amplitude modulation (AM) is that the waves are easily disrupted by any kind of electrical interference in the atmosphere. This can be caused by natural electrical arcing in the atmosphere (lightning, for example) or by man-made devices like automobiles. While such arcing is annoying when we are trying to listen to the radio, it may also be of benefit if used to detect an approaching thunderstorm and serve as an early warning.

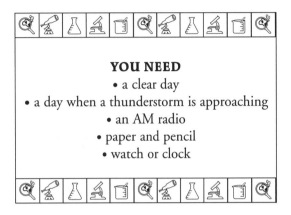

YOU NEED
- a clear day
- a day when a thunderstorm is approaching
- an AM radio
- paper and pencil
- watch or clock

HYPOTHESIS Hypothesize that you can use an AM radio to detect the approach of dangerous thunderstorms.

PROCEDURE On a clear day, when no storms are in the forecast, tune an AM radio to a spot on the dial where no stations can be heard. For five minutes, monitor the sound on that frequency. Make a record describing any sounds you hear. If there are loud "cracks," record the number heard within the five-minute observation period.

On a day when a thunderstorm is approaching, again turn on the AM radio and tune it to a spot on the dial where no stations can be heard. (in the same position as you did for the clear-day observations). Monitor the sounds you hear for five minutes. Record the number of times during the five minutes that loud, sharp cracks are heard.
WARNING: Do not go outside when there is the threat of a thunderstorm. Perform this experiment indoors only!

Note the types of sounds and the frequency of their occurrence (the number of times they are heard in a given period of time) on the clear day and the day of an approaching electrical storm. Use your recorded data to make the comparison.

RESULTS & CONCLUSION Write down the results of your experiment. Come to a conclusion as to whether or not your hypothesis was correct.

SOMETHING MORE
1. Does the loudness and/or the number of cracks heard increase as a lightning storm gets closer to you? Use a tape recorder.
2. What sounds, if any, are heard on an AM radio when a severe storm is approaching but it does not contain any visible lightning?
3. Is TV as good an indicator of an approaching electrical storm as an AM radio? Is an FM radio as good an indicator of an approaching electrical storm as is an AM radio?
4. Can you use an AM radio to tell storm direction by knowing where the radio station is located? Does a station to the east sound clearer than one to the west?

Too "Clothes" for Comfort

Static electricity in clothing material

PURPOSE With clothes dryers in many modern homes today, you may have observed some pieces of clothing sticking together as you remove them at the end of the drying cycle. Could this static electricity be caused by the hot, dry, tumbling environment of the dryer?

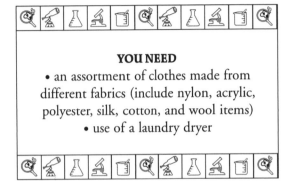

YOU NEED
- an assortment of clothes made from different fabrics (include nylon, acrylic, polyester, silk, cotton, and wool items)
- use of a laundry dryer

OVERVIEW The ancient Greeks were aware of the power of amber. When rubbed with certain materials, such as fur, this mineral can attract some objects that are small and light in weight. Ben Franklin first proposed the concept that static electric charges were not created nor destroyed, but were caused by a transfer of "electric fluid," as he called it, between objects. He believed in a conservation law that stated that when an amber rod is rubbed with fur, "electric fluid" is transferred from one object to the other. Although Ben did not know this "electric fluid" as "electrons," he was correct in his principle of the conservation of charges. The charges were not created or destroyed, only moved.

HYPOTHESIS Hypothesize which types of materials are more apt to become statically charged in the clothes dryer.

PROCEDURE Gather an assortment of clothing for washing and drying. Include as many different types of fabric materials as you can. Along with cotton, wool, and silk, add such synthetic-fiber fabrics as polyester, nylon, and acrylic. Wash them and then dry them in a dryer. *Note:* Some laundry products are designed to remove static electricity. Record which types of materials appear to have a static charge. Note which materials attract and repel other materials. Remember that like charges repel and unlike charges attract.

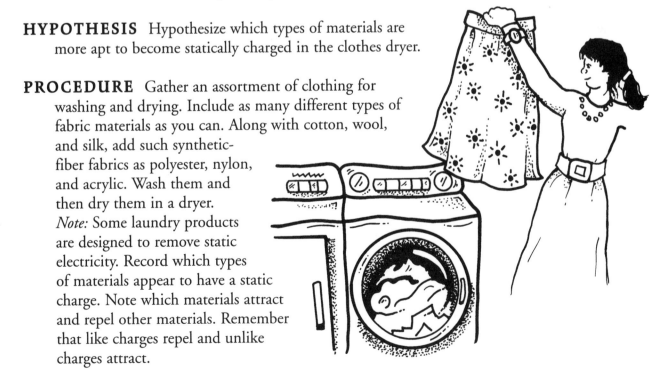

RESULTS & CONCLUSION Write down the results of your experiment. Come to a conclusion as to whether or not your hypothesis was correct.

SOMETHING MORE

1. Since unlike charges attract and like repel, can you determine which types of material are similarly charged and which have opposite charges?

2. Are there any natural substances that you could stick in the dryer to reduce static cling, other than the commercially available "static-free" products? How effective are these various products for the dryer that are designed to make clothing static-free? Are they effective in reducing static electricity in all types of fabrics?

3. It has been said that dish towels don't absorb moisture as well once they are put through a drying cycle in which a commercial static-free product was used. Can you confirm this?

4. When two pieces of clothing stick together when you remove them from the dryer, do the static charges soon equalize so that the two articles of clothing lose their attraction?

5. Do clothes in a dryer develop the static charge as moisture leaves, or would dry clothes put through a cycle develop a charge, too?

GROUNDED AGAIN

REMOVING STATIC CHARGES IN CLOTHING BY GROUNDING

PURPOSE When clothes are removed from the laundry dryer, some fabrics have an annoying static buildup in them. Will touching such fabrics with a conductor connected to an earth ground drain the static electricity from the clothing? Wouldn't it be great if this static could be discharged simply and quickly without the use of commercial products or chemical sprays?

OVERVIEW The ground (earth's surface) is considered to be a point of zero volts. When we "ground" a piece of electrical equipment, it means that an electrical connection is made from the piece of equipment to the earth. This is often done for safety reasons, for example, connecting a washing machine's metal cabinet to a ground point. Then, if a "hot" electric wire in the washer, one carrying a high voltage, should come in contact with the cabinet, the person using the washer would not receive an electric shock or be electrocuted. The high voltage drains off to the earth grounding.

Each electrical outlet box in your home is supposed to be connected to a wire that goes to a grounding point. Lightning rods on houses are grounded by means of thick wire from the rod on the roof to a metal pipe or copper rod driven several feet into the ground.

HYPOTHESIS Hypothesize whether or not an Earth ground can be used to remove static electricity from clothing.

PROCEDURE Wet several articles of clothing made from such synthetic materials as nylon, polyester, rayon, and acrylic, materials which commonly display static cling when removed from a dryer. Place the clothes in the dryer and turn it on.

Using a hammer, drive a 2- to 3-foot-long (61–91 cm) metal pipe into the ground, leaving only a few inches extending above ground. Cut a 4- or 5-foot (122–152 cm) length of solid-core hookup wire. Strip about ¾ inch (2 cm) of insulation from

both ends of the wire. Install an alligator clip on each end. Connect one alligator clip to the metal pipe and the other to a metal coat hanger.

Remove the static-charged clothing from the dryer. Slowly wipe the grounded metal coat hanger over each clothing item. Did the hanger remove any of the static? Did garments that were clinging together separate?

RESULTS & CONCLUSION   Write down the results of your experiment. Come to a conclusion as to whether or not your hypothesis was correct.

SOMETHING MORE
1. Can you quantify the amount of static built up in a garment by measuring the distance of an arc? (This might best be seen, and enjoyed, in a darkened room or outside at night.)
2. How might the pipe-ground connection be improved? Would soaking the ground around the pipe with water make it ground better?
3. Are some fabric materials harder to discharge than others?

TEA FOR TWO

ELECTROSTATIC GENERATION
(VAN DE GRAAFF GENERATOR)

PURPOSE Let's explore the properties of static electricity and the workings of an electrostatic generator.

OVERVIEW Electrostatic fields are used in many applications, such as the removal of particles from the air (dust, pollen, or other particulate matter in industrial chimneys) and to direct the flow of sprayed paint.

YOU NEED
- Van de Graaff generator
- cellophane adhesive tape
- 2 tea bags with strings and tags

A common device found in many school science rooms is the "electrostatic generator," also known as a "Van de Graaff generator." This device is used to build up a high electrical charge ranging from about 200,000 volts from a relatively small unit, to much higher voltages for bigger ones. A motor drives a belt made of gum or other material inside a tube. A smooth round dome is placed on the top. The dome is made large so that the electricity does not leak off easily. As the belt moves at high speed, a grounding wire drains negative charges off the belt at the bottom of the device, thus leaving a positive charge on the top dome. The Van de Graaff generator is a good continuous source of static electricity.

Note the Van de Graaff generator is capable of giving anyone who touches it an unpleasant shock , but because there is little current, it is not harmful. Avoid touching the generator while it is on. If you must touch it, use a long stick, such as a broom handle or a wooden back-scratcher.

HYPOTHESIS Hypothesize that, since like charges repel, two strings taped to the top of a Van de Graaff dome will repel each other because they will be charged to the same potential.

PROCEDURE Remove the string and tags from two tea bags. Place the tags next to each other and tape them to the top of the Van de Graaff generator's dome. Turn the generator on. Do the strings appear to stand up straight? Are they standing perpendicular to the dome? Do they lean toward each other, or away from each other?

RESULTS & CONCLUSION Write down the results of your experiment. Come to a conclusion as to whether or not your hypothesis was correct.

SOMETHING MORE

1. Wet the strings. What effect, if any, does this have?
2. What happens when you bring another object into the field, such as a wooden back-scratcher?
3. Is the three-dimensional static field surrounding the dome symmetrical? Is it higher than it is wide?
4. Light a candle and place it next to the generator. Why does the flame bend as though a steady wind was blowing from the dome?
5. Blow soap bubbles across the top of the generator. Hypothesize that the bubbles will be attracted to the dome or repelled as they approach it.

SECTION 3
CURRENT FLOW

Electricity is described using two terms, potential and current. Current flow is the movement of electrons (negatively charged particles) through a medium. The medium is called a "conductor" because it conducts, or carries, the current along a path. Ordinary wire, with which you are familiar, is a conductor of electricity. We often use the phrase "the flow of electricity" to mean the flow of current, both terms being identical. Current is measured in "amperes." Small current flows are measured in "milliamperes," a milliampere being 1/1,000th of an ampere. Amperes and milliamperes are commonly shortened to simply "amps" and "milliamps" when writing or talking about electricity. These are measures of the strength of the electricity's flow.

"Electrical potential" is a measure of stored electrons with the possibility of doing work. There may be no work being done, but there is the "potential" to do it. Electrical potential is measured in "volts." A new flashlight battery sitting on the table has a difference in electrical potential of 1.5 volts across its positive and negative terminals.

Current flows when there is a difference in "electrical potential" between two points and a conductor is connected between them. The conductor provides a path for electrons to move. One point has too many electrons gathered and another has too few. Similar to water seeking its own level, electrons move along from an area where there are a lot of electrons to where there are less.

VOLTS AND AMPS

UNDERSTANDING THE CONCEPTS OF VOLTAGE AND AMPERAGE

PURPOSE Before a person can undertake more involved electrical projects, it is important that there be a good understanding of the two terms "potential" and "current flow." This project, aimed at lower grade levels, is a demonstration which will help fellow classmates understand these two terms.

PROCEDURE Connect a battery to a switch and a small lamp (flashlight bulb). Voltmeters measure the difference in potential across two terminals. Place the positive probe of the voltmeter on the top of the battery and the negative on the bottom. The meter is said to be "in parallel" with the battery. It will read about 1.5 volts, regardless of whether the lamp is lit or not. The milliammeter must be placed "in series" (in the path) with the current flow. It measures how much current is flowing through the circuit. In this setup, the lamp is drawing the power to light it. That power is measured by the milliammeter.

    Throw the switch to "open" the path. The voltmeter will still show potential but the milliammeter will drop to zero.

YOU NEED

- 1.5-volt "D" flashlight battery
- "D" cell battery holder
- incandescent "flashlight" bulb
- bulb socket/holder
- insulated jumper leads, with alligator clips on each end
- voltmeter
- milliammeter
- on/off switch

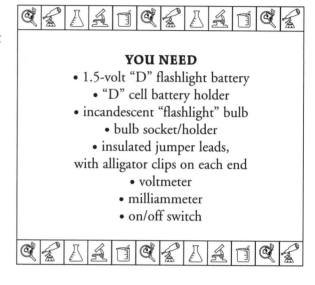

WET-CELL BATTERY

TESTING ELECTROLYTES TO MAKE WET-CELL BATTERIES

PURPOSE To test liquids for their abilities as electrolytes.

OVERVIEW Electricity can be produced by chemical action. Take a piece of paper and wet it. Make a sandwich by placing a nickel on the bottom, the wet piece of paper in the middle, and a penny on top. Here we have two dissimilar metals (called "electrodes") and an "electrolyte" substance between them. An electrolyte is a liquid solution which conducts electricity and, when used with certain metals, can generate electricity. Electrolytes are typically made up of weak sulfuric acid or dissolved salt. Place a milliammeter probe on the penny and the other probe on the nickel. The meter's needle will move, indicating a current flow.

YOU NEED
- a piece of zinc
- a piece of carbon
- 1 pint (500 milliliters) of citric acid (lemon juice)
- a glass beaker or wide-mouth jar
- insulated jumper leads with alligator clips on each end
- a milliammeter
- distilled water
- spring water

HYPOTHESIS Hypothesize that while pure water is best for drinking, it is among the worst electrolytes.

PROCEDURE Place a piece of zinc and a piece of carbon in a beaker or wide-mouth jar. These will be the electrodes. You may wish to use a little masking tape to secure the electrodes to the side of the beaker. Attach jumper wires with alligator clips from one electrode to a terminal on a milliammeter and another from the meter to the other electrode. The zinc electrode will have a negative charge and the carbon will be positive. The flow of electricity is in one direction. Will it matter which terminal on the meter (the positive "+" or the negative "−") is connected to the zinc or carbon electrodes?

Fill the beaker with 16 ounces (500 millilitres) of lemon juice. Read and record the milliammeter reading. This is 100% lemon juice.

Pour out 8 ounces (250 millilitres) of the juice, and replace it with 8 ounces of distilled water. Stir. This makes a 50% lemon-juice solution. Record the meter reading.

Rinse the beaker and fill it with 16 ounces (500 millilitres) of distilled water. Record the meter reading.

Can this device be used as a water tester? Is pH (the measure of alkalinity/acidity) a factor in determining a good electrolyte? Try raising the pH of the water with potash or some other alkaline solution. Is it true that the purest drinking water makes the poorest battery?

RESULTS & CONCLUSION Write down the results of your experiment. Come to a conclusion as to whether or not your hypothesis was correct.

SOMETHING MORE

1. Try many different electrolyte solutions: club soda, spring water, lake or sea water, apple juice, orange juice, vegetable oil. Crystals of these substances can also be dissolved in water to make electrolytes: potassium chloride, sodium chloride (table salt), as well as bromium chloride (sea salt).

2. Can you construct several wet-cell batteries and place them in series (similar to the two batteries in flashlights) to increase the overall voltage potential?

3. Hypothesize that larger electrodes produce more current than smaller ones because there is more electrode surface area in contact with the electrolyte.

After the Warm-Up

THE EFFECT OF TEMPERATURE ON BATTERY LIFE

PURPOSE To test the effect of temperature on batteries.

OVERVIEW When the icy cold winter winds howl, you will undoubtedly hear someone complain that he couldn't get his car started that morning. Often the cause is a bad car battery, affected by the cold. Does temperature affect the dry cell batteries found in flashlights, toys, and portable radios? Does operating them in the cold enable them to generate energy longer than at room temperature? If so, does heat have the opposite effect?

HYPOTHESIS Hypothesize that heat extends the hours of useful energy produced by a flashlight battery and a decrease in temperature causes a decrease in battery life (or hypothesize that the exact opposite happens).

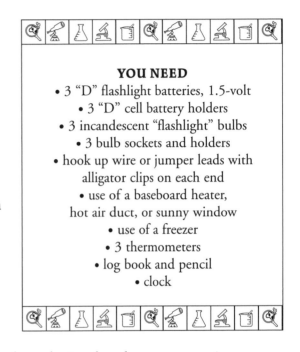

YOU NEED
- 3 "D" flashlight batteries, 1.5-volt
- 3 "D" cell battery holders
- 3 incandescent "flashlight" bulbs
- 3 bulb sockets and holders
- hook up wire or jumper leads with alligator clips on each end
- use of a baseboard heater, hot air duct, or sunny window
- use of a freezer
- 3 thermometers
- log book and pencil
- clock

PROCEDURE Connect a light bulb (lamp) to a battery. The hookup wire between them should be about 1 foot (31 cm) long because we are going to place one of the batteries inside a refrigerator's freezer, but we want the bulb to stay outside at room temperature. Construct two other similar setups to give a total of three battery/lamp devices.

Place one device on a table at room temperature. Place the other in an area of higher temperature, such as a sunny window or on a hot-air duct. You can put it near an electric baseboard heat unit or radiator, but not too close. (For safety, have an adult help you place this battery device in an appropriately warm area.) The third battery will be placed inside a freezer. Let the hookup wires from the battery to the bulb extend out the freezer door and connect to the bulb outside, which will remain at room temperature. It may not make a difference, but generally the electrical resistance of wire is decreased as temperature decreases. The short piece of wire and small range of temperatures we are dealing with should not make enough difference in wire resistance to affect the results of your project. But the filament of a light bulb is a special kind of wire so we will keep the bulb out of the cold (and the other bulb out of the direct heat) to give our experiment the most accurate result.

When you construct the three battery/lamp devices, make one of the wires easy to connect and disconnect. If you use a battery holder, you can easily disconnect the wire, as you can if you use alligator clips.

Place the three devices at their locations (room-temperature table, freezer, and warm area). Connect the batteries to the lamps. In a log book, record the time on the clock that the experiment begins. Every half hour, check each lamp to see if it is still burning. Since this project will take several days, disconnect all the batteries from the lamps (only one wire needs to be disconnected to open the circuit) when you want to stop to go to school or to bed because it is necessary to constantly observe the performance of each set. If you forget, and one battery stops just after you go to bed, and another stops just before you get up, you would not know which one lasted longer. Note the time you disconnect the batteries in your log book and calculate the number of hours each has been lit. The next time you will be home for a while, continue your experiment by hooking all the batteries back up and start your half-hour monitoring again.

RESULTS & CONCLUSION Record which battery gives out first, second, and third. Come to a conclusion as to whether or not your hypothesis was correct.

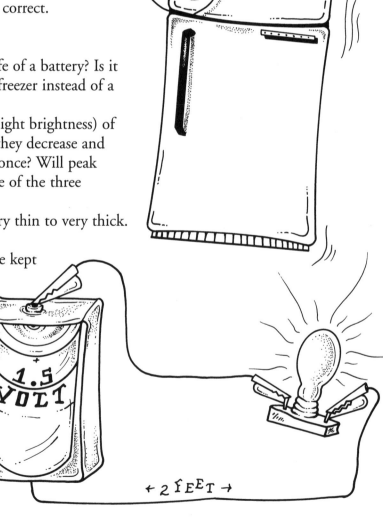

SOMETHING MORE
1. Does temperature affect the shelf life of a battery? Is it better to store new batteries in the freezer instead of a cabinet drawer?
2. Measure the lumens (a measure of light brightness) of each lamp using a light meter. Do they decrease and slowly die out or just die out all at once? Will peak output be maintained longer by one of the three batteries?
3. Alter the gauge of the wire from very thin to very thick. Hypothesize an effect.
4. In the above project, the lamps were kept out of the warm and cold areas. Repeat the project with the lamps in the warm and cold areas as well as the batteries.
5. Increase your sample size (use six batteries instead of three).
6. Does intermittent use of a battery extend its life? Maybe a battery recovers a little if it is given a rest period every hour, which could mean a longer total useful life.

KEEPS ON KEEPING ON

COMPARING POPULAR BRANDS OF BATTERIES

PURPOSE Do you believe that some popular name-brand batteries really do run longer than other brands?

OVERVIEW All battery commercials and ads boast that their brand is the best. But they can't all be the "best." One might have the best price. Another might have the best shelf life. Yet another may be best at providing power for a longer period of time.

HYPOTHESIS Hypothesize which batteries you believe produce useful power for the longest time. This project assumes that all batteries are equally new and fresh.

YOU NEED
- 3 "D" cells, 1.5-volt, from different manufacturers (All battery brands used in test—Duracell, Eveready, Radio Shack, Mallory, Ray-O-Vac, or other—must be made of same material, such as alkaline.)
- "D" cell battery holders
- incandescent flashlight bulbs (lamps), one for each battery
- bulb socket/holders, one for each battery
- hook-up wire or insulated jumper leads with alligator clips on each end
- log book and pencil
- clock

PROCEDURE Connect a lamp to a battery. Do this for each battery you have. Turn all the lamps on at the same time. After many hours (or days) of operation, watch for dimming. When the lamps begin to dim, start checking every half hour. Since this project will require several days, disconnect each lamp from its battery during periods when you cannot monitor them (such as while you sleep or are at school). In a log book, record the time you start and stop the project each day so that you can work out the total operating time for each battery when they do finally give out.

RESULTS & CONCLUSION Study your log book records and determine if the most popular brand-name batteries really do last the longest. Come to a conclusion as to whether or not your hypothesis was correct.

SOMETHING MORE

1. Are the results the same if you use standard-formula batteries rather than alkaline (or vice versa)?

2. Are the results the same for batteries of other sizes: "C" cells, "AA," "AAA," "N," or 9-volt?

3. Compare cost effectiveness. Do the batteries that last the longest also have the best price? Determine the cost per hour to light your lamp for each battery manufacturer.

4. Is the discrepancy in usage greater within the brand or from one brand to another? In other words, are there greater differences among one manufacturer's batteries compared to differences among many manufacturers?

LIVE-WIRE WOOD

INSULATORS BECOME CONDUCTORS UNDER CERTAIN CONDITIONS

PURPOSE To determine whether insulators become conductors under wet conditions.

OVERVIEW Some objects that are normally insulators can become conductors of electricity under certain circumstances. If someone were trapped by a downed "live wire" from a telephone pole, a person might think a tree branch or broom handle could be used to safely push the electric wire away, since wood is an insulator. But wood soaked from being in a storm or lying in water will conduct electricity.

YOU NEED
- toothpick
- wax candle
- piece of rubber
- ohmmeter
- jumper leads with alligator clips on each end
- log book, pencil
- tap water

HYPOTHESIS Hypothesize that objects which normally insulate can become conductors when wet and, therefore, may not be safe to use in handling electricity.

PROCEDURE Using an ohmmeter, check the resistance of objects that are normally insulators. Use as many objects as you can think of, such as a toothpick or pencil (representing wood), a wax candle, and a piece of rubber (rubber glove used to wash dishes). Record their resistance in a log book or chart. They should all have such a high resistance that the meter's needle will read infinity. This means they will have a very low conductivity rate (poor conductors). The higher the resistance, the lower the conductivity.

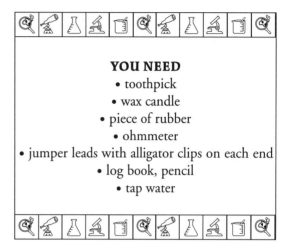

Soak the objects in water for a few minutes. Again, read the resistance of each object and record the results. Try moving the meter probe points close together on the objects and at opposite ends. Note if there is any change in resistance with distance across the surface of the object.

RESULTS & CONCLUSION Write down the results of your experiment. Come to a conclusion as to whether or not your hypothesis was correct.

SOMETHING MORE

1. Repeat the experiment adding salt to the water. What would happen if these objects had become wet from salty sea water?
2. Weigh a small piece of wood. Soak it for an hour in tap water (place a brick or other weight on it to keep it under water). Weigh it again. Let the wood thoroughly dry out for several days, perhaps placing it in a sunny window. Again, weigh the wood when it is dry. Repeat the procedure with another piece of wood using salt water. Does the wood absorb more salt water then fresh water?
3. Try balsa wood, pine, oak, and an assortment of wood densities. Does the density of the wood affect the conductivity when wet?

CURRENT EVENT

FUSES PROTECT FROM EXCESS CURRENT FLOW

PURPOSE Learning about fuses.

OVERVIEW A "short" in an electrical circuit can cause an excess amount of current to be drawn from the power source. A "short" circuit is when the resistance of a circuit falls from its normal value to a very low value. This may occur when an electrical component fails. Appliances such as electric heaters, microwave ovens, and hair dryers, normally draw a considerable amount of current. A short circuit in such an appliance could cause an excess amount of current to be drawn from the electrical outlet. This condition, if allowed to continue, could cause the AC power cord on the appliance (and even the wiring in the walls of the house) to heat up. Such heat places surrounding materials in danger of being set on fire.

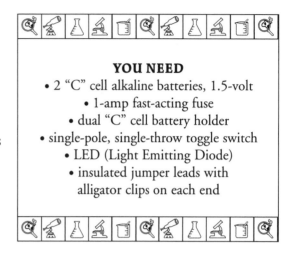

YOU NEED
- 2 "C" cell alkaline batteries, 1.5-volt
- 1-amp fast-acting fuse
- dual "C" cell battery holder
- single-pole, single-throw toggle switch
- LED (Light Emitting Diode)
- insulated jumper leads with alligator clips on each end

To prevent an appliance or electronic device from drawing too much current, a safety component, the "fuse," is often used. Fuses, which are also used in electrical panels to protect the wiring in homes, can protect the power supply from having too much current "pulled" from it. It can also protect other components inside the electrical device from damage.

Fuses in electronic devices come in many shapes and forms. The most common is a small glass tube, looking like a one-inch length of soda straw, with a metal cap on each end. Inside the tube a strand of wire, made of an alloy which melts at a low temperature, completes the circuit, and allows current to pass. If too much current flows, the wire begins to heat up. When the wire reaches a certain temperature it melts, and the electrical path is broken. This open circuit safely stops the current flow and protects the power source as well as other components inside the appliance or electronic device. Fuses are rated by the number of amperes they will allow to flow through them before they open and stop the flow.

HYPOTHESIS Hypothesize that a fuse can safely protect a circuit from overloading the power source to which it is connected.

PROCEDURE Construct the circuit shown in the illustration. Be sure the toggle switch is in the open (turned off) position before the batteries are connected to the circuit. Upon connecting the batteries, the LED will light. Under this normal condition, the LED requires less than one ampere of current to illuminate it. When closed (turned to the on position), the toggle switch placed across the LED will "short out" the LED, that is, it will cause the LED to be bypassed, and current will no longer flow through the LED. This is due to the fact that electricity takes the path of least resistance. The switch provides a path of almost no resistance. Closing the switch removes the "load" (the power-absorbing device), which was the LED, and the circuit becomes a "dead short." Effectively, there is now no resistance in the circuit to impede the flow of current.

Therefore, the circuit will try to draw as much current as the batteries can supply, and alkaline batteries are capable of delivering a heavy supply, more than one ampere. As the current rises above one ampere, the fast-acting fuse will "open," breaking the flow of current, and the batteries will be protected from being drained.

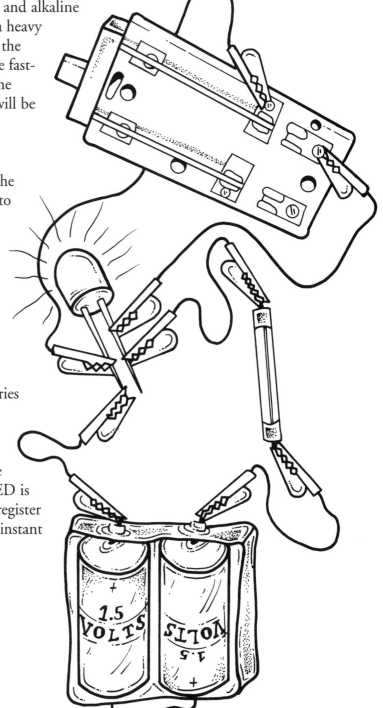

RESULTS & CONCLUSION
Write down the results of your experiment. Come to a conclusion as to whether or not your hypothesis was correct.

SOMETHING MORE

1. What happens if the 1-amp fuse is replaced with a 2-amp fuse? A 3-amp fuse? A 10-amp fuse?

2. Place a 500 milliammeter in series with the fuse and batteries. How many milliamperes does the circuit draw normally when the LED is lit? When the switch that shorts across the LED is closed, does the milliammeter register an increase in current flow the instant before the fuse blows?

SECTION 4
ELECTROMECHANICAL DEVICES, MOTORS

We are living in a machine age. Motors are everywhere. In the home, they can be found in swimming pool pumps, refrigerators, washing machines, clothes dryers, hair dryers, VCRs, electric lawn mowers, fans, and water pumps. All motors operate due to electromagnetic principles. Basically, a motor converts electricity into motion; a conversion of energy. A generator does the opposite. Motion produces electricity.

Magnetism is a force that acts between certain materials (or devices). When electricity passes through a wire, a magnetic field is created surrounding the wire. A magnetic field in motion will produce a voltage potential in a wire. We can cause some metal materials, such as soft iron, to become permanently magnetized by placing them in an electromagnetic field.

ALL COILED UP

EFFECT ON CURRENT FLOW BY MAGNET MOVING PAST A COIL

PURPOSE Is it enough to simply move a magnet near a wire or coil of wire to induce an electrical flow?

OVERVIEW Scientists had long suspected that there was a connection between magnetism and electricity, because both have similar properties. Polarity is one of these properties. There are north and south poles in magnetism just as there are positive and negative polarity in electricity. Also, in both cases, opposites attract.

In 1820 Hans Christian Orsted, a Danish physicist, discovered that a compass needle moved when brought into the presence of a wire in which current was flowing. The reverse also happens. Electrical energy is induced in a wire when that wire moves through a magnetic field.

> **YOU NEED**
> • cardboard toilet-tissue or towel roll
> • spool of solid core hookup wire
> • DC milliammeter capable of measuring to several milliamperes
> • a rectangular magnet just small enough to fit through a cardboard toilet tissue roll regardless of how it is positioned
> • wire cutters or wire strippers
> • insulated jumper leads with alligator clips on each end

HYPOTHESIS Hypothesize that moving a magnet near a wire or coil of wire is not enough to induce a flow of electricity. The polarity of the magnet in relation to the wire's position is an important factor, too.

PROCEDURE Using a cardboard toilet-tissue roll or a section cut from a paper-towel roll, wrap 50 turns of solid-core hookup wire around the roll in a spiral pattern. Strip about 1 inch (2.5 cm) of insulation off both ends of the hookup wire. Connect each end of the coil of wire to the terminals on a DC milliammeter using insulated jumper cables with alligator clips.

Hold the magnet in a horizontal position and drop it down through the cardboard roll. Record the number of milliamperes that registered on the meter. Rotate the magnet 90 degrees (hold it vertically) and drop it again. Record the number of milliamperes that registered on the meter. When the meter's needle moves, it will only jump for the briefest second. Record the highest number the needle reaches during its momentary jump.

Compare the readings of the current from both drops through the tube. If a higher reading occurred when the magnet was dropped in one particular position, then your hypothesis was correct.

RESULTS & CONCLUSION   Write down the results of your experiment. Come to a conclusion as to whether or not your hypothesis was correct.

SOMETHING MORE
1. What results are obtained when the number of turns of wire is increased to 100 turns?
2. What results are obtained when thicker wire is used to make the coil?

MARVELOUS MAGNETIC MEASURER

DETECTING MAGNETISM

PURPOSE How can you detect magnetism in an object?

OVERVIEW A strong magnet can, of course, attract soft-iron nails, paper clips, and may even adhere itself to a refrigerator. But there may be times when you want to detect even weak magnetism in an object. The project on page 276, for example, demonstrates an attempt to magnetize an iron nail. To do this, the nail is stroked many times with a permanent magnet. How many times must it be stroked before it displays *any* observable magnetic effect? To answer this, a device sensitive to even a small amount of magnetism is needed.

YOU NEED
- soft-iron nail
- permanent magnet
- spool of thread
- desk stapler with staples
- several scraps of wood (to construct a small swing stand)
- wood screws or nails
- screwdriver or hammer
- scissors
- hand saw (optional, adult supervision required)

HYPOTHESIS Hypothesize that you can create a testing device that will detect small amounts of magnetism in objects.

PROCEDURE Using several wood screws or nails and some short lengths of wood, construct a small stand about 1 to 2 feet (31–61 cm) high. Take a desk stapler and crimp a staple onto the end of a piece of thread. Unroll a length of thread about 2 feet (61 cm) long and cut it off the spool. Tie it around the top of the wood stand so that staple hovers suspended about 1 inch (2.5 cm) from the stand bottom.

The mass of the staple is very small, and since it is suspended on a thread, it doesn't require much force to make it move laterally (sideways in any direction). This makes it very sensitive.

Slowly bring a soft-iron nail near the staple. The staple should not move in reaction to the nail. If it does, then the nail has already been magnetized and you must replace it with another nail.

Once you have established that the nail has no observable effect on the staple, it is ready to be stroked with a permanent magnet. Stroke the nail once, starting at the top of the nail and stroking downward. Bring the nail close to the staple and see if it has taken on any signs of magnetism. Stroke it a second time, and repeat the test. Be sure to use the same pole on the magnet each time you stroke. Continue stroking and testing until the staple is moved by the nearness of the nail. How many strokes does it take before the proximity of the nail has an observable effect on the staple?

RESULTS & CONCLUSION Write down the results of your experiment. Come to a conclusion as to whether or not your hypothesis was correct.

SOMETHING MORE Quantify the amount of magnetism in your test samples by measuring the distance the staple is deviated from plumb (moved from the center hanging point).

CURRENTLY SET UP

MAGNETIC INDUCTION

PURPOSE To explore magnetic induction.

OVERVIEW When electric current flows through a wire, a magnetic field is established around the outside of the wire. If another wire is brought into the magnetic field, electric current is induced into the second wire by magnetic induction.

In this project, a coil of wire is wound around a nail and a second wire is coiled over it. When a battery is connected to the first coiled wire, known as the "primary" winding, a sensitive DC milliammeter connected across the "secondary" winding will register a jump; ever so slightly and for only an instant, but it will be detectable.

YOU NEED
- spool of solid-conductor hookup wire
- sensitive DC milliammeter
- soft-iron nail
- 6- or 12-volt lantern battery
- insulated jumper leads with alligator clips on both ends
- single-pole, single-throw, normally open, momentary contact switch
- wire cutters

Although only a slight momentary movement of the meter's needle occurs, the discovery of this effect ranks among the most important of the electrical age. The concept of electromagnetic induction enabled the invention of coils, transformers, motors, and generators.

Although two scientists, Michael Faraday and Joseph Henry, working independently, discovered this electromagnetism effect at the same time, it is Faraday who receives the credit as he was the first to publish his findings.

The year was 1831, when Faraday wound two unconnected coils of wire onto a donut-like ring made of iron. Iron was used to intensify the magnetic field. When a battery was connected across the first coil, the needle of his galvanometer (a gauge that measures current flow), which was connected across the second winding, reacted with a momentary jump. The amount of current induced into the secondary winding was very tiny, but he had proven that current could be induced in a wire through the use of magnetism.

HYPOTHESIS Hypothesize that you can duplicate Faraday's results, inducing the momentary current flow in a wire and thereby prove, again, the magnetic-induction process.

PROCEDURE Construct the circuit as shown in the illustration on the opposite page. Wrap 50 turns of wire around a soft-iron nail and strip about ¼ inch (1 cm) of the

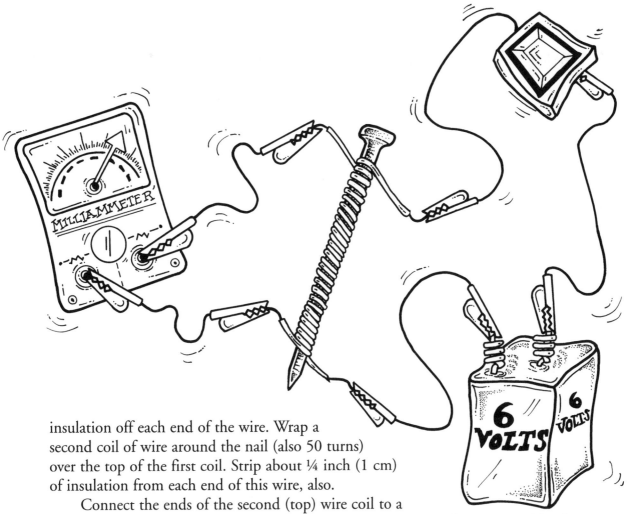

insulation off each end of the wire. Wrap a second coil of wire around the nail (also 50 turns) over the top of the first coil. Strip about ¼ inch (1 cm) of insulation from each end of this wire, also.

Connect the ends of the second (top) wire coil to a sensitive DC milliammeter. Connect a momentary contact switch in series with a battery and the first (under) coil. Push the button. What happens to the needle on the gauge at the moment the button is pushed? What does the meter's needle do when you continue to hold the button down? What happens when you release the button?

RESULTS & CONCLUSION Write down the results of your experiment. Come to a conclusion as to whether or not your hypothesis was correct.

SOMETHING MORE
1. What can be done to increase the deflection of the meter's needle, to make the effect more pronounced? Does increasing the number of turns of the wire help? What happens if the number of coil turns of the primary winding is more or less than that of the secondary winding? Does placing two batteries in series or in parallel make the meter's needle jump a farther distance?
2. Confirm Lenz's law. What is known as Lenz's law states that the direction of the induced current in the secondary winding is opposite to the direction of the primary. Heinrich Lenz, a Russian scientist, developed this principle in 1834.

Double Throw to Second Base

RELAYS TO REMOTELY CONTROL OTHER CIRCUITS

PURPOSE To learn about the relay, an electrical device that allows current flowing in one circuit to control the current flowing in another circuit.

OVERVIEW The relay consists of a coil with an iron core, forming an electromagnet. A metallic plate is placed in position over the electromagnet and kept at a distance from it by a spring. Connected to this plate are one or more switch contacts. When the electromagnet is at rest, some of the switch contacts may be touching (making a "closed" circuit) and some may not (making an "open" circuit). When the electromagnet is energized, those switch contacts that were open now become closed, and vice versa.

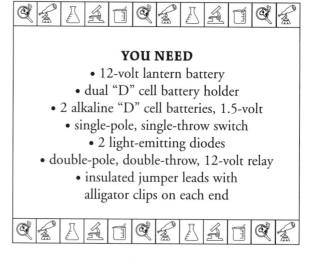

YOU NEED
- 12-volt lantern battery
- dual "D" cell battery holder
- 2 alkaline "D" cell batteries, 1.5-volt
- single-pole, single-throw switch
- 2 light-emitting diodes
- double-pole, double-throw, 12-volt relay
- insulated jumper leads with alligator clips on each end

Relays are often used in situations where a small current flow can turn on a machine that requires a large current flow, or high voltage. This makes such a system safer. If only a little voltage is needed to turn the relay on, a switch, or button, that a human must come in contact with to activate the larger system would present no shock hazard. It would only have to hold enough current to turn on a relay. The contacts on the relay, however, can be

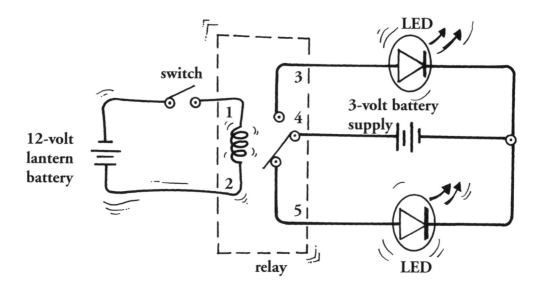

designed to handle much larger amounts of current and voltage, thus the user is indirectly controlling the more dangerous circuit safely. A good example of this kind of relay system is a doorbell.

Since the contacts on the relay can be normally open or normally closed when the relay is at rest, relays can be used to complete one circuit when the electromagnet is off and another when the electromagnet is energized. As you know, you can connect a battery to a switch and a small lightbulb and the bulb will light when you turn on the switch to close (complete) the circuit. But what if you wanted to turn a lightbulb on when the switch was in the open position? A relay can be used to perform this task. This application is used in industrial electronics as well as in some remote-controlled TV sets.

HYPOTHESIS Hypothesize that, by opening a switch, you can close another circuit through the use of a relay.

PROCEDURE Assemble the circuit shown in the illustrations. Two power sources, in this case two separate battery supplies, are required for this circuit. The 12-volt battery supply delivers power to the relay coil when the switch is turned on. The 3-volt battery supply, made up of two 1.5-volt batteries in series, is used to light the LEDs (light-emitting diodes). Which of the two LEDs are illuminated depends on whether the relay's coil is powered or not. Notice that the two battery-powered circuits are electrically independent of each other.

One LED should be lit when the switch in the relay coil circuit is off, and the other LED should be lit when the switch is on. Label the switches to indicate whether the switch is on or off.

RESULTS & CONCLUSION
Write down the results of your experiment. Come to a conclusion as to whether or not your hypothesis was correct.

SOMETHING MORE What applications, or uses, can you envision for this type of circuit? How does a thermostat in your living room control the furnace in your basement?

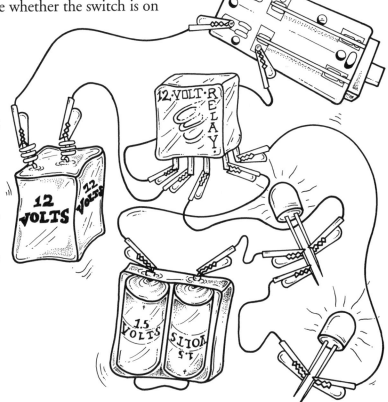

MOTORING YOUR GENERATOR

MOTORS ARE THE OPPOSITE OF GENERATORS

PURPOSE Learning the difference between motors and generators.

OVERVIEW When an electrical conductor passes through a magnetic field, an electric current is induced in the conductor. The opposite is also true. A conductor carrying an electric current creates a magnetic field around it.

An electric motor consists of a magnet and an "armature," which is a coil of wire mounted on a shaft that rotates inside the magnet's magnetic field. A generator and a motor are similar in construction, but opposite in purpose. In a motor, electricity is put in and the armature turns, yielding a mechanical force. In a generator, a mechanical force is used to turn the armature and the output is electricity.

HYPOTHESIS Hypothesize that, when the armatures of two identical motors are connected together and electricity is supplied to one, one motor will turn the electrical energy into mechanical energy and the second motor will turn mechanical energy into electrical energy. (An electric motor is the opposite of a generator.)

PROCEDURE On a small piece of wood, mount two 3-volt DC miniature hobby motors facing each other. Use screws or other mounting hardware to secure the two motors firmly to the wood. The gears on the motor shafts must mesh so that when the shaft of one motor turns the other will also turn.

YOU NEED

- 2 identical, 3-volt DC, miniature hobby motors, with small gear on shaft
- 2 "D" cell alkaline batteries
- dual "D" cell battery holder
- sensitive DC milliammeter
- insulated jumper leads with alligator clips on each end
- small piece of wood, screws, and hardware to mount motors

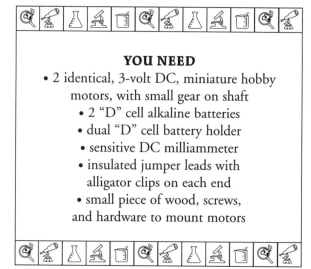

Connect two 1.5-volt "D" cell batteries in series, creating a 3-volt power source. Connect the power to one of the motors. Determine whether electricity is flowing from the second motor by connecting a sensitive DC-milliammeter to the generator.

RESULTS & CONCLUSION Write down the results of your experiment. Come to a conclusion as to whether or not your hypothesis was correct.

SOMETHING MORE

1. Will the energy conversion become more efficient if more voltage is applied? Efficiency is equal to voltage out divided by voltage in. Do this computation for several different voltage inputs.
2. Can friction be reduced by lubricating the gears? Is it measurable?

SECTION 5
RESISTANCE & CAPACITANCE

Resistors and capacitors are perhaps the most common passive components used in electronic circuits. They perform dozens of tasks, depending on how they are used in a circuit.

As the name implies, a resistor "resists" the flow of electrons, making their travel difficult. Resistors can limit the flow of current and drop voltage down to a desired level. The amount of resistance a resistor has is measured in "ohms."

Capacitors are storage devices. They consist of two metal plates separated by an insulating material, called a "dielectric." They do not generate electricity but they can store a small amount of it. Capacitors are used in many ways such as filters, temporary storage devices, and as blocks to DC (direct current) flow while passing AC (alternating current) signals. The amount of capacitance a capacitor has is measured in "farads." The most commonly used values, however, are only in millionths of a farad, called "microfarads."

WIRED TO MELT

RESISTANCE IN WIRE CAN PRODUCE HEAT

PURPOSE To learn about resistance in wire.

OVERVIEW Often, heat is an undesirable side effect of electricity passing through a wire, for example in motors or such electronic appliances as TVs and stereos. But there are times when we can put the heat coming from electric current traveling in a wire to good use.

We have all seen the wires inside a kitchen toaster glowing orange as we make breakfast, and we know not to touch the toaster while it is glowing. The heating-element wire inside a toaster is made of metal wire called nichrome, an alloy of nickel, iron, and chromium. It has a high electrical resistance and warms up quickly. If DC (direct current) were applied to a piece of nichrome wire, would the part of the wire closest to the negative pole of the battery heat up before the side opposite? The negative pole of a battery supplies the electrons that flow through the wire as they travel toward the positive pole, which is lacking electrons.

> **YOU NEED**
> - a 6-inch piece of thin nichrome wire (from a discarded toaster)
> - 2 alkaline "D" cell batteries
> - dual "D" cell battery holder
> - insulated jumper leads with alligator clips at each end
> - candle
> - matches
> - a piece of scrap paper
> - 2 sections of 2 × 4 wood about 4 or 5 inches (10–12 cm) long
> - 2 nails about 2 inches long
> - hammer
> - wire cutters

HYPOTHESIS Hypothesize that when DC voltage is applied to a piece of nichrome wire, the end of the wire closest to the negative source of the battery will heat faster than the other side.

PROCEDURE Lay two pieces of 2 × 4 board on a workbench or old table so that the widest part is lying flat. Hammer a nail partway into each, leaving about ½ inch to 1 inch (1.25–2.5 cm) of the nail extending above the board. These will be terminal posts, where the nichrome wire can be wrapped and alligator clip leads from the batteries can be connected.

Cut a 6-inch (15 cm) piece of nichrome wire. Request some wire from your school's science teacher or ask an adult help you remove a piece from an old, discarded toaster. (An old toaster might be found at a yard sale for a dollar or two.)

Wrap one end of the nichrome wire around the nail in one of the pieces of wood. Wrap the other end around the nail in the other piece of wood. Gently push the two pieces of wood away from each other until the nichrome wire is slightly taut, so that the wire is straight and level.

Place a piece of scrap paper on the table under the nichrome wire to catch liquid wax. Have an adult light a candle, and drip a thin coat of wax onto the whole length of the wire.

Use an insulated lead with alligator clips to connect the positive terminal of a dual "D" cell battery holder to one of the nail terminal posts. Take the other clip lead and connect one end to the negative battery terminal. Clip the other end to the remaining nail terminal and observe the wax on the ends of the nichrome wire. Does the wax near the negative nail terminal begin to melt before the wax on the opposite end?

To check your project for validity, light and use the lit candle again to recoat the nichrome wire evenly with wax and repeat the procedure, but this time reverse the positive and negative clip leads. The wax will always melt first by the negative clip lead.

RESULTS & CONCLUSION Write down the results of your experiment. Come to a conclusion as to whether or not your hypothesis was correct.

SOMETHING MORE

1. How do kinks in the wire affect heating? Tie a knot in the wire and repeat the experiment. Does the knot heat faster, slower, or the same as the wire near the negative battery terminal?

2. Cut an "H" shape in a piece of wood and suspend a piece of nichrome wire across the top two legs in the "H." Use clip leads for connection to a battery and use this tool as a candle cutter or a Styrofoam cutter.

3. Place a DC ammeter in series with the nichrome wire. Hypothesize that when current is first applied to the wire and the wire is cold, its resistance is low, and there will be a great amount of current flow. But as the wire begins to heat, its resistance increases and the current flow will decrease slightly.

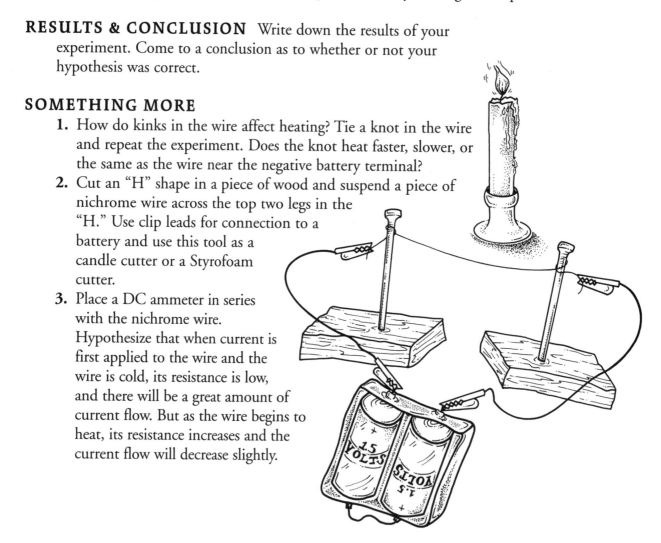

TWO KINDS OF SHARING

COMPARING RESISTORS IN SERIES AND PARALLEL

PURPOSE Resistors can be placed either in series (in line with) or parallel (across each other) in a circuit. Does the resistor placement in a circuit, parallel or in series, affect the amount of resistance?

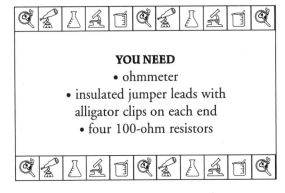

YOU NEED
- ohmmeter
- insulated jumper leads with alligator clips on each end
- four 100-ohm resistors

OVERVIEW Electric current flows through a path of wire and other components that make up an electric circuit. In a circuit powered by a battery, the negative terminal on the battery is the source of the electrons that will work their way through the circuit to get to the positive terminal of the battery.

A resistor is an electrical component that "resists" or cuts down the amount of electrons that flow through it. Imagine driving a car at a fast highway speed on a smooth road and then suddenly hitting a rough and bumpy section of roadway. You would have to reduce your speed. Similarly, a resistor gives electrons a tough time and reduces the current flow.

Resistors come in different amounts of resistance, which is measured in units called "ohms." A low ohm value indicates that the resistor presents only a little hindrance to the electrons while a high number severely limits current flow.

HYPOTHESIS Hypothesize that resistors placed in series will make the total resistance of the circuit equal to the sum of the resistances, but resistors placed in parallel will share current flow. Therefore, the total resistance of a parallel circuit will be less than the lowest value resistor.

PROCEDURE Use an ohmmeter to measure the resistance of four 100-ohm resistors. The value of a resistor may be a little less than or a little greater than the actual amount listed. The value of resistors may either be typed onto the resistor itself or indicated by bands of color. The first three bands indicate the resistor's value in ohms. If there is no forth band, then its accuracy is plus or minus 20 percent. That would

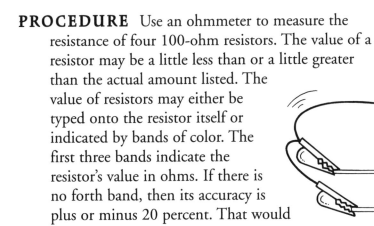

mean that a 100-ohm resistor could really be as little as 80 ohms or as much as 120 ohms. A silver forth band means 10 percent "tolerance" (accuracy), and a gold band means 5 percent. Record the actual value of each resistor.

Twist one end of a 100-ohm resistor with one end of another. Using insulated jumper wires with alligator clip ends, connect the two 100-ohm resistors in series. Put the probes of an ohmmeter on the other ends of the resistors. Record the reading on the ohmmeter. Is the measured resistance the same as the individual resistances of the two resistors added together?

Twist both ends of two resistors together to put them in parallel (across) each other. Using insulated jumper wires with alligator clip ends, connect an ohmmeter. Record the circuit's resistance as measured by the meter. Is the resistance less than the lowest individual resistor value? (Note: When two resistors of the same value are in parallel, the total circuit resistance will be half the value of the resistors. In this case, half of 100 ohms is 50 ohms.)

RESULTS & CONCLUSION Write down the results of your experiment. Come to a conclusion as to whether or not your hypothesis was correct.

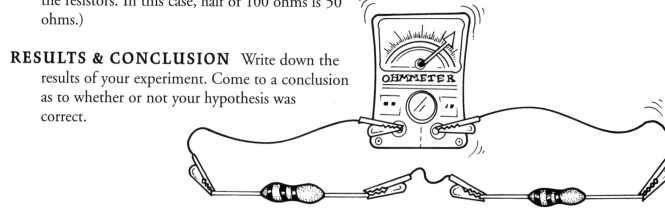

SOMETHING MORE

1. There is a formula for determining the total resistance for two resistors placed in parallel:

$$R \text{ total} = (R1 \times R2) / (R1 + R2)$$

For example, if the first resistor is 100 ohms and the second is 50 ohms, the total resistance would be:

$$R \text{ total} = (100 \times 50) / (100 + 50)$$
$$R \text{ total} = 5000 / 150$$
$$R \text{ total} = 33.3 \text{ ohms}$$

If there are more than two resistors, the formula is:

$$R \text{ total} = 1 / (1/R1 + 1/R2 + 1/R3 \ldots)$$

2. A potentiometer is a variable resistor, as is the volume control on your TV set. Use a potentiometer in parallel with a known resistor and measure the total resistance. Hypothesize that you can indirectly determine the resistance of the potentiometer in any position by measuring the circuit's total resistance and using the formula to calculate the unknown value.

BROWN OUT

POWER LOSS IN ELECTRIC TRANSMISSION LINES

PURPOSE Demonstrating the concept of wasted power by transmission line resistance, using high resistance wire to simulate miles of transmission lines.

OVERVIEW A tremendous amount of electricity that power plants generate is wasted by resistance in the transmission wires that carry the electricity from the plant to our homes. While the resistance of the wires is very low, the total resistance in thousands of miles of wire becomes very significant. When Thomas Edison wired a town to bring electric lights to every home, he noticed that the lights

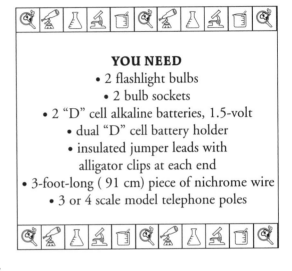

YOU NEED
- 2 flashlight bulbs
- 2 bulb sockets
- 2 "D" cell alkaline batteries, 1.5-volt
- dual "D" cell battery holder
- insulated jumper leads with alligator clips at each end
- 3-foot-long (91 cm) piece of nichrome wire
- 3 or 4 scale model telephone poles

were brighter near the power plant than those across town from it. The resistance in the long runs of wire reduced the amount of power available to homes located far from the plant.

Today, improvements have been made that reduce wasted electricity in transmission wires, but significant losses still remain a problem. Power companies use AC (alternating current) instead of DC (direct current). Transformers can be used with alternating current to step voltage up or down. As current travels through a wire, resistance creates a power loss in the form of heat. The amount of power wasted is determined by the following formula:

$$power = current^2 \times resistance$$

As you can see, if either the current or the resistance figures can be reduced, then the power consumed will be reduced. Also, because:

$$power = voltage \times current$$

the same amount of power can be carried in the wires by either a high voltage with a low current or a low voltage with a high current. The power formula above suggests making current low to reduce wasted energy as heat. Therefore, power companies use transformers to step up the voltage at the power plant, thus reducing the current traveling in the wires. The voltage can then be stepped down by another transformer once it reaches your home, and higher current will be available for your use.

To further minimize resistance loss in wire, the diameter (thickness) of the wire can be increased. This works up to a certain point, after which further increasing offers no improvement. Imagine water rapidly flowing through a small hose compared to a larger hose. There is less resistance to the flow of water in the larger hose.

HYPOTHESIS Hypothesize that, because wire has resistance, electric power is wasted by the wires that carry it from the power plant to our homes.

PROCEDURE Gather the materials listed on the previous page. Nichrome wire can be purchased through a scientific supply house or obtained from a discarded toaster. (You may be able to pick up an old toaster for a dollar or two at a yard sale.) Have an adult help you remove the wire, which is the toaster's heating element. Three or four scale model telephone poles may be obtained from a hobby shop carrying model-train supplies. If you choose, use balsa wood and construct your own telephone poles.

Drape the nichrome wire along the model telephone poles. Use alligator clips to connect all components in the circuit, as shown in the illustration. One lightbulb will be connected near the battery supply and another 3 feet (91 cm) away, at the end of the nichrome wire. Which light is brightest?

RESULTS & CONCLUSION Write down the results of your experiment. Come to a conclusion as to whether or not your hypothesis was correct.

SOMETHING MORE

1. Use an ohmmeter to check the resistance of the wire when it is cold and again immediately after the bulbs have been operating for several minutes.
2. If the nichrome wire is kept cooled (run it through ice cubes), does the bulb at the far end appear any brighter?

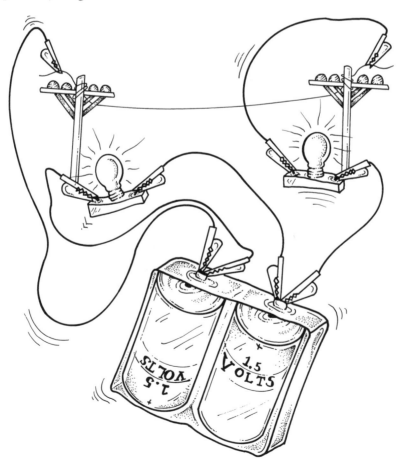

SECRET RESISTANCE

DETERMINING RESISTANCE BY INDIRECT MEASUREMENT AND COMPUTATION

PURPOSE We know that a lit bulb gets hot, but how can the resistance of the hot bulb be determined?

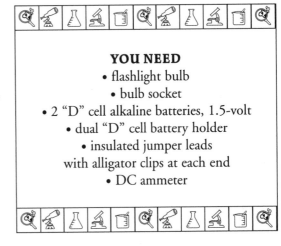

YOU NEED
- flashlight bulb
- bulb socket
- 2 "D" cell alkaline batteries, 1.5-volt
- dual "D" cell battery holder
- insulated jumper leads with alligator clips at each end
- DC ammeter

OVERVIEW It was in 1827 that Georg Ohm, a German high school teacher, discovered a very simple relationship, but one of the most valuable in the field of electricity. This relationship was among resistance, voltage, and current. Through experimentation, he discovered that the current flowing in a conducting device was directly proportional to the voltage across it. He developed a formula which is now known as "Ohm's law": voltage = current × resistance, where voltage is expressed in volts, current in amperes, and resistance in ohms. People in the field of electronics remember the formula as

$$\frac{\text{VOLTS}}{\text{AMPS} \times \text{OHMS}}$$

If two of the variables are known, the third can be determined by placing your hand over the variable you want to know and covering it. For example, to determine the voltage if the current and resistance are known, place your hand over VOLTS and you get the formula AMPS × OHMS. To find the amps (amperes), the formula becomes volts/ohms.

What is the resistance of a flashlight bulb when it is lit? An ohmmeter can only be used to read the resistance across the bulb when it is off and the filament is cold. But in order to light the bulb, voltage must be applied to it. An ohmmeter cannot read the resistance of any device that has power applied to it.

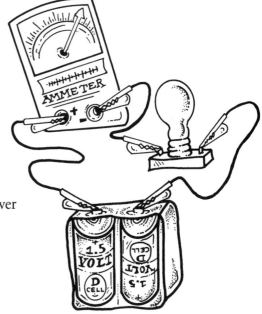

HYPOTHESIS   Hypothesize that, by the use of indirect measurement and Ohm's law, the resistance of a hot, illuminated flashlight bulb can be determined.

PROCEDURE   Construct the circuit as shown in the illustration on the previous page. Record the reading on the DC ammeter. The voltage across the bulb is 2 × 1.5 volts (or 3.0 volts), since there are two batteries in series and their voltages add together. Using Ohm's law, the bulb's resistance is equal to the voltage (3.0) divided by the ampere reading on the meter.

RESULTS & CONCLUSION   Write down the results of your experiment. Come to a conclusion as to whether or not your hypothesis was correct.

SOMETHING MORE   What is the difference in resistance between the cold bulb and the bulb when the filament is hot?

DIVIDE AND CONQUER

VOLTAGE DIVIDER CIRCUITS

PURPOSE A "potentiometer" is a special type of resistor whose resistance can be varied by moving a wiper arm across a resistive material, such as carbon. Whether you are aware of it or not, you are quite familiar with potentiometers and their use. Volume controls on your TV and stereo are potentiometers whose resistance is changed by turning a knob attached to a shaft. Other controls on TVs and stereos, such as color, brightness, treble, and bass, are also potentiometers. Is there a way to determine the resistance of a pententiometer?

YOU NEED
- 10k ohm resistor
- 10k ohm potentiometer
- DC ammeter
- dual "D" cell battery holder
- 2 "D" cell batteries, 1.5-volt
- insulated jumper leads with alligator clips at each end
- DC voltmeter (able to accurately show ¼ volts or less)
- ohmmeter

OVERVIEW When several resistors are placed in series with each other, each resistor "drops" a part of the total "supply" voltage across it. For example, suppose a 12-volt battery was connected across two resistors of equal value that were in series. Then each resistor shares in dropping a portion of the total voltage across it. The diagram shows the circuit. The total voltage is 12 volts. If both resistors are equal in their value of resistance, then the voltage measured from Point A to Point B will be 6 volts, and the voltage measured from Point B to Point C will also be 6 volts. The total voltage across the resistors is, of course, 12 volts. In a series circuit, the sum of the voltage dropped across each resistor is equal to the supply voltage. This resistor arrangement is called a "voltage divider."

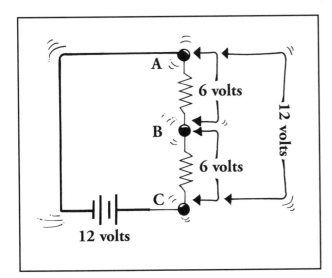

HYPOTHESIS Hypothesize that, by using the concept of a voltage divider, the resistance of a potentiometer can be determined by measuring the voltage drop across the potentiometer, measuring the current flowing in the circuit, and then mathematically applying Ohm's law.

PROCEDURE Construct the circuit illustrated. Potentiometers have three lugs (connection points) on them as shown. Only two are needed here. Use the center lug and one of the end lugs (it doesn't matter which one) in this project. Turn the shaft on the potentiometer to approximately the middle of its range. Using a DC voltmeter, measure the voltage drop across the potentiometer. As seen in the illustration, this would be measured between Point A and Point B. Record the voltage registering and the reading on the DC ammeter.

Using Ohm's law, where resistance in ohms = volts/amps, calculate the resistance of the potentiometer at its present shaft position.

Remove the potentiometer from the circuit. Without disturbing the shaft position, place the probes of an ohmmeter across the two lugs that were previously connected to the circuit. Measure the resistance. Is the measured resistance about the same as you calculated?

RESULTS & CONCLUSION Write down the results of your experiment. Come to a conclusion as to whether or not your hypothesis was correct.

SOMETHING MORE

1. Confirm that the sum of both voltage drops is equal to the supply voltage by measuring the voltage drop across both resistors then adding the two readings together.
2. What happens if there are three resistors in series? Can you still determine the resistance of each one by knowing the current flow and the voltage drop across each one?

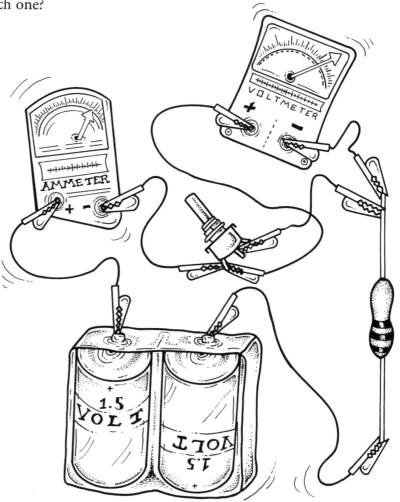

CHARGE IT!

CHARGING TIME IN A RESISTIVE/CAPACITIVE CIRCUIT

PURPOSE Determining how the value of the capacitance in a restive/capacitive circuit affects the charging time of the capacitor or capacitors.

OVERVIEW One of the factors that determines the electrical-storage capability of a capacitor is the surface area of the two plates that make up the capacitor. When voltage is placed across a capacitor that has no previous charge stored in it, electrons rush from the negative terminal of the power source (such as a battery) to one plate in the capacitor, while electrons on the other plate rush to the positive terminal of the power source. The electrons continue to flow until the voltage across the capacitor approaches the voltage supplied by the power source.

> ### YOU NEED
> - 9-volt battery
> - 9-volt-battery clip connector
> - two 220-microfarad, 35-volt capacitors
> - voltmeter
> - insulated jumper leads with alligator clips at each end
> - 10k ½-watt resistor
> - switch (such as: slide, toggle, or knife)
> - stopwatch or watch with a second hand
> - a friend

If a resistor is placed in series between the power source and the capacitor, the time it takes to charge the capacitor increases. This is called an "RC" circuit, meaning a "resistive/capacitive" circuit. Interestingly, electrical engineers have determined that the time it takes a capacitor in this kind of a circuit to charge to 63.2 percent of the power source voltage can be calculated by multiplying the value of the resistor (expressed in megohms) by the value of the capacitor (expressed in microfarads). This charging time, expressed in seconds, is called a "time constant."

HYPOTHESIS Hypothesize that the larger the value of capacitance in the resistive/capacitive circuit, the longer it will take to charge the capacitor (or capacitors) because of the increased overall plate surface area.

PROCEDURE Construct an RC circuit as shown on the following page. Observe the polarity of the meter, battery, and capacitor when connecting them.

Here is where a friend will be needed. When the on/off switch is closed, the voltage indicated on the meter will slowly rise. Have a friend begin a stopwatch the moment you close the switch and call out each second. Quickly, write down the voltage reading at that moment. After a short time, the voltage will stop increasing and appear to level off.

Draw a graph, with time in seconds on the X axis and voltage on the Y axis, and plot the data collected.

Next, take an insulated jumper wire and connect it across the capacitor, holding it there for at least one minute. This discharges the capacitor.

Connect another 220-microfarad capacitor across the one already in the circuit, placing the two capacitors in parallel to each other. Repeat the charging and recording procedure, recording the time versus the voltage across the capacitor.

RESULTS & CONCLUSION Graph the data collected. Write down the results of your experiment. Come to a conclusion as to whether or not your hypothesis was correct.

SOMETHING MORE

1. Place a milliammeter in series with the resistor and capacitor. When the switch is closed, observe what happens to the voltmeter reading and the milliammeter reading. The capacitor acts as a direct short the moment the switch is closed. All voltage is dropped across the resistor. Current leads the voltage when the capacitor is charging. On graph paper, chart both the charging current and the voltage with respect to time.

2. What happens to the charging time of the capacitor if the value of the resistor is increased or decreased? Try values of 100 ohms, 1k (1,000 ohms), 100k, 1 meg (1 million ohms).

3. Try placing different values of resistors across the capacitor to lessen the discharge time.

4. What happens to the charging time when two capacitors are placed in series instead of parallel?

SECTION 6
GENERATING ELECTRICITY

Human beings first used their own muscles to accomplish the tasks they needed to do. As time went on, various tools that could utilize animal power were invented. A poem written in 85 BC mentions the use of a waterwheel to harness the power of flowing water. The wind, too, has long been used to fill the sails of ships. Windmills were probably developed around the 700s in Persia.

Today, electricity is one of our main sources of energy, but it has to be generated and sent over transmission lines to our homes and businesses. Power utility companies generate electricity in several ways, including burning fossil fuels, harnessing moving water (hydroelectric generators), and nuclear energy.

Electricity can also be generated in other ways. In nature, lightning is a most powerful display of electricity. The electric eel, a fish that lives in the muddy waters of the Amazon River in South America, can generate shocks as strong as 300 volts, enough to stun a full-grown man.

Chemicals can be combined to form batteries that supply electric current. A thermocouple is a device made of two dissimilar metals which, when in contact with each other and heated, produces electricity. The electromotive force that is produced from a thermocouple, however, is in such small quantity that it is not used as a source of electricity, but as a temperature sensor in various devices. Solar cells convert sunlight to electrical potential. Piezoelectric energy is generated when crystals of certain materials are subjected to pressure, which makes it ideal for such applications as in microphones.

But, for supplying great amounts of electricity, the magneto concept is most widely used. This is where a coil cuts through a magnetic field, generating an electromotive force in the wire.

A SALT AND BATTERY

DETERMINING PEAK POWER
FROM WET-CELL BATTERY AS LOAD IS APPLIED

PURPOSE Are wet-cell batteries able to produce a steady current flow, or do they fluctuate? Does a wet-cell battery accumulate a charge over time? When a milliammeter is bridged across two electrodes (two dissimilar metals) suspended in an electrolyte solution, does the current flow build to a peak, or does it start at its peak output and fall off?

OVERVIEW When a certain pair of dissimilar metals are suspended in an electrolyte (a liquid solution that conducts electricity), a voltage potential is generated across the metals (making a "wet-cell" battery).

Different combinations of metal electrodes and electrolyte solutions will yield different electrical results. Some combinations may not produce any electricity, while others are good producers.

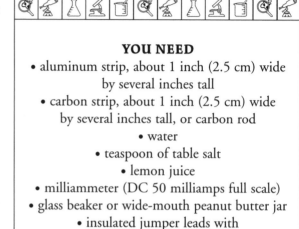

YOU NEED
- aluminum strip, about 1 inch (2.5 cm) wide by several inches tall
- carbon strip, about 1 inch (2.5 cm) wide by several inches tall, or carbon rod
- water
- teaspoon of table salt
- lemon juice
- milliammeter (DC 50 milliamps full scale)
- glass beaker or wide-mouth peanut butter jar
- insulated jumper leads with alligator clips on each end

HYPOTHESIS Hypothesize that the peak current delivered by a wet-cell battery which uses salt water as an electrolyte will either build up or fall off but does not stay steady after the circuit is initially closed to allow current flow.

PROCEDURE Place a strip of aluminum and a carbon rod in a glass beaker or wide-mouth peanut butter jar. Attach one end of an insulated jumper wire to the aluminum strip and one end of another jumper to the carbon rod. Fill the beaker with water and stir in a teaspoon of table salt. Attach one end of one of the jumpers to a terminal on a milliammeter. Observing the meter's needle, touch the other jumper to the other meter terminal. (Note: If the needle moves backwards, to below zero, reverse the two jumpers on the milliammeter terminals marked + and −. Since we are measuring direct current, we must consider polarity, which is the direction of current flow.)

Record the initial meter reading. After a few seconds, note and record the meter reading again. Continue to monitor the current flow, watching for a trend, steadily falling, rising, leveling off, and so on.

Repeat the procedure but this time replace the electrolyte solution (salt water) with a solution of lemon juice and water. Are the results different? Did both wet-cell batteries deliver a steady current flow, or did it quickly change once current began to flow?

You may wish to try other combinations of electrodes in salt water; such as zinc, lead, iron, and tin.

RESULTS & CONCLUSION Write down the results of your experiment. Come to a conclusion as to whether or not your hypothesis was correct.

SOMETHING MORE
1. How long will each wet cell continue to generate measurable current flow: aluminum and carbon with a lemon-juice electrolyte; with a salt water electrolyte? Make a graph showing time on one axis and milliamperes on the other.
2. Hypothesize which direction electrons flow for each pair of dissimilar metals used in making wet-cell batteries (zinc and carbon, carbon and aluminum, or lead and iron, for example).
3. Does the resistance of the electrolyte change by heating it? Does this have any effect on the voltage generated by the wet-cell battery?
4. Is the temperature of the electrolyte in a wet-cell battery a factor in voltage potential generated? If so, could the sun's rays be used to warm an electrolyte to make a better battery?
5. Try different electrolyte solutions: water, lemon juice, etc. Hypothesize that the greater the electrical resistance of the electrolyte (measured with an ohmmeter), the less voltage will be generated by the wet-cell battery (measured by a voltmeter).
6. How long will the wet-cell battery continue to generate current flow? Make a graph showing time versus milliamperes.

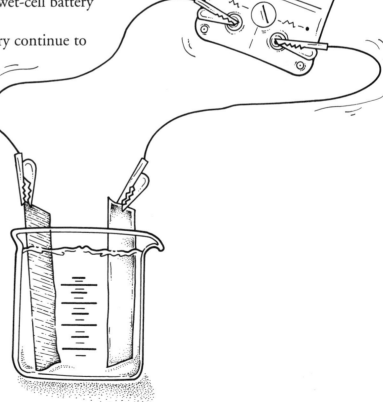

IDAHO ELECTRIC COMPANY

ELECTROLYTES IN POTATOES

PURPOSE Bet you thought french fries were only for eating! Do you have a problem seeing a potato as a power source? It is possible though, but quite a large number of potatoes would be needed to power even the smallest electrical device.

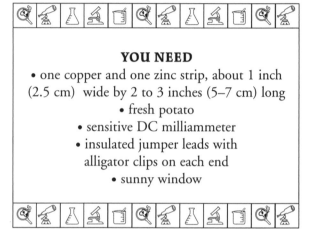

YOU NEED

- one copper and one zinc strip, about 1 inch (2.5 cm) wide by 2 to 3 inches (5–7 cm) long
- fresh potato
- sensitive DC milliammeter
- insulated jumper leads with alligator clips on each end
- sunny window

OVERVIEW Electricity can be produced by chemical action between two dissimilar metals with an "electrolyte" substance in between. An electrolyte is a liquid solution that conducts electricity and is used with certain metals to generate electricity.

Since a potato is made up largely of water, a "potato battery" is actually a type of wet-cell battery.

What happens to the electric-generating ability of a potato as it gets old, loses moisture, and begins to shrivel up? Do you think it will lose the ability to produce as much electricity as a fresh potato, because there is less water? Or do you think that, since there is less water, the substances in the water that make it an electrolyte are more concentrated and the potato will be capable of creating more electricity?

HYPOTHESIS Form a hypothesis based on either of these theories.

PROCEDURE Carefully cut a fresh potato in half and discard one section. Push a small copper strip into one side of the potato half and a small zinc strip in the other side. Use alligator clip leads to connect each metal strip to the terminals on a sensitive DC milliammeter. Measure and record the current indicated on the meter. Remove the metal strips.

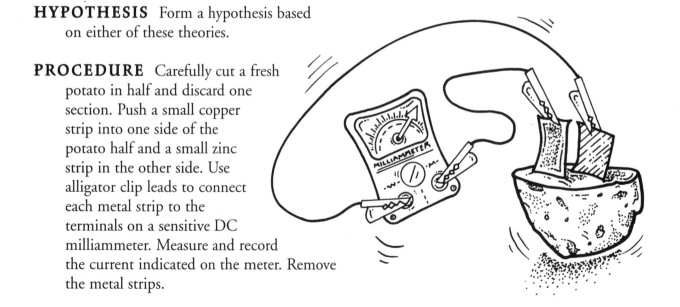

Place the potato in a sunny window. At the end of each day, insert the metal strips and record the amount of current indicated on the meter. Continue to check the output of the potato battery daily for several weeks.

RESULTS & CONCLUSION Compare the daily readings. Has the battery output risen, fallen, or remained the same over the several-week period? Reach a conclusion about your hypothesis. Do you think pH was a factor?

SOMETHING MORE

1. Perform this experiment with different types of potatoes, such as red skin, sweet, even cooked french fries.
2. Measure the output from a potato battery. Then microwave the potato until it is cooked. Measure the output again. Compare the cooked and uncooked outputs.
3. Perform the battery experiment using electrolytes other than potatoes, such as apples, oranges, or vegetables.
4. Is there a relationship between carbohydrate content and the ability of different potatoes to produce current?
5. Replace the copper and zinc strips in the potato battery with strips of other types of metals. Which combinations give the best results?

LIGHTEN UP

SOLAR CELLS

PURPOSE Learning about solar cells.

OVERVIEW The space age would have had a big setback had it not been for the invention of the "photovoltaic cell," commonly called a "solar cell." A solar cell is a semiconductor device that converts light into electricity. Satellites in orbit around the earth depend on solar cells to convert sunlight into electricity to power the equipment on board. Solar cells are also useful when a small electrical source is needed in a remote area where no electric power lines exist; for example, an isolated weather station that transmits data to scientists at a distant location.

> **YOU NEED**
> • 4 or more small solar cells
> • DC ammeter
> • DC voltmeter
> • insulated jumper leads with alligator clips on each end

Often you will see small mushroom-shape lights outlining walks and driveways of homes. To avoid the need for burying wire and making connections between a power source and each lamp, some light sets are completely self-contained. They require no external power connection because solar cells on the top of the lamps collect sunlight during the day and convert it to electricity. Rechargeable batteries store the electricity and, when the sky is dark at night, power the lamps.

The problem with solar cells has been that a small cell produces very little electrical power. A small cell (measuring about 1 × 2 inches or 2 × 4 centimeters) may be capable of delivering only about 0.3 amperes at ½ volt in full sunlight. A typical two-cell flashlight, by comparison, requires about 3 volts and 450 milliamperes to yield a bright light. For solar cells to be truly put to work, their power output needs to be increased.

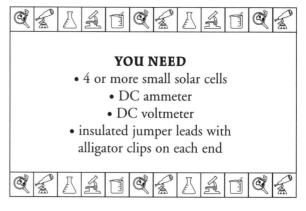

HYPOTHESIS Hypothesize that solar cells can be arranged and connected in various ways (combinations of series and parallel) to produce a variety of voltage and current requirements and thus make them useful for powering many devices.

PROCEDURE For series connections, the positive terminal of one cell is connected to the negative terminal of the next. For parallel connections, all the positive terminals are connected together and all the negative terminals are also tied together. Show that by connecting solar cells in series, the voltage is increased (use a voltmeter). Show that connecting solar cells in parallel increases the amount of current the cells are able to deliver (use a DC ammeter). Connect two sets of cells in series and then place both sets in parallel. Measure the total voltage and the total available current.

RESULTS & CONCLUSION Write down the results of your experiment. Come to a conclusion as to whether or not your hypothesis was correct.

SOMETHING MORE You may wish to enhance your science fair display by having the solar-cell assemblies power light-emitting diodes, small bulbs, and miniature motors.

NIAGARA SINK

HYDROELECTRIC POWER

PURPOSE Can water create electricity? Let's learn about hydroelectric power.

OVERVIEW To generate electricity, barrier dams are built across rivers to direct the flowing water past huge, water-catching mechanisms that rotate the armatures of generators. These great turbines generate tremendous "hydroelectric power" (electricity from flowing water) which does not use up our natural resources, as does energy derived from burning oil and coal—resources that are not renewable. The faster the armature of a generator rotates, the more power it provides.

HYPOTHESIS Hypothesize that increasing the velocity of water hitting paddle-wheel fins attached to a generator will increase the voltage output.

YOU NEED

- dual "D" cell battery holder
- sensitive DC voltmeter, capable of reading less than 1 volt
- insulated jumper leads with alligator clips on each end
- very thin balsa wood
- utility knife or wood cutting tool
- an adult
- sink with tap
- varnish or shellac
- paint brush
- glue

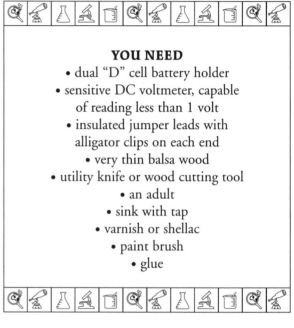

PROCEDURE Have an adult with a utility knife, or other balsa-wood cutting tool, cut out a small disk about 1¼ inch (3 cm) in diameter. You may want to place something round, such as the top of a small jar, on the wood and trace it. Into the edge of the wheel, cut six equidistant slots about 1¼ inch (3 cm) deep. Cut six small flat squares to act as the blades of a paddle wheel. Insert these blades into the disk's slots.

The wood should now be sealed to make it waterproof. Varnish or shellac the wheel assembly. When dry, make a small hole in the center of the wheel for the shaft of the motor (which will be our generator). Use glue to secure the wheel to the shaft. Connect the probes of a sensitive voltmeter (one capable of reading below

1 volt) to the generator. Hold the paddle-wheel device under a sink tap and turn the water on slightly. Watch the voltmeter readings as you slowly increase the amount of water coming from the tap. Does the voltage increase as you increase the velocity of the water?

RESULTS & CONCLUSION Write down the results of your experiment. Come to a conclusion as to whether or not your hypothesis was correct.

SOMETHING MORE
1. What happens if the water falls from higher up?
2. Research the Niagara Falls generating plant, Boulder Dam, and other hydroelectric plants.
3. Can you get your generator to produce enough power to illuminate a light-emitting diode (LED)?

METER MADE

PERIODS OF PEAK USE OF ELECTRIC POWER IN THE HOME

PURPOSE Does your home use more energy during the day or the night? Consider that during the day, parents may be at work and children at school and no one may be home. If the house uses electric heat, sunshine entering windows during the day may reduce the need for electric heat, while the sunless, colder evenings may need more.

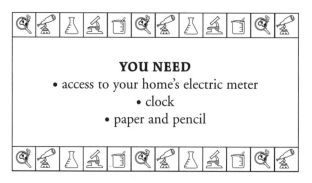

YOU NEED
- access to your home's electric meter
- clock
- paper and pencil

OVERVIEW We often take the convenience of electrical energy for granted. If we want to see in a dark room, we simply switch on the light and the room is filled with brightness. But using electricity costs money. Utility companies place an electric meter on each house to measure the amount of electricity used, so they know how much to bill. The utility companies measure the power used in "kilowatt-hours," one kilowatt being equal to 1,000 watts. It takes one kilowatt-hour of energy to operate ten 100-watt light bulbs for one hour.

HYPOTHESIS Choose two 12-hour periods, one during the day and one at night. The day hours, for example, may run from 8 a.m. to 8 p.m. and the night period from 8 p.m. to 8 a.m. Hypothesize in which period (day or night) most electric power is used in your home.

PROCEDURE Electric meters have dials on their faces that are used to measure electric power consumption. Similar to the car odometer, which measures mileage, the numbers continue to count upward. The meter is not reset by the utility company "meter reader" who comes by each month.

To determine the amount of energy used over a given period of time, you need to record the number showing on the dials at the beginning and at the end of the time period and subtract to get the difference. The dials on an electric meter are read from right to left. From right to left, the dials indicate the ones, tens, hundreds, and thousands places.

In the morning, at 8 a.m. (or whatever time you have decided to use) read and record the number indicated by the dial on the electric meter. At 8 p.m., or twelve hours later, read and record the number again. Subtract the morning from evening number to get the number of kilowatt-hours of energy used during the day.

At 8 a.m. the following morning, read and record the meter dials and subtract this number from the one recorded when you read the meter at 8 p.m. the night before. The result is the number of kilowatt-hours used during the twelve-hour night period. Compare the two numbers.

RESULTS & CONCLUSION   Write down the results of your experiment. Come to a conclusion as to whether or not your hypothesis was correct.

SOMETHING MORE

1. How much does it cost for the electricity used in your home during a typical 24-hour period? From the monthly electric bill, you can find the cost per kilowatt-hour. Depending on where you live, this may be 5 cents to 15 cents per kilowatt-hour. Record the electric meter reading at 8 a.m. and again 24 hours later. Find the difference between the two numbers. Multiply this number by the cost per kilowatt-hour to determine the cost for the 24-hour period. Do this for 7 days and calculate the average cost per day. Which day of the week had the highest use of energy? Which day had the least? Why do you think the readings on those days differed?

2. Determine the cost to run each electrical appliance in your home for one hour. Make a list of each electrical device: TV, computer, toaster, refrigerator, hair dryer, iron, and others. Use the stickers and tags on the back of the appliances or refer to the owner's manual to find its power consumption. For example, if the utility company in your area charges 12 cents per kilowatt-hour and the sticker on the back of the TV set lists energy consumption as 125 watts (which is .125 kilowatts), then:

$$0.12 \times 0.125 = 0.015$$

or 1½ cents per hour. Watching TV for 4 hours, then, would cost

$$4 \text{ hours} \times 1½ \text{ cents} = 6 \text{ cents}$$

Which electrical appliances are the heaviest users of electric power? Which cost the most to operate over the period of one year? An iron may be a heavy user of electricity but if it is only used to iron clothes once a week, it may not be the most costly appliance to operate over the period of a year.

3. Can you reduce your home's monthly electric bill by practicing electrical conservation? What ways do you think you might be able to lower consumption and save kilowatt-hours?

4. Electric meters have a round disc that rotates as electricity is used. A mark on this disc and the use of a stopwatch, or watch with a second hand, can be used to determine how many revolutions per minute the disc is rotating (count them). Reduce the electrical consumption in your home to as low as possible. Ask everyone not to use anything electrical while you are observing the meter. Be sure the refrigerator compressor is off while observing. Compare the number of revolutions per minute at this point with the number observed at other times, such as when a toaster, clothes dryer, air conditioner, or steam iron is running. The faster the disc rotates, the more energy is being used.

5. Household safety: What appliances should not be plugged into the same receptacle and used at the same time?

SECTION 7
SOLID-STATE ELECTRONICS

In our homes are many work-saving appliances: washing machines, dryers, refrigerators, swimming pool pumps, and vacuum cleaners. These are "electrical" appliances. Within the electrical field of study is a special branch called "electronics." Electronics is the science and practice of using special electrical components to perform tasks that are not possible with other electrical devices. The key devices in electronics are diodes, transistors, and integrated circuits, which make up a group called "semiconductors." Vacuum tubes also come under this category, but are seldom used today. The unique behavior of these electronic components makes possible radio, TV, long-distance phone service, computers, space travel, satellite communications, and advances in science, industry, and medicine.

The invention of the vacuum tube ushered in the age of electronics. But these devices were bulky, expensive, and inefficient. The next technological advance came in 1948 at Bell Telephone Laboratories with the invention of the transistor. Transistors performed the same electrical tasks as vacuum tubes, but they were inexpensive to make, were extremely small, required little energy, and could work in a wide range of temperatures. Thus began the era of miniaturization.

As technology improved, scientists were able to integrate thousands of transistors into one electrical component called an "integrated circuit." These "integrated circuits," sometimes affectionately referred to as "chips," make possible many of the appliances we enjoy today: computers, VCRs, microwave ovens, cordless phones, video games, and camcorders, to name a few.

ONE-WAY STREET

USING LEDS TO PROVE DIODES ESTABLISH DIRECTIONAL CURRENT FLOW WHEN AC SOURCE IS SUPPLIED

PURPOSE The diode is an extremely useful electronic component. Let's learn about diodes.

OVERVIEW In the early days of this industry, electronic tubes were used to perform the tasks that small semiconductor diodes do today. Semiconductors are materials that are classified between conductors and insulators. They exhibit unique electrical characteristics and are used in a wide variety of applications.

YOU NEED
- 9-volt AC transformer
- rectifier diode
- 1,000-ohm, ½-watt resistor
- 3 LEDs (light emitting diodes)
- low-wattage soldering tool and solder
- spool of solid conductor hookup wire
- wire cutters
- an adult, to solder and supervise

In electronic circuits, diodes can be used to convert AC (alternating current) to DC (direct current) through a process called "rectification," as well as to perform a number of other tasks. When the task is to change current from alternating to direct, the diode is sometimes called a "rectifier."

This project involves constructing a circuit that will use a diode to convert AC to DC. In AC circuits, the polarity of the power source is constantly changing. In the United States, the rate of polarity change in the electricity supplied to homes is 60 times per second, an amount determined by the power utility company. In DC circuits, the polarity remains constant, and current flows only in one direction. The "anode" is the positive terminal on the diode and the "cathode" is the negative. When a positive voltage is applied to the anode and a more-negative voltage on the cathode, then current flows through the diode.

HYPOTHESIS Hypothesize that a diode will establish a single-directional flow (DC) when an alternating current (AC) source is applied.

PROCEDURE Construct the circuit as shown in the illustration on the following page. This project requires some soldering. If you have never used a soldering tool before, ask someone experienced with soldering to show you the proper technique. You can then practice by twisting two pieces of bare hookup wire together and soldering them. **Caution:** The tip of a soldering tool gets very hot. Use the special stand made to safely hold the soldering tool when you aren't working with it. Place an old piece of cardboard or wood on your work area to catch any solder that drips. Be alert! Have an adult supervise.

As soon as you are finished soldering, unplug it. Remember that, although it may not look it, the tip will stay quite hot for a few minutes after the plug is disconnected.

In the circuit to be constructed, the AC power transformer provides the AC source of voltage to the circuit, stepping down the higher voltage in the wall outlet to 9 volts. This voltage is not only safer to work with, but LEDs (light emitting diodes) only need a few volts to work. A resistor is also added to further reduce the voltage which powers the circuit.

LEDs are a special type of diode. Similar to other diodes, they only let current flow through them in one direction. But when the polarity is correct and current flows through them, they glow like small lightbulbs. Different-colored translucent plastic cases let the light shine out. The most popular colors are clear, red, yellow, and green.

In our circuit, an LED is placed on the AC side of the diode being used as a rectifier. This LED will detect the presence of alternating current. Every time the polarity changes favorably for the LED, it will light; and when the polarity is reversed, which happens many times per second, it will not light. Our eyes, however, cannot even detect the flickering, since the 60 cycles are so fast.

Next in line is a diode that will only let current flow when the polarity of the voltage reaching it though the resistor is positive. In this instance, the diode becomes a conductor. When the AC polarity swings in reverse, the diode will stop conducting and it will act like an open circuit.

To prove the hypothesis, two LEDs are placed on the output side of the rectifying diode. Note the polarity of these LEDs. In reference to their polarity, one is connected in a way opposite to the other. Remembering that the rectifying diode will only conduct when the positive part of the AC cycle reaches its anode, which LED do you think will light? If one of the LEDs on the output side of the diode lights and the other does not, your hypothesis is correct.

RESULTS & CONCLUSION Write down the results of your experiment. Come to a conclusion as to whether or not your hypothesis was correct.

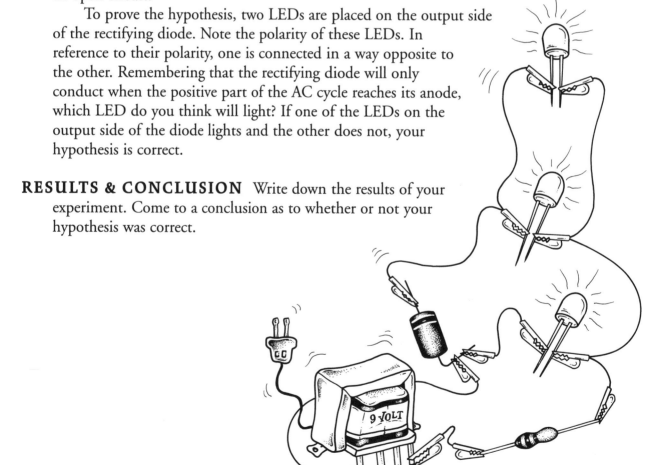

CUT THE SINE IN HALF

SPEAKER CAN DETECT DIODE'S ABILITY TO CHANGE WAVE FORM

PURPOSE What affect does a diode have on the shape of a wave form?

OVERVIEW The AC (alternating current) voltage supplied to our homes by the electric utility companies changes its polarity many times each second. The "frequency" of these changes is measured in "cycles" or "Hertz." In the United States, the frequency is 60 times per second, or 60 Hertz. The wave form that is created by this change is called a "sine wave." A sine wave shows graphically how the AC voltage changes polarity. The amplitude (size) of the voltage increases in one direction, then decreases and begins increasing in the opposite direction, completing the cycle by returning back to the starting point. The swing of a simple pendulum traces a sine wave.

YOU NEED

- speaker (preferably 6-inch diameter or larger)
- 9-volt AC transformer
- rectifier diode
- 1,000-ohm, ½-watt resistor
- low-wattage soldering tool and solder
- spool of solid conductor hookup wire
- insulated jumper leads with alligator clips on each end
- wire cutters
- an adult

By using a transformer, the higher AC voltage (120 volts in the United States) coming from an electrical wall outlet can be stepped down to a lower voltage. When a low-voltage AC sine wave is applied to a speaker, we hear a pure, low tone. When a diode is used as a rectifier to convert AC to DC, it changes the shape of the AC sine wave. Since the diode will only conduct when the voltage coming into it is of the correct polarity, the wave form coming out of the diode will be missing half of the sine wave each cycle. This will alter the sound we hear if that wave form is applied to a speaker.

HYPOTHESIS Hypothesize that a diode changes the shape of an alternating current wave form and this can be detected by a change in sound.

PROCEDURE Construct the circuit shown in the illustration. This project will require a little soldering. If this is new to you, ask someone with experience at soldering to show you the proper technique. You can practice by twisting two pieces of bare hookup wire together and soldering them. *Caution:* The tip of a soldering tool gets quite hot. Place the tool in a stand that holds it safely when you aren't soldering with it. An old piece of cardboard or wood placed on the work area will catch any solder that drips. Be very careful. In addition to doing soldering jobs, the hot soldering pencil tip can cause a painful burn. Have an adult supervise and, as soon as you are finished using the tool, pull the plug. Be aware that the soldering tip, though it may not look hot, will stay hot for several minutes after the electric plug is disconnected from the wall outlet.

The speaker needed for this project is not critical, but the larger it is, the better. We are dealing with a low frequency, and large speakers reproduce this lower frequency better than smaller speakers do. To save you money, a local TV-repair shop may be willing to sell you a used speaker from an old stereo, or you may be lucky enough to find one at a flea market, or one that someone has discarded.

In the circuit to be constructed, the AC transformer provides the AC voltage, stepping the voltage in the wall outlet down to 9 volts. The resistor helps to further decrease the voltage and limit the amount of current passing through to the speaker to prevent damage to it.

Connect jumper leads with alligator clips on each end to the terminals on the speaker. Connect the other ends to the resistor and transformer at points A and B. Listen to the sound that is coming from the speaker.

Disconnect the speaker lead at point A and connect it instead to point C. Listen again to the sound coming from the speaker. Does it sound different than it did before? Describe the sound difference you hear.

RESULTS & CONCLUSION Write down the results of your experiment. Come to a conclusion as to whether or not your hypothesis was correct.

SOMETHING MORE This project uses one diode and makes a half-wave rectifier circuit. Get a basic book on electronics and construct a full-wave rectifier using four diodes. Does the sound coming from the speaker appear any different?

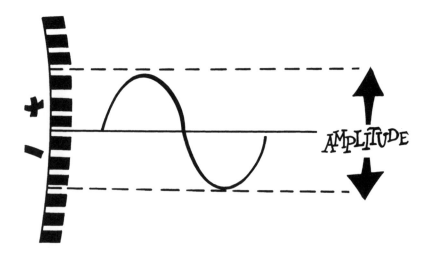

YES OR NO

AND and OR computer logic circuits

PURPOSE Many of the electronic circuits that make up a computer can be represented as single "blocks" that perform a handful of operations. Such blocks include storage of data, "flip-flops," and "gates." Inside the computer, these blocks actually consist of many electronic components: resistors, transistors, capacitors, and integrated circuits.

    Just as a gate in a fence will let an animal through if it is open and will prevent it from passing through when it is closed, a "logic gate" refers to a circuit that will allow passage of a signal *under certain conditions*.

YOU NEED
- 2 dual "D" cell battery holders
- 4 "D" cell batteries, 1.5-volt
- 4 single-pole, single-throw, toggle switches
- 2 LEDs (light-emitting diodes)
- solid-core hookup wire
- low-wattage soldering tool and solder
- printed circuit board for mounting components

OVERVIEW The two most common types of computer logic gates are the AND gate and the OR gate. Consider a cow pen that has two fence gates in series with each other. Let's represent a closed gate condition by the number zero, meaning no cows can pass. If one gate is open, the condition is represented by the number one. All information stored in a computer is in the form of binary numbers (base two), either a 1 or a 0. As you can see from the illustration, both gates must be open for the cows to pass out of the pen.

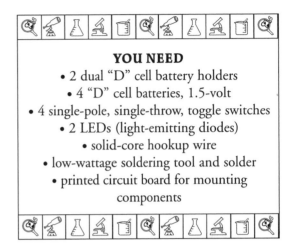

AND

OR

    Computer logic gates have two or more "inputs" and one "output." The accompanying chart for AND and OR gates shows the status of the outputs for each possible input condition. Both inputs of an AND gate must have a 1 present in order for the output to be 1. Similarly, both the first fence gate and the second fence gate must be open in order for any cows to pass through.

    The second illustration shows how the OR gate relates to our cow-pen analogy. In the AND gate scenario, both gates have to be open before cows can pass. In the OR configuration, either the first fence gate or the second gate can be open to let cows pass.

HYPOTHESIS Hypothesize that you can use toggle switches to represent the concept of AND and OR computer logic gates.

PROCEDURE   This project will require a little soldering. If you have never not done this before, ask someone experienced with soldering to show you the proper technique. You can practice by twisting two pieces of bare hookup wire together and soldering them.

Caution: A soldering pencil tip gets quite hot. Use a stand to safely hold the hot soldering tool when you aren't actually using it. A piece of cardboard or wood under your work will catch any solder that drips. Be alert that the tip of the soldering tool can burn you. Have an adult supervise. As soon as you are finished using the tool, unplug it, but still be careful of the tip. Although it may not look hot, it will stay hot for some minutes after you disconnect it from the outlet.

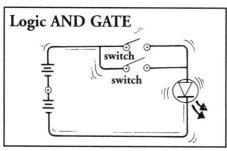

Logic AND GATE

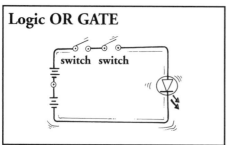

Logic OR GATE

Construct two circuits, one in which two switches are placed in series and the other in which two switches are placed in parallel. Be sure to observe the correct polarity when wiring the batteries and the LEDs into the circuit, since these components will not work if they are installed incorrectly.

The circuit in which the two switches are in parallel with each other represents the OR computer logic gate. If either the first switch or the second switch is placed in the "on" position, the LED will light.

The circuit in which the two switches are wired in series with each other represents the AND computer logic gate. Both the first switch and the second switch must be on before the LED will light.

Compare all possible combinations of on/off positions and the switches with the AND and OR logic tables shown in the chart. Replace each 0 with the word "off" and each number 1 with the word "on." Try each switch combination as shown on the chart, placing the switches in various on and off positions and making note of whether the LEDs are lit or not.

RESULTS & CONCLUSION   Write down the results of your experiment. Come to a conclusion as to whether or not your hypothesis was correct.

SOMETHING MORE

1. Some computer logic and gates have more than two inputs. How would the above AND switch circuit be modified to simulate a 4-input computer logic and gate?

2. There are other logic gates used in electronics: NAND, NOR and XOR. Research the logic tables for them. Can similar circuits using switches, batteries, and LEDs be used to illustrate the concept of these gates?

Gate Logic Tables		
AND		
Input A	**Input B**	**Output**
0	0	0
0	1	0
1	0	0
1	1	1
OR		
Input A	**Input B**	**Output**
0	0	0
0	1	1
1	0	1
1	1	1

REPULSIVE ATTRACTION

USING SOUND WAVES TO REPEL INSECT PESTS

PURPOSE Can sound repel flying insects?

OVERVIEW During the spring, summer, and autumn months, many of us are bothered by insect pests. Some insects, such as gnats, are so tiny that even well-screened doors and windows don't keep them out. Do nocturnal insects respond to sound? Are they either attracted to the source of it or repelled by it?

HYPOTHESIS Hypothesize whether or not you think sound has any effect on common flying nocturnal insects in your area.

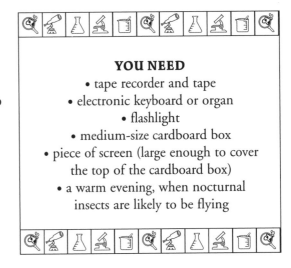

YOU NEED
- tape recorder and tape
- electronic keyboard or organ
- flashlight
- medium-size cardboard box
- piece of screen (large enough to cover the top of the cardboard box)
- a warm evening, when nocturnal insects are likely to be flying

PROCEDURE Leave the first 15 minutes of an audio tape blank, with no sound on it. Then record 10 minutes of a continuous, very-low note, sustaining the key on a electronic synthesizer or organ. Follow that with 10 minutes of a continuous high tone.

Open out or remove the top flaps from a cardboard box about 2-feet square (3,600 square cm). On a warm evening after dark, when insects are out, place the box outside. Put a lit flashlight and the tape recorder, containing the tape of low and high notes, into the box. Turn the recorder on and place a piece of screen over the top of the box.

The light from the flashlight will attract all kinds of nocturnal insects. Many will gather on the screen, where they can be roughly counted. The first 15 minutes of the tape has no sound, therefore, the light should be the only thing that is attracting the insects. Toward the end of this quiet period, count the number of insects on the screen, doing it as accurately as you can. As the tape continues to play, the 10 minutes of the low note will be heard. After several minutes, count the number of insects now on the screen. Several minutes after the high note starts to play, count the number of insects on the screen again.

RESULTS & CONCLUSION Write down the results of your experiment. Come to a conclusion as to whether or not your hypothesis was correct.

SOMETHING MORE

1. Does volume have an effect?
2. Use smaller incremental changes in frequency, perhaps recording five minutes of each key played on the organ or keyboard in an attempt to find a frequency that either attracts or repels insects.
3. Can you identify any of the type of species of insects that have gathered on the screen (beetles, butterflies, mosquitos, and so on)?
4. Instead of placing a tape recorder in the box, play a radio tuned to a station playing music. This would generate a wide range of frequencies at once.

SECTION 8
RADIO-FREQUENCY ENERGY

Radio frequency waves, commonly called RF energy, are electromagnetic waves resembling light waves in their behavior. They travel at the speed of light. Radio waves are produced by an electronic high-frequency oscillator, a circuit that causes voltage to swing back and forth many times a second. This vibrating rate (the number of cycles per second) is called the "frequency" of the wave. There are various frequency "bands." These bands, or groups of frequencies, are used for different types of communications. On your radio, you may recall seeing the number KHz at one end of your AM dial (KHz means 1,000 "Hertz" or cycles per second). Radio waves in the "AM broadcast band" are called "long waves." The "short wave" band begins where the other leaves off and is commonly used for foreign radio broadcasts. FM radio and television stations broadcast at much higher frequency bands, up in the millions of cycles per second. Extremely high frequencies in the gigaHertz range (1 billion cycles per second) are called "microwaves." Home satellite TV dishes and microwave ovens work at these frequencies.

Radio waves can be used to carry sound and pictures through the air. At a radio station, the music and announcer's voice is electronically combined with a "carrier wave," which is a high frequency radio wave. This wave is then transmitted from the station's antenna and it travels many miles through the air until it reaches the receiving antenna on your radio. The circuitry inside the radio allows you to tune in one station at a time and separate the sound from the radio-wave carrier. The transmission of television pictures, although much more complex, is handled in a similar manner.

The carrier wave can be amplified, made much more powerful, to increase the distance it can cover. Listen to your AM radio during the day and during the night. Log the stations you hear. Do you receive some stations at night that you can't bring in during the day?

INTERFERENCE: FOILED AGAIN!

ATMOSPHERIC RADIO-FREQUENCY NOISE GENERATED BY ELECTRICAL DEVICES AROUND THE HOME

PURPOSE How can we reduce the amount of radio-frequency noise given off by electronics?

OVERVIEW One of the problems with electronic appliances with circuitry that operates at very high speeds is that they radiate RF (radio frequency) energy. Such appliances usually have a type of filter system or shielding to suppress RF radiation, but some energy may leak out and can often be detected in close proximity to the appliance.

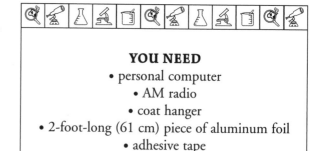

YOU NEED
- personal computer
- AM radio
- coat hanger
- 2-foot-long (61 cm) piece of aluminum foil
- adhesive tape

One such offending electronic device is the personal computer. Computers, especially the newer models, operate at very high speeds, in—the megaHertz range (1 megaHertz is 1 million cycles per second). If radiation is too strong, this can pose a problem. If someone in your home is using a personal computer that is radiating a strong RF signal, it may interfere with someone else there trying to listen to a radio or watch television.

HYPOTHESIS Hypothesize that radio-frequency interference generated by an electronic appliance can be reduced by the proper use of shielding.

PROCEDURE Turn an AM radio on and set the tuning dial to a position where no station can be heard and the background noise is fairly quiet. Place a personal computer on a table or desk and turn it on. Bring the AM radio close to the computer. Do you hear a whistling sound from the radio? To be sure the RF signal being heard is radiating from the computer, turn the computer off. The whistling sound will disappear if its origin is the computer.

Using adhesive tape, tape a 2-foot-long (61 cm) piece of aluminum foil to the bottom of a coat hanger. Holding the coat hanger, slowly pass the foil sheet between the computer and the radio. Keep the foil close to the radio to reduce the amount of RF signal that leaks around the foil. Observe and record any changes in sound coming from the radio.

RESULTS & CONCLUSION Write down the results of your experiment. Come to a conclusion as to whether or not your hypothesis was correct.

SOMETHING MORE
1. What happens to the whistling sound heard in the AM radio as you do different functions on the computer, such as access a disk drive or press keys on the keyboard?
2. Is the interference stronger on one part of the AM band than the other? (Is it stronger at the lower or higher frequencies, or doesn't it make any difference?)
3. Could this setup be used as a metal detector?
4. Try using other materials to shield the radio-frequency interference, such as plastic, glass, and wood.

ONLY WAY OUT

LIMITING THE DIRECTION OF RADIO-FREQUENCY RADIATION

PURPOSE Is it possible to limit the direction of RF (radio frequency) waves transmitted by a walkie-talkie?

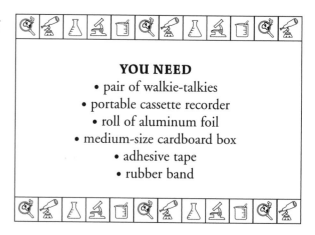

YOU NEED
- pair of walkie-talkies
- portable cassette recorder
- roll of aluminum foil
- medium-size cardboard box
- adhesive tape
- rubber band

OVERVIEW When RF waves are transmitted by a walkie-talkie, the waves leave the tall rod antenna in an "omnidirectional" pattern, that is, they radiate out in all directions equally. This is similar to the waves that ripple out when a stone is dropped into a pond. In this project, we will try to limit the direction of the energy's travel.

HYPOTHESIS Hypothesize that it is possible to limit the direction of a radio wave.

PROCEDURE Record your voice on a portable tape recorder, talking for about 10 minutes. You could read part of a book or the daily newspaper.

Tear the flaps off of a cardboard box about 2 to 3 feet square (61 to 91 cm square). Cover all the sides of the box, including the closed bottom, with aluminum foil, taping it to the box.

Lay the box on its side outside so that the open side, the top, faces out. Place the cassette recorder with the tape of your voice in the box. Near the recorder's speaker, place one of the walkie-talkies, to catch the sound. If your walkie-talkie has a high, telescoping antenna, reduce the size of it so that will fit inside the box. Use a rubber band to depress the walkie-talkie's transmit button, holding it "on." Start the cassette recorder playing.

With the second walkie-talkie tuned to the channel on which the other walkie talkie is transmitting, walk all around the box and listen for any changes in the sound you hear. Does the sound become weaker when you walk behind the box or along the sides that have the aluminum-foil shielding?

RESULTS & CONCLUSION Write down the results of your experiment. Come to a conclusion as to whether or not your hypothesis was correct.

SOMETHING MORE Stake out the strong reception area in front of the box. Measure the angle of the strong signal coming out of the box.

GLOSSARY

AC alternating current, current that changes polarity (direction) rapidly.

acceleration an increase in speed. To accelerate means to go faster. Physicists define acceleration as a measure of the rate of change of velocity over time.

acid is a characteristic describing a chemical substance. Substances that are strongly acidic may "burn" your skin or dissolve other substances. A pickle tastes sour because it is an acid. The opposite of an acid is an alkaline. Chemists use a scale called a pH scale to determine whether a substance is an acid, an alkaline, or neutral.

acoustics the study of how sound behaves, usually in rooms, halls, and auditoriums. The volume, quality, and amount of reverberation of sound are often important acoustic characteristics about a room.

alloy a metal made from a mixture of different metals or a combination of a metal and another substance, which gives the metal new qualities.

ampere the unit of measure for current flow, often referred to simply as "amp."

amplitude the size or amount of wave form or signal. In electronics, often measured in volts.

anode the positive terminal on a battery or electronic component (such as a tube or a diode).

apparatus equipment used in a chemist's laboratory; the tools of the trade include flasks, beakers, test tubes for handling small amounts of substances, scales and balances, and Bunsen burners.

armature a rotating wire coil placed in a magnetic field. Armatures are found in generators and motors.

assumption In doing science experiments, scientists often make assumptions that certain things are true. An assumption is something that is believed to be true.

base substances that are strongly alkaline in the measure of their pH. Alkaline substances may "burn" the skin.

buoyancy The buoyancy of an object is its ability to float on the surface of water (or any fluid). Water gives an upward push on any object in it. The amount of force pushing up is equal to the weight of the water that the object "displaces" (takes the place of).

calibrate to make a correction or adjustment, often to a measuring device. When two thermometers are used in an experiment, it is important that both report temperatures accurately. When they are in the same place, they should both read the same temperature. If one reads higher than the other, it must be noted and the difference in temperature must be added or subtracted from the other one in all experiments where the temperatures on the two thermometers are compared.

calories For the human body to function, it needs energy. We get energy for our bodies by eating foods. The amount of energy we can get from a particular food is measured in units called calories.

capacitor an electronic component that stores an electrical charge. It consists of two metal plates separated by an insulating material. The unit of measure of capacitance is the farad. They are often used in television sets, computers, radios, and other electronic devices.

carbon One of the basic elements of matter, carbon combines with many other substances to take on different forms. Carbon can combine with oxygen to form carbon dioxide, a gas that plants absorb to make food for the plant. Carbon is also a residue of burning.

catalyst something that can speed up, slow down, or cause a change in a chemical reaction. The catalyst substance itself does not change.

cathode the negative terminal on a battery or electronic component (such as a tube or diode).

caustic can damage or destroy (corrode or burn) from a chemical reaction.

centrifugal force a force that pushes outward when an object is moving in a curve.

chemical change When a chemical change takes place, a new substance with different properties is formed. Rust is produced when oxygen and iron combine. This is different than a physical change, which is the change of a substance from one form to another without a change in its composition; freezing and melting are examples of a physical change.

chemical equation the use of chemical symbols in a formal statement to represent the complex factors that are the result of chemical reaction.

chemical symbols one or two letter "abbreviations" that represent the elements. Elements are substances that cannot be chemically broken down into simpler basic substances.

colloidal A colloidal substance is a gelatin-like substance in which the small particles that make it up do not dissolve, but stay suspended in the fluid. The substance may be more like a liquid in one state and more solid like a putty in another state.

compound A chemical compound is a substance made up of two or more elements in a certain proportion to each other. Compounds often do not have the characteristics of the elements that compose them. Water is a compound containing two parts of hydrogen to one part of oxygen. Oxygen makes fire burn, yet water (H_2O) puts fires out.

conductor a material that makes an easy path through which current can flow. Metal is a good conductor of heat, making an easy path for heat to be carried along; it is also a good conductor of electricity.

control When doing experiments, a control has all the variables maintained. For example, to test the effects of carbon monoxide on plants, you must have two equally healthy plants. Both plants would receive exactly the same care and conditions (soil, sunlight, water). The experimental plant only would receive additional carbon monoxide. The other plant would be the control plant. The control plant would receive maintained conditions while the experimental plant receives the variation. Larger experiments often require a "control group."

crystals Some substances have a characteristic shape of smooth, flat sides with sharp edges and corners. Table salt and sugar are crystals, with grains shaped like three-dimensional cubes.

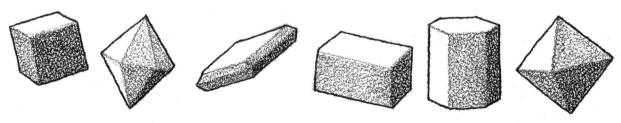

current flow the transfer of energy along a conductor by the movement of electrons.

cycle Every time a voltage or signal reverses polarity and then changes back again constitutes one cycle. The polarity in the electrical outlets in the United States changes 60 times a second. Another term often used to describe a cycle is the "Hertz." One million cycles per second may also be referred to as 1 million Hertz, or 1 megaHertz. The number of cycles per second is called "frequency."

DC direct current, unchanging current as supplied by a battery.

dead short an electrical path that has almost no resistance to impede current flow. This term is traditionally used to describe an electrical path of extremely low resistance (near zero ohms), where normally there would be a higher resistance. This signals a problem such as a failed electrical component or a faulty electrical path.

density The density of a material refers to how closely packed together the matter is that makes up that material. If two objects are exactly the same size, one will weigh more if it is denser than the other. Objects that are less dense than water will float in it; objects that are denser will sink.

diameter the distance across an object measured as if a straight line was drawn from one side to the other through the middle.

dilute the addition of liquid to make something thinner or weaker.

dissolve to break down a substance into a liquid. You can dissolve salt in water.

distillation a method of extracting or purifying a substance.

distilled water water totally free of impurities. It can be purchased at supermarkets and pharmacies.

drag an aviation term meaning the resistance by air to the forward motion of an aircraft. Drag is a force that tries to slow down a plane as it moves faster through the air, causing it to use more fuel energy.

echo a distinct repeat of a sound. If the ear hears two sounds that are the same but the second sound is at least 65 milliseconds later than the first sound, the brain will interpret them as an echo or as separate sounds. An echo is caused by sound reflecting off of a surface and returning back to the ear.

elasticity the material's ability to be stretched or compressed and then return to shape.

electric circuit various electrical components connected and arranged in a way to allow at least one closed path for current to flow.

electrical potential a measure of the ability of a battery or other power source to do work. Electrical potential is measured in volts.

electrode the terminal of an electrical source. The electrode with the positive charge is called the anode, and the electrode with the negative charge is the cathode.

electrolyte a liquid solution that conducts electricity and, when used with certain metals, can generate electricity. Typical electrolytes are a solution of salt water and a solution of diluted sulfuric acid.

electromagnet a magnet that only attracts when electric current is connected to a power source.

electromagnetic field (EMF) an induced field around a moving electric device or current through a conductor.

electromotive force (EMF) another term for "voltage," the electrical potential to do work.

element a substance that cannot be separated into different substances (except by nuclear disintegration). All matter is made up of elements. There are currently 111 known elements.

endothermic reaction a chemical change requiring heat for a reaction to take place.

exothermic reaction a chemical change where heat is given off when the reaction takes place.

experiment a planned operation designed to test a hypothesis.

farad the unit of measure of capacitance.

fermentation a chemical change involving the breaking down of a combination of starch and sugar. The combination is turned into alcohol and carbon dioxide gas. When cider ferments, vinegar is formed.

fluorescent bulb See **incandescent bulb**.

flux See **magnetic flux**.

force a push or a pull on an object. It is an action that can change the motion of a body. Sources of force include gravity, electricity, magnetism, and friction.

frequency the number of times per second an alternating current completes a full cycle, going from a positive polarity to negative, and back to positive again.

friction Friction is the resistance to motion when two things rub together. Friction keeps a car on the road. It makes your hands warm when you rub them together quickly. Melting ice reduces friction, which makes it hard to walk on it without falling.

fulcrum the supporting object around which a lever (a simple machine) pivots.

fuse an electrical safety device which stops the flow of current in a circuit if the current flow increases beyond a desired level. Fuses are rated by the maximum number of amperes they will allow to flow before they "blow" and open the circuit.

germination The short time period when a seed begins to sprout a root and a leaf (using its own stored energy) but before it is able to make food on its own.

gravity a force of attraction between two objects

ground electrical ground is a point in a circuit where there is a zero volt potential in reference to the earth. The earth always has a potential of zero volts.

heat sink usually a specially shaped piece of metal used to carry heat away from an object. In electronics, heat sinks are attached to transistors and integrated circuits to keep them cooler.

hertz another term for "cycles," named in honor of Heinrich Rudolph Hertz (1857–1894) who discovered electromagnetic waves, the basis for radio and TV communications.

hydraulics a branch of physics that studies the laws of liquids in motion.

hypothesis a thoughtful, reasoned guess about something, based on what is known. A hypothesis must be proven by experimentation.

incandescent bulb The most common types of electric lights used in our homes are incandescent and fluorescent bulbs. In both kinds of light, electrical energy is turned into light energy. In an incandescent light bulb, electricity passes through a small wire, called a filament, which glows brightly. In a fluorescent light bulb (which is often in the shape of a long, straight tube or a circular tube), the inside of the bulb is filled with a gas. The inside glass of the bulb is coated with materials called phosphors. When electricity is passed through a heating element in the bulb, the gas gives off rays which cause the phosphors to fluoresce (glow).

inorganic chemistry deals with substances that do not contain carbon. Carbon is the chemical of life.

insulator a material through which electricity will not flow.

kilowatt-hour a unit of measure of electrical power consumption used by power companies in determining how much to charge their customers for the electricity they use. A kilowatt is 1,000 watts. It takes one kilowatt-hour of electrical energy to operate ten 100-watt light bulbs for one hour.

kinetic energy the energy of work being done; the energy of motion. A bowling ball rolling down an alley is an example of kinetic energy. See **potential energy**.

LED, or **light emitting diode** an electronic component that produces a small light from a semiconductor material. LEDs are commonly used in watches and as light indicators on home stereos, computers, and other home electronic appliances.

litmus paper is a device used by chemists to measure the pH of a substance; that is, its acidity or alkalinity. It is a dye made from certain plants. A substance which is an acid will turn blue litmus paper red. Alkalines turn red litmus blue or deep violet. If the solution is neutral, it will not change the color of the paper. Litmus paper is inexpensive to buy. You can make your own by boiling cabbage.

load the power absorbing device in a circuit.

magnet a material which exhibits the unique property of attracting pieces of iron and steel.

magnetic flux a field in the space surrounding a wire carrying an electric current or the field surrounding a magnet.

magnetism a force exhibited by certain objects that attract iron.

mass how much "stuff" an object is made of. The more mass it has, the heavier it is. A Ping-Pong ball and a golf ball are about the same size and shape, but a golf ball has more mass.

micro a prefix meaning one millionth. A microfarad is one millionth of a farad.

microfarad a unit of measure of electrical storage used to indicate how large an electric charge can be stored by an electrical component called a capacitor.

microwaves Microwaves are a kind of radio frequency energy. They are electromagnetic waves. Their frequency (the number of times the wave vibrates each second) is much higher than most other types of radio and TV waves. Microwaves are used for telephone and satellite communications as well as for cooking in "microwave ovens."

milli a prefix meaning one thousandth. A milliampere is one thousandth of an ampere.

mixture When two or more elements or compounds are combined but do not chemically combine to form new substances, the substance is called a mixture. Orange juice, air and sea water are mixtures. The proportions of each element or compound can be in different amounts.

nano a prefix meaning one billionth. A nanosecond is one billionth of a second.

nichrome wire an alloy of nickel, iron, and chromium which has a high electrical resistance as it heats and is used as a heating element in toasters.

noise random electrical voltages in the atmosphere and in electronic circuits which are usually undesirable. Noise may interfere with the operation of electronic equipment. Lightning causes electrical noise in the atmosphere which can be heard as sharp cracks in an AM radio.

nuclear energy is a type of energy that is released when the nuclei of atoms are either combined together (called fusion) or split apart (called fission). The energy released, called nuclear energy, is in the form of heat, light, or some other type of radiation. Nuclear energy is used to make electricity by heating steam that drives giant turbine generators.

observation using your senses—smelling, touching, looking, listening, and tasting—to study something closely, sometimes over a long period of time.

ohm the unit of measure of resistance.

Ohm's law Georg Simon Ohm discovered a relationship between voltage, current, and resistance in 1827, with the equation: current × resistance = voltage, where current is expressed in amperes, resistance in ohms, and voltage in volts.

open circuit an electrical circuit where there is a break in the path, preventing current from flowing.

organic chemistry deals with all substances that contain carbon; the chemistry of life. The opposite is inorganic chemistry.

oxidation is a process that occurs when oxygen combines with other substances and changes them. Oxidation can happen quickly as when a log burns in a fireplace, or it can happen slowly as when a metal object oxidizes and turns to rust. Heat is given off whether the process happens quickly or slowly. When oxidation occurs rapidly, a lot of heat is given off and sometimes light is given off, too.

parallel circuit an electrical circuit where components are connected across one another rather than connected end to end.

pendulum A weight hung by a wire or string tied to a fixed point (one that doesn't move) is called a pendulum. If the weight is pulled to one side and then released to fall freely, it will swing back and forth. Gravity pulls it down, and then momentum keeps it moving past the "at rest" hanging point. Eventually, the weight stops swinging back and forth because air friction slows it down.

pH is a measure of the acidity of a substance. On the pH scale, pure water is in the middle of the range, with a pH of 7. A lower number means the substance is an acid. A higher reading means it is an alkali. Litmus paper is a device which turns red when dipped in a substance that is an acid and blue when it is an alkali. The abbreviation pH stands for "potential of electricity for positive hydrogen ions."

photosynthesis The process of a plant making its food by gathering light energy from the sun is called photosynthesis. Also needed in the process are carbon dioxide, water, chlorophyll (which gives leaves their green color), and trace amounts of minerals.

photovoltaic cell a semiconductor device that converts light into electricity (also referred to as a **solar cell**).

piezo electric certain crystal materials, such as quartz and Rochelle salts, that generate electricity when their surface is subjected to physical force or sound pressure.

polarity the direction of current flow, which results in the condition of positive or negative. One terminal on a battery is positive and the other is negative. Regarding magnets, the term polarity describes the property of the material having magnetic poles, one positive (attracting) and the other negative (repelling).

potential energy stored-up energy; the ability to do work. A rock resting high on a hilltop has potential energy; the ability to do work because of gravity. See **kinetic energy**.

potentiometer a variable resistor, like the volume control on a TV or stereo.

power Power is defined as the rate of doing work or energy used. Power equals work divided by time. Units of measure of power are the watt and horsepower.

quantify to measure an amount, or "how much" of something.

radio frequency energy electromagnetic waves used to carry TV and radio signals.

RC circuit resistive/capacitive circuit, an electrical circuit with a resistor and capacitor placed in series. When a resistor is placed in series between a capacitor and a power source, the time it takes to charge the capacitor increases as the value of the resistor increases.

reaction A chemical reaction is where the bonds that hold atoms together in molecules are broken and rearranged to form different bonds, making new substances. Chemical changes can take place when elements come in contact with each other, when they decompose, or when there is a change in temperature or pressure. Chemical reactions may cause energy to be given off in the form of electricity, light or heat.

rectifier a device that changes alternating current to direct current. A diode used to convert AC to DC is said to be acting as a rectifier.

relay a device in which one circuit can open or close a current path in another circuit. An electromagnet and spring are used to open and close switch contacts.

residue solid material remaining or deposited after a liquid containing the material has gone or evaporated.

resistor an electronic component that impedes the flow of electrons. The unit of measure of resistance is the ohm.

reverberation the sound of thousands of echoes washing together, each echo having a different delay. The ear doesn't hear any one particular echo, but rather a mixture of indistinguishable sounds.

sample size the number of items being tested. The larger the sample size, the more significant the results. Using only two plants to test a hypothesis that sugar added to water results in better growth would not yield a lot of confidence in the results. One plant might grow better simply because some plants just grow better than others.

saturated solution When a substance that is being dissolved in a liquid can no longer be added to the liquid and dissolved, the liquid solution is called a saturated solution. It is easy to tell when a solution has reached saturation, as the substance to be dissolved will start becoming visible in the container, since it can no longer be dissolved in the mixture, no matter how much stirring is done.

schematic diagram a pictorial drawing of electronic components and how they are arranged and connected together in a circuit. Symbols are used to represent the components.

scientific method a step-by-step logical process for investigation. A problem is stated, a hypothesis is formed, an experiment is set up, data is gathered, and a conclusion is reached about the hypothesis based on the data gathered.

semiconductor a material that falls into a classification between conductors and insulators and exhibits unique electrical characteristics. Semiconductor components in electronics include diodes, transistors, and integrated circuits.

series circuit an electrical circuit in which there is only one current path and all components are connected end to end.

short circuit the falling of a circuit from its normal value to a very low value, which usually causes the electrical device to fail or a fuse to blow. Electricity takes a short cut through the circuit instead of flowing normally throughout all the components. If the resistance has become so low that it approaches zero ohms, it is said to be a "dead short."

simple machines tools—such as levers, inclined planes, pulleys, wedges, screws, and wheel and axles—that make it easier to do work. All complex mechanical machines are made up of simple machines. Simple machines provide a way to change a force to a distance, a distance to a force, or to change direction. A pulley on a flagpole changes the downward force on a rope to an opposite, upward, movement of a flag.

sine wave the fundamental wave form from which all others are derived. The amplitude (size) increases in one direction, then decreases and increases in the opposite direction, completing the cycle by returning back to the starting point. The swing of a simple pendulum traces a sine wave form. In the United States, the AC power delivered to homes by electric utility companies takes the form of a sine wave, with the voltage building positive then swinging negative 60 times per second.

solar cell See **photovoltaic cell**.

solution a specific type of mixture where the substances are uniformly (evenly) mixed. Sugar in ice tea is an example. The sugar dissolves and is distributed throughout the whole glass of tea. See **mixture**.

solvent a substance that can dissolve another substance, or turn it into yet another substance.

static electricity an electrical charge on an object giving it potential energy. The friction from rubbing a hard-rubber rod with fur causes electrons to be transferred from the piece of fur to the rod, giving the rod a negative charge and the fur a positive charge.

surface area the amount of outside area of an object.

surface tension On the surface of a liquid in which molecules are close enough together, they attract one another to create a skin-like condition called surface tension. Place a drop of water on a piece of wax paper and it will form a tiny sphere. A pin placed gently on the surface of water in a bowl will float on the water because the surface tension has created a tough "skin." Soap changes the surface tension of water.

tare weight The tare weight is the weight subtracted from a gross weight to allow for the weight of the container. The result gives the weight of the contents of the container or holder. If you want to know how much your cat weighs, but he or she won't sit still on a scale, weigh yourself holding the cat. Then just weigh yourself. Subtract your weight (the "tare" weight) from the weight of both you and the cat and the answer is the weight of the cat.

tensile strength how strong something is, and how much tension or pressure it can take before it breaks. Steel has great tensile strength.

thermistor a device made of certain semiconductor material (such as uranium oxide, nickel-manganese oxide, and silver sulfide) which is sensitive to temperature. As temperature increases, resistance decreases, behavior opposite to that of other metal conductors.

tolerance-resistor band The color of the fourth band on resistors indicates its "tolerance" or accuracy. A resistor marked 100 ohms with a silver fourth band (indicating 10% tolerance) could have an actual value between 90 ohms and 110 ohms.

torque a twisting force, or the force used to rotate an object.

trace a barely detectable amount of something.

trajectory the path of an object as it travels through the air.

transformer an electrical component consisting of two or more coils which can step voltage up or down.

unbalanced force a push or pull on an object that is stronger in one direction than any push or pull in the opposite direction.

variable something that can be changed.

velocity speed with a direction of the motion assigned to it.

viscosity the ability of a fluid to flow. A fluid that has a low viscosity flows easily and quickly. Water has a low viscosity; cold molasses has high viscosity.

voltage the potential difference in electric charge between two points. This potential difference is the force which drives electric current through a conductor.

wafting a technique used to safely sample the scent of something without taking a deep breath of it. Holding the object away from your face, wave you hand over it, blowing a few of the vapors toward your nose.

watts a unit of measure of electrical power. An equation for watts: watts = volts × amperes.

wave form the shape of an electric signal.

wavelength Energy can travel in the form of a wave. You are familiar with rolling waves in the ocean. Other types of energy waves, such as sound waves and radio waves, would look similar to ocean waves, if we could see them. A wave has a crest, or peak, the highest part of the wave, and it has a trough, the lowest part. The length from crest to crest (or trough to trough) is called the wavelength. The wavelength of a tsunami (a tidal wave) can be 100 miles (161 kilometers) long! The wavelength of a 550 Hertz (cycles per second) sound wave, which is a note that is a little higher than "middle C" on a piano, is 2 feet.

weight the force of gravity pulling on an object downward toward the earth.

wet-cell battery a container with two dissimilar metals immersed in a liquid solution causing a voltage potential to be produced across the two metals. Typically, the metals might be copper and zinc and the liquid a dilute solution of sulfuric acid.

windbreak an object that reduces the force of the wind. Trees are sometimes planted around a house to act as a windbreak, protecting the house from strong winds.

work the measure of the motion-producing effects of a force. The formula in physics for work is WORK = FORCE × DISTANCE.

SCHEMATIC SYMBOLS
FOR COMMON ELECTRONIC COMPONENTS

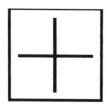

**wires intersecting
(connected)**

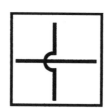

**wires intersecting
(not connected)**

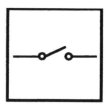

switch

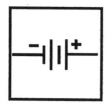

battery

capacitor

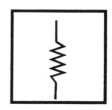

resistor

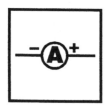

ammeter

light bulb

diode

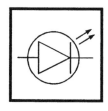

LED

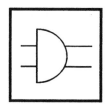

AC plug

transistor

volt meter

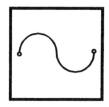

speaker

fuse

integrated circuit

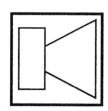

solar cell

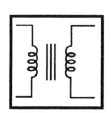

transformer

METRIC CONVERSION CHART

Inches to Centimeters
(12 inches = 1 foot   3 feet = 1 yard)

⅛	0.3	9	22.9	30	76.2
¼	0.6	10	25.4	31	78.7
⅜	1.0	11	27.9	32	81.3
½	1.3	12	30.5	33	83.8
⅝	1.6	13	33.0	34	86.4
¾	1.9	14	35.6	35	88.9
⅞	2.2	15	38.1	36	91.4
1	2.5	16	40.6	37	94.0
1¼	3.2	17	43.2	38	96.5
1½	3.8	18	45.7	38	99.1
1¾	4.4	19	48.3	40	101.6
2	5.1	20	50.8	41	104.1
2½	6.4	21	53.3	42	106.7
3	7.6	22	55.9	43	109.2
3½	8.9	23	58.4	44	111.8
4	10.2	24	61.0	45	114.3
4½	11.4	25	63.5	46	116.8
5	12.7	26	66.0	47	119.4
6	15.2	27	68.6	48	121.9
7	17.8	28	71.1	49	124.5
8	20.3	29	73.7	50	127.0

INDEX

radio-frequency,
     limiting direction of, 350
     solar, 210–211
radio-frequency energy, 347, 357
     See Energy: radio waves
     See Microwaves
RC circuit, 325–326, 357
reaction, action and, 257
reactions, 357
     acid–base, 108
     endothermic, 124–125, 354
     exothermic, 126–127, 354
rectification, 339
rectifiers, 339, 357
recycling, 58–59, 77
reflection
     of light, 198–199, 238, 243
     of sound, 216
relays, 310–311, 357
residue, 144, 357
resistance
     determining by indirect
          methods, 321–322
     heat production from, 315–316
     to motion. *See friction*
resistors
     defined, 314, 357
     in parallel circuits, 317–318
     in series circuits, 317–318, 323
reverberation, 216–217, 357
RF energy. *See Radio-frequency
     energy*
ripening, of fruit, 132–133
rust, magnetic properties of, 274

S
safety, 9
sample size, 177, 357
saturated solution, 357
schematic diagrams, 266, 357
schematic symbols, 360–361
science fair projects, 9–10
scientific method, 9, 357
screwdriver, 202–203
semiconductors, 338, 357
series circuits, 357
     resistors in, 317–318, 323

shape, balancing point and, 234–235
short, in electrical circuit, 301–302
simple machines, 202, 358
     levers, 204–205
     wedge, 250–251
     wheel and axle, 202–203
sine wave, 341–342, 358
sinks, heat, 194–195
siphon, 253
slope angle
     kinetic energy and, 212–213
     overcoming friction and,
          186–187
smell
     in food identification, 150–151
     of natural substances, 98–99
     process of, 154
     releasing fragrance with heat,
          154–155
     strong substances safely, 100
snow, melting, 14, 210–211
soap
     adding to water, 130–131
     changing shape/density of,
          156–157
     solution, for monster–bubbles,
          140–141
soda drinks, reducing carbonation
     from, 116–117
sodium bicarbonate, releasing
     carbon dioxide from, 162–163
solar (photovoltaic) cells, 66–67,
     327, 332–333, 356
solar energy, 28, 62, 76
     collection, 24–25
     dispersion, 25
     distribution, 30–31
     heating the body, 85
     loss, 56
     protection, 54
     radiation, 29
     storage, 23, 29
solar heat, transfer, 190–191
solar radiation, 210–211
solid-state electronics, 338
solute, 109, 120–121
solution, 109, 358

solvent, 109, 358
sound
     amplifying, 220–221, 240–241
     focusing, 240–241
     pleasant, vs. noise, 218–219
     qualities, 216–217
     speed of, 249
     transmission, 214–215
     travel, 249
     waves, as insect repellent,
          345–346
sounding board, piano, 240
speaker, for detecting diode wave
     form changing ability, 341–342
speed
     of light, 249
     momentum and, 188–189
     rate changes, 193
     of sound, 249
     wind, 232
spoke, 202
spores, 110
starch, in fermentation, 138–139
static electricity
     defined, 280, 358
     generation of, 289–290
     grounding, 287–288
static interference, 86
steam, 230
steel, tensile strength of, 192
strength, tensile, 192
stretching, elasticity and, 260–261
string instruments, 262–263
sugar
     energy food, 37
     in fermentation, 138–139
     natural forms, 37
     natural vs. artificial sweetener,
          134–135
     ripening process and, 132–133
     sweetness of, 164–165
sun
     beams, 90
     heat protection, 14
     light energy rays, 90
     light into heat, 13
     light reflection, 90